D1004726

EAST-WEST PASSAGE

To
Marjorie Hope Nicolson

EAST-WEST PASSAGE

A STUDY IN LITERARY RELATIONSHIPS

by

DOROTHY BREWSTER

GEORGE ALLEN & UNWIN LTD

RUSKIN HOUSE MUSEUM STREET LONDON

First published in 1954

PRINTED IN GREAT BRITAIN
in 12-point Fournier type by
SIMSON SHAND LTD.
LONDON, HERTFORD AND HARLOW

FOREWORD

THIS STUDY in literary relationships has grown out of a long professional academic interest in the Russian influence on English literature and a more general interest in the cultural interchange between Russia and the West, which since the 1917 Revolution has become increasingly complicated by political conflicts. Part of the study, therefore, is specifically literary, and part introduces social and political considerations bearing on literary questions.

Knowledge of Russian literature in England and the United States grew slowly in the nineteenth century, rapidly in the twentieth. By 1880–1890 a number of English and American critics were already sufficiently familiar with Russian fiction to contrast it with French fiction in the hotly debated arguments over the nature of Realism. The story up to that point of what one may risk calling Russian penetration was already quite a long one, but relatively simple; after that point, it became more and more complex. To follow it calls for the examination of material that may be roughly classified thus:
(1) Doctoral dissertations recording the results of research in special fields, with such titles as *Turgenev in England and America*, *Dostoevsky's English Reputation*, *Gogol's First Century in England and America*, *Tolstoy's Fiction in England and America;* and in a class with the dissertations, such special articles in learned periodicals as *The Influence of Turgenev on Henry James*, *Victorian Comment on Russian Realism*, and so forth. (2) Books written by scholars, interpreting Russian literature on the sound basis of a study of both the language and the culture; especially the biographies of Gogol, Pushkin, Tolstoy, Turgenev, Dostoevsky, Gorky and Chekhov, and the histories of Russian literature, written in English or translated from the Russian. The scholars supplement and correct one another, as new material has come to light. (3) Informed and perceptive essays of general literary criticism, concerned with Russian writers. As these writers slowly became known in the West, acceptable principles of interpretation and evaluation were formulated. But noticeable in these essays are the changes in taste over the years and the disagreements resulting from both different critical sensibilities and different social philosophies. The list of essayists is

long and distinguished: from Henry James and William Dean Howells, Matthew Arnold and George Moore, on down through the Garnetts, Edward and Constance, Havelock Ellis, Lafcadio Hearn, Edmund Gosse, William Lyon Phelps, Bernard Shaw, Percy Lubbock, E. M. Forster, Edmund Wilson, Virginia Woolf, D. H. Lawrence, Middleton Murry, V. S. Pritchett, and many others. And finally (4) countless articles, reviews, incidental comment, introductions, notes, letters, advertisements, in the magazines and newspapers of over a century in England and the United States; offering us the day-by-day, year-by-year accumulation of fact and falsehood, opinion and speculation, set down by travellers, diplomats, journalists, churchmen, generals, doctors, scientists, tourists, translators, propagandists, secret agents, exiles, engineers, and any other vocal human beings that may come to mind.

The challenge of this material is that of putting together a coherent account of cultural interpenetration in one of its many aspects. The aspect considered here is that of the influences coming from Russia to England and the United States: it is the East-West, not the West-East, passage. Parts of the story have been told, but no general survey exists. In Part I the treatment is mainly chronological, but flexible enough to permit some digressions on special topics; in Part II it is mainly topical, as the chapter headings indicate. The reasons for the shift of emphasis in organizing the material are explained in the text. Many of the conclusions are tentative, and some questions are raised which are not answered or even fully formulated. In a study of this length, there could be no attempt at complete discussion of all the issues. That there are so many issues and that they are so intricately interwoven has been one of the interesting discoveries resulting from work on the material. The intention of the author has been to bring together widely scattered but relevant facts and opinions, to stimulate further examination, to provoke dissatisfaction with the easily accepted dogmas of the moment, and to provide a convenient framework within which more intensive research can be conducted.

DOROTHY BREWSTER

Columbia University, New York, 1953

CONTENTS

PART ONE

CHAPTER I

FROM *LOVE'S LABOUR'S LOST* TO *ALICE THROUGH THE LOOKING-GLASS*

i

Travellers' Tales – Sixteenth and Seventeenth Centuries

LONG BEFORE there were any translations into English of Russian literature, there were notions current about Russian culture, Russian traits, Russian history, Russian climate. Travellers and traders brought back information and misinformation, beginning with the picturesque contributions of the Elizabethans. The Russian Bear appeared upon the scene long before the Russian Soul. No reader of the translations that began to be published in considerable numbers after the middle of the nineteenth century could have been free of preconceptions about Russia and her people, which had been familiar for generations. What some of these preconceptions were can be suggested by going back to the Elizabethans, and picking up a few of the typical and recurrent notions, down through the decades and the centuries.

Russians appear masqued—a sinister touch?—in *Love's Labour's Lost*. Or more accurately, the King of Navarre and his courtiers disguise themselves as frozen 'Muscovits', looking pale, 'sea-sick, I think', says Rosaline, 'coming from Muscovy'. The date of the play is not later than 1591. The allusion is to an event in 1582, when the Russian ambassador came to arrange a treaty and to take back a wife for the Tsar from among Elizabeth's kinswomen. The lady selected was presented to the ambassador in the gardens of York House, with a ceremony that 'may have given a hint for the masque of the Muscovites in V. ii, 158 ff.—especially as the episode was long remembered as a joke'. (Cambridge edition of Shakespeare's Works, ed. W. A. Neilson.) Thomas Nashe, in *Have With You to Saffron Walden* (1596), contributes a Russian pun on his own name and a bit of information about a 'chiefe office in the Emperour of Russiaes court', known as the 'grand commander of silence'. Nashe threatens those who may curse and rail upon him with being compelled to fall down and worship him, 'crying upon their knees *ponuloi nashe*, which is in the Russian tongue, Have mercie upon us'.

There are many such examples of garbled Russian words in the works of Elizabethan poets and playwrights. Both Elizabeth and not a few of her subjects were interested in the Russian tongue. When Jerome Horsey in 1587 presented her with certain documents of privileges, granted to English subjects in Russia, the queen perused the 'lyminge and characters of the privilege, having some affinity with the Greek'; asked if such and such letters and asseverations had not this signification; said she, 'I could quickly learn it,' and prayed my lord of Essex to learn 'the famoust and most copius language in the world; after which commendation his honor did much affect and delight it, if he might attain thereunto without paiens-takinge and spending more time than he had to spare'. This 'if' has deterred many since his Honour; one cannot help wondering if Essex might not have kept his head on his shoulders, had he taken to the study of Russian instead of to more dangerous adventures.

The Russian Bear, real, not symbolic, since bear-baiting was a good Elizabethan sport, is used to point a retort in *Henry V*, when Orleans, answering Rambures, who has praised the island of England for breeding valiant creatures and mastiffs of unmatchable courage, says—'Foolish curs, that run winking into the mouth of a Russian bear, and have their heads crushed like rotten apples.' And the rugged Russian bear joins the armed rhinoceros and the Hyrcan tiger as shapes Macbeth would prefer to meet, rather than the ghost of Banquo.

It is a task for the industry of graduate study to collect all the passing references in the literature of the period to Russia, its language and drinks and fauna. They prove, if nothing else, the currency of the travellers' tales. To put together anything like a summary of these narratives and comment upon them would make several books, and would take us into history, geography, trade relations, diplomacy and politics. It is not the accurate information and the historical documentation with which we are concerned here, but rather the picturesque episodes, the broad generalizations about a people and its culture, which pass into the common stock of English notions about Russia.

We have early poetic generalizations from the pen of Master George Turberville, in 'certaine letters in verse, written out of Moscovia'. Turberville went to Russia as secretary to Master Thomas Randolph, her Majesty's Ambassador to the Emperor, in 1568. Three letters appear in Hakluyt's *Voyages*, 1589, addressed to his especial friend, Master Edward Dancie, to Spenser and to Parker. He finds that the Russes drink too much:

> A people passing rude, to vices vile inclinde,
> Folke fit to be of Bacchus traine, so quaffing in their kinde.
> Drinke is their whole desire, the pot is all their pride,
> The sobrest head doth once a day stand needfull of a guide.

He describes kvas—

> . . . whereby the Mousike lives,
> Small ware and waterlike, but somewhat tart in taste.

Their beasts are like to the English, but the beef is not firm, like the English beef, and he thinks little of their cooking. They are given over to Idoles:

> The house that hath no god or painted Saint within
> Is not to be resorted to, that roofe is full of sinne.

He tells in quaint detail what both men and women look like and what they wear:

> The Russie men are round of bodies, fully fac'd,
> The greatest part with bellies bigge that overhang the waste.
> Flat headed for the most, with faces nothing faire
> But browne, by reason of the stove and closeness of the aire.

He describes their collars set with pearl, their long shirts, the furred shuba over all, notes the absence of the codpiece—that rich source of Elizabethan jest; observes that women, 'against our use', bestride the horse and is shocked by their excessive use of cosmetics, wondering what madness makes them paint when they 'keepe the stove' and are seldom seen abroad.

She pranks and paints her smoakie face, both brow, lip, cheeke and chinne.
Yea, those that honest are, if any such there bee
Within the land, doe use the like.

Some lay it on too thickly,

But such as skilful are, and cunning Dames indeede,
By dayly practise doe it well, yea sure they doe exceede.

The cold deeply impressed him, a cold so severe that the dead had to be left unburied till spring because of the hard-frozen ground, but wood being very plentiful, everyone was assured of a coffin. The cattle—sheep, colts, cows—come right in and lodge fast by the Mowsike's bed, and 'weare the winter with the Mowsike and his wife'. He was not pleased with the beds, and couldn't understand why there were no bolsters, when plenty of down was available. He and Stafford 'lay upon a beare'—skin, one supposes.

In short, the country is too cold, the people are beastly, and he could tell a lot more, if he chose:

The colde is rare, the people rude, the prince is full of pride,
The Realme so stored with Monks and nonnes and priests on every side.
The manners are so Turkie like, the men so full of guile,
The women wanton, Temples stuft with idols that defile
The Seats that sacred ought to be, the customes are so quaint
As if I would describe the whole, I feare my pen would faint.

In his final judgment he makes a comparison (which is also made by Edmund Spenser, in *A View of the Present State of Ireland*):

Wilde Irish are as civill as the Russies in their kinde,
Hard choice which is the best of both, ech bloody, rude and blinde.

But the Russies are good chess players:

The common game is chesse, almost the simplest will
Both give a checke and eke a mate, by practise comes their skill.

Perhaps that was something not to forget, down through the changing centuries.

Trade and diplomacy are the important themes in the narratives of Jerome Horsey and of Giles Fletcher, father of the poets Phineas and Giles. Horsey was factor of the English Russia Company (founded in 1563), and had obtained large concessions for the English from the Protector, Boris Godunov. Fletcher, in the diplomatic service, was sent in 1588 to the court of the Tsar Theodore, to conclude an alliance between England and Russia, restore English trade, and obtain better conditions for the English Russia Company. The threat of the Spanish Armada made the diplomatic going tough, but the English victory cleared the skies, and Fletcher returned in the company of Horsey, having secured exclusive rights of trading on the Volga, and security of English traders from the infliction of torture. In 1591 Fletcher published *Of the Russe Commonwealth*, 'a comprehensive account of Russian geography, government, law, methods of warfare, Church and manners' (*Encyclopaedia Britannica*).[1] Horsey's narrative of his travels was published in *Purchas His Pilgrimes*, 1626. Many Russian translations were made of Fletcher's book. The Russian historian Karamzin frequently quotes from Horsey's narrative, never expressing distrust of it as an authority.[2]

Horsey had gone to Russia first in 1573 as clerk of the Russia Company. When selected in 1580 as messenger from the Tsar to Queen Elizabeth, he was familiar with the Russian language. 'Though but a plaine gramarian, and having som smake in the Greek, I ateyned by the affinitie therof in shortt tyme to the readie and famillier knowledge of their vulgar speach, the Sclavonian tonge, the most copius and elegent language in the world.' The more copious and elegant the language, the more credit to him for mastering it. Had his mastery been less, he might not have kept himself alive in that court, in the midst of intrigue and violence. Horsey's account begins with the wars of Ivan the Terrible about 1570, and the burning of Moscow by the Crimean Tartars in 1571. He describes a Tartar ambassador who 'chaffes with a hellish hollow voice, lokinge fearce and grimly'. He cuts short an account of tortures, forbearing 'to trouble the modest eyrs and Christian pacience of such as shall read it'. About 1576 he carried a letter from the Tsar to Queen Elizabeth, through countries at war with Russia, concealing it in the false side of a wooden bottle of brandy, hanging under the horse's mane. Arrived in England, he took the letter out and 'sweetened' it as well as he could, but the Queen had a good nose and smelt 'the savier of the aqua vita'.

Horsey's last visit to Russia, 1589–91, was troubled by jealousies and calumnies. The Protector, Boris Godunov, was his friend, and continued to assure him privately that he would not suffer a hair to fall from his head, but Horsey, with the scepticism of experience, called the assurance a 'phrace'. He had to answer complaints made against his Queen, and did so 'pithely'. But things happened: 'my water to dres my meat withal was poisoned; my drink and herbs and mush-millians sent, poisoned; my laundress hired to poison me, which she confessed, by whom, when, and how; still I had good intelligence. My cook, my butler died, both of poison'. One of his servants, the son of a Dantzig lord, 'burst out with 20 blaines and boyells and narrowly escaped. Boris sends me word I should not fear'. All this ended one night when he was roused by a messenger from the palace where the young prince, Demetrius, son of Ivan the Terrible, had just had his throat cut. The mother of Demetrius was stricken with poison, and Horsey, besought for a remedy, gave the messenger a specific against poison, which with great foresight he had brought from England.

Horsey returned to England in 1591 and settled down in a condition of some affluence. He served above thirty years in Parliament. He wrote that 'all the known nations and kingdoms of the world are not comparable for happiness to this thrice blessed nation, the angelical Kingdom of Cannan, our England'. Yet after all his years in the angelical kingdom, he wrote: 'The experience of this wicked world, both at home and abroad, makes me now the more willing to live in a better.'

Giles Fletcher dedicated his *Russe Commonwealth* to Queen Elizabeth—'a prince of subjectes, not of slaves, that are kept within duetie by love, not by feare'—quite otherwise than in the tyrannical state he is describing, 'without true knowledge of God, without written law, without common justice, save that which proceedeth from their speaking law, to wit the magistrate'. Fletcher was wrong about the law, as the editor of the 1856 Hakluyt Society edition points out, referring to the known fact that Ivan Grozny (or the Terrible) composed a body of law, founded on the code of Ivan III, highly esteemed and promulgated in 1550. In general, Fletcher lives up to his professed aim of noting things 'of more importance than delight, and rather true than strange'. He is sparing of comment and generalization. Under Cosmography, he tells of the breadth and length of the land, the soil, climate, rivers, chief cities, native commodities; under Policy, he explains the ordering of the State, judicial proceedings, warlike provisions, ecclesiastical system; and under Economic or Private Behaviour, he includes the emperor's domestic manners, his household and offices, and the manners and customs of the people. There are lively descriptions of the installation of a new emperor, marriage and baptismal ceremonies, the mustering and equipping of troops, the governing of colonies, and the infliction of torture. There are a few novelties in torture, but surely little to surprise Elizabethan citizens, who in 1594 had flocked to see Dr Lopez castrated, disembowelled and quartered. His characterization of the common people is rather favourable: they have 'natural wittes in the men and very children', but are kept from learning that they may be fitter for their servile condition; they have reasonable capacities, 'if they had those means that some other nations have to train up their wits in good nurture and learning'. Their tyrannous Government is to blame; they are kept from travelling, that they may learn nothing nor see the fashions of other countries abroad; nor are strangers suffered willingly to come into the realm, except for trading. All this falls familiarly upon a twentieth century ear. Cruelly treated, they in turn become cruel to others. As for their honesty, 'it may be saide truely (as they know best who have traded most with them) that from the great to the small (except some few that will scarcely be founde) the Russe neither beleeveth anything that an other man speaketh, nor speaketh anything himself worthie to be beleeved.'

The Russian soldier is thought to be better at his defence within some castle or town than he is abroad at a set pitched field. Fletcher speculates upon the possibility of overthrowing the tyrannical Government. But the common people are robbed, and unpractised in the use of arms, the nobility unable to make head, and the emperor well-supplied with his own special forces; and 'this desperate state of things at home maketh the people for the most part to wish for some forreine invasion, which they suppose to bee the onely means to rid them of the heavy yoke of this tyrannous Government'. Later centuries, one reflects, produced Napoleon and Hitler as foreign invaders, but their fate has not noticeably discouraged modern speculation on this theme.

The snow and the wolves are played up—as they continued to be by later travellers—snow so severe from November on 'that it would breede a frost in a man to looke abroad at that time and see the winter face of that countrie'; and wolves that issue in troops out of the woods in extreme winters and enter villages, tearing and ravening. But Fletcher sounds a note seldom heard about the 'sommer time', when 'you shall see such a new hew and face of a countrie, the woods (for the most part which are all of fir and birch) so fresh and sweet, the pastures and medowes so greene and well growen (and that upon the sudden), such varietie of flowres, such noyse of birdes (especially of nightingales, that seeme to be more lowde and of a more variable note than in other countries), that a man shall not lightly travell in a more pleasant countrie'. But it was the wolf and not the nightingale that continued to impress the popular imagination.

Fletcher, interestingly, does not present as an atrocity Ivan the Terrible's killing of his son: 'That he meant him no such mortal harm when he gave him the blow may appear by his mourning and passion after his son's death, which never left him till it brought him to the grave. Wherein may be marked the justice of God, that punished his delight in shedding of blood with this murder of his son by his own hand, and so ended his days and tyranny together with the murdering of himself by extreme grief, for this his unhappy and unnatural fate.'

There is an anecdote (mentioned by Bond in his introduction to the 1856 Hakluyt) that Fletcher was as thankful to return safe to England as Ulysses was to come out of the den of Polyphemus. Yet he did not have too secure a time after his return. Though in 1596 he was saved by Essex from imprisonment as surety for his brother's debts, he was actually imprisoned in 1601, 'apparently for attributing Essex's disgrace to Raleigh'. (*Encyclopaedia Britannica.*)

The travel books of Purchas, Hakluyt, Chancelor, Willoughy, and half a dozen other sources led Milton, at some period before he lost his sight, to compile his brief history entitled *Muscovia*, published in 1682. It is rather dry reading, with some nice touches, like the description of the Abbey of St Nicholas, far to the north—built of wood, 'wherein are twenty Monks; unlearned, as then they (the English voyagers) found them, and great Drunkards; their Church is fair, full of Images and Tapers'. One would have liked Milton's opinion on the marriage and divorce customs which he records in detail: 'When there is love between the two, the Man among other trifling Gifts, sends to the Woman a Whip, to signify, if she offend, what she must expect; and it is a Rule among them, that if the wife be not beaten once a week, she thinks herself not belov'd and is the worse; yet are they very obedient, and stir not forth, but at some seasons. Upon utter dislike the Husband divorces; which Liberty no doubt they receiv'd first with their Religion from the Greek church and the Imperial laws.' Fletcher, unlike Milton, expressed disapproval of the position of women, saying that the ordinary Russian is of a barbarous condition in living with his wife, using women as servants rather than as wives, and he calls it a 'fowle abuse' that upon dislike of his wife or other cause whatsoever, a man may go into a monastery and 'shire himself a frier by pretence of devotion' and so leave his wife to shift for herself.

These early accounts may be taken here as illustrating the gradual accumulation of fact and fancy and opinion about Russian ways. Travellers in the sixteenth and seventeenth centuries brought back, besides tales, books and manuscripts: the Gospels, psalm books, Slavonic primers, charters, fragments from Russian chronicles. In 1618, for example, Richard James, the chaplain who accompanied Sir Dudley Digges, founder of a company for trade with Russia, brought back some transcriptions of Russian oral literature—songs; and these MSS. anticipated by a century the first written Russian records of these songs.

Two years before Peter the Great visited Oxford in 1698, the Oxford Press published the Russian grammar of Henry William Ludolf. And so began (in badly handicapped competition with travellers' tales) the extremely slow process of learning to know a people through its language and literature.

ii

Facts and Opinions – Eighteenth Century

WHAT OF eighteenth-century travellers, and eighteenth-century speculation on Russian character and customs? Out of much material we select a traveller and a philosophic 'citizen of the world'—Dr Bell, and Oliver Goldsmith.

Dr John Bell was a Scotsman, whose *Travels from St Petersburgh in Russia to Divers Parts of Asia* was published in 1763, and highly recommended to Boswell by Dr Johnson. Dr Bell made a journey from St Petersburg to Ispahan and back, with an embassy from Peter the Great to the Sophy of Persia in 1715–1718; another from St Petersburg to Pekin through Siberia in 1719–1721; another from Moscow to Derbent in Persia in 1722, when Peter himself went; and still another from St Petersburg to Constantinople in 1737–1738. He is an interesting writer, and the accompanying maps are entrancing. Bell reached Cronstadt in October 1714, and lodged that winter at Mr Noy's, an English shipbuilder in the Tsar's service. He often saw the Tsar, who was easy of access on the streets—he liked to go to fires, and they were frequent—and who readily received and acted on petitions. As a man of business, he won Bell's admiration. Bell absolves him from the charge of excessive drinking; at least on the trip to Persia, he was abstemious. Among the things done by Peter that impressed Dr Bell was the importation of a flock of sheep and a German shepherd to a region near Viatka, good for pasturage. He pays tribute to 'the unbounded genius of this great and active prince who spares no expense and overlooks nothing' that can contribute to the honour and advantage of the empire. He has little to say about the extent to which human beings, too, were expendable by Peter.

Like many a later reporter, Dr Bell has a word on prisoners. These were Swedish prisoners of war whom he found in Siberia, scattered about in a not too uncomfortable exile, cultivating some of the sciences and music and painting, and helping to civilize the inhabitants, teaching French and German to young ladies and gentlemen in Tobolsk. He corrects some mistaken notions, such as that spread by certain 'grave German authors' about the plant called Tartarian lamb, used to face the caps of Armenians and Tartars; it was supposed to partake of both animal and vegetable life, 'eating' grass and weeds. Dr Bell found just a plant, subsisting like other plants. He travelled down the Volga with a party in barques. 'In the night one of our boats was driven by the rapidity of the current among the woods and stuck fast between two trees, up which the people climbed, being apprehensive of danger.' Next morning they climbed down from their roost and the vessel was extricated. Altogether Dr Johnson showed his usual good judgment in recommending this book.

Oliver Goldsmith at about the same time—1762—in his *Letters of a Citizen of the World* has his fictional Chinese correspondents exchange views on the Russians. They have lost their Elizabethan remoteness. Letter 87 is critical of the wisdom of Europe in applying to the Russians—'their neighbors and ours'—for assistance in war; Russian auxiliaries or mercenaries had been hired in some of the wars of the period, and the wise Chinese observer notes how this employment strengthens the Russians, already too powerful. 'I cannot,' writes Fum Hoam to Lien Chi Altangi, 'avoid beholding the Russian Empire as the natural enemy of the more western parts of Europe; as an enemy already possessed of great strength, and from the nature of the government every day threatening to become more powerful.' Occupying nearly a third of the Old World, it has increased in wealth and extent since the time of Johan Basilides (Ivan III); it has internal peace, learns military art at the expense of others abroad, will grow more powerful and, in future times, perhaps, as formerly, will be called *officina gentium*—a manufactory [or workshop] of peoples. Had Peter the Great succeeded in his ambition to establish a fort in the western part of Europe, he would have been in possession of a floodgate, and 'whenever ambition, interest, or necessity prompted, they (the Russians) might then be able to deluge the whole Western world with a barbarous inundation'. They have now reached a period between refinement and barbarity most adapted to military achievement, and 'if once they happen to get footing in the Western parts of Europe, it is not the feeble efforts of the sons of effeminacy and dissension that can serve to remove them'. The fertile valleys and soft climate of the West will draw whole myriads from their native deserts, the trackless wild or snowy mountain. One notes in this geographical rhetoric no vegetation, no summer, no nightingales. The letter concludes with comparisons to famished locusts and myriads of ants issuing from the southern desert and bringing desolation; and with references to the migrations of savage hungry men issuing wild from their forests and dens—Goths, Vandals, Tartars, Saracens—the usual list of 'hordes'.

These dire prophecies should give to present-day readers of whatever political persuasion satisfaction in their convictions either (1) that the Russians have always been like that, or (2) that the fears of the West have always been like that.

Lien Chi Altangi, in Letter 62, turns from politics to women, and in a portrait of the wife of Peter the Great, Catherine Alexovna, implies the existence of a good deal of civilization of a sort, in that reservoir of ants, locusts and hordes. Catherine is praised as a fair woman who properly confined herself within the 'narrow limits of domestic assiduity and softened the cares of man'. 'While the extraordinary prince, her husband, laboured for the reformation of his male subjects, she studied in her turn the improvement of her own sex. She altered their dresses, introduced mixed assemblies, instituted an order of female knighthood; and at length, when she had greatly fulfilled all the stations of empress, friend, wife and mother, bravely died without regret, regretted by all.' Goldsmith's Chinese gentleman fails to mention what the *Encyclopaedia Britannica* terms a dangerously familiar flirtation, which created a great scandal, between Catherine and her gentleman of the bedchamber, William Mons; he was decapitated and his severed head, preserved in spirits, was placed in her apartments. A little disturbance like this did not prevent this 'uncommonly shrewd, sensible and good-tempered woman' from attending Peter in his last illness and closing his eyes.

In another letter, discussing Russian marriage customs, Goldsmith notes with approval the gift of a cudgel to the husband from the father of the bride. And comparing English and Russian methods of dealing with adulterous wives, he considers the Russian very wise—the wife promising the husband never to let him see her transgressions of this nature; if detected, she is beaten and forgiven, and all goes on as before.

iii

Two Russian Rulers: Catherine the Great and Peter the Great – Eighteenth and Early Nineteenth Century Fact and Fancy

IVAN THE TERRIBLE (Grozny) corresponded with Queen Elizabeth —and even offered her a refuge in case of need—a contingency much more present to Ivan's mind than to Elizabeth's. But to the West he was a shadowy and remote figure compared to Peter the Great, who opened his windows to the West, and himself came as far as Oxford.

Defoe is credited with *An Imperial History of the Life and Actions of Peter Alexowitz, Czar of Muscovy*, published in 1723. The account is presented as the work of a British officer in the service of the Tsar, and is a routine job, describing among other things Peter's voyage to England, where he was shown the manner of a naval engagement, and 'all the ways of taking advantage of an enemy in fight'. The Citizen of the World, just quoted, could hardly have approved of that. The account breaks off during the war with Sweden, leaving to other hands to continue the story so that 'the glories of our August Emperor of Russia may be handed to Posterity in a manner suitable to his Fame and to the Merit of the greatest Prince in all the Eastern Part of the World. Amen'.

Peter's glories had already been celebrated by a minor English poet, Aaron Hill, at the outset of a career as playwright, journalist, 'projector' and friend of Pope and Richardson. Hill published a long poem, *The Northern Star*, in 1718, which must have been read, for a fifth edition appeared in 1739. A Latin translation included in the 1724 edition reached Peter himself and produced for Hill a gold medal, sent by the Empress after Peter's death in 1725, but by his order, and a promise of papers to be used in a biography. Some papers actually arrived; Hill refers to them in a letter to Pope and declares that they throw 'the noblest and most beautiful colors on a circumstance which the malice of some great courts in Europe has taken pains to misrepresent and blacken'. This no doubt is a reference to the violent end of Peter's son Alexis. But the Empress died, no more papers came, and the biography was not undertaken, though Pope wrote in flattering terms of what Hill would be able to make of the material. What he might have made of it we can guess from the poem. Young, enthusiastic, bursting with magnanimity, Hill felt it his duty to search out and exalt virtue wherever he found it—even outside his own nation, even in a Russian Tsar.

> Perish that narrow pride, from custom grown,
> That makes men blind to merits not their own.
> Briton and Russian differ but in name.

We are clearly moving into the Age of Enlightenment. The poet credits Peter with civilizing his own people, making the Dane, the Swede and the Turk tremble, and the lords of China shrink behind their famous wall. He has thawed the icy influence of the North Pole and

The shaggy Samoid, shaking off the snow,
Warms his cold breast with new desire to know.

The 'virgin Caspian' is even more seriously affected. Wooed by this bold lover, not vainly, and 'grasped to his wish',

. . . she has her love confessed
And given him leave to wander o'er her breast.

And wander on, it seems, to Persia's heaped wealth, and to India, whose sovereigns will kneel to her lord. In lines dimly—very dimly—prophetic of the last chorus of Shelley's *Hellas*, Hill foresees the final overthrow of the Crescent by the Cross and the rebirth of Greece:

Shall we behold earth's long-sustained disgrace
Revenged in arms on Osman's haughty race?
Shall Christian Greece shake off a captive's shame,
And look unblushing at her pagan fame?
'Twill be. Prophetic Delphos claims her own,
Hails her new Caesars on the Russian throne.
Athens shall teach once more, once more aspire!
And Spartan breasts reglow with martial fire.
Still, still, Byzantium's brightening domes shall shine,
And rear the ruined name of Constantine.

In the long and checkered history of the power struggle over Constantinople, both poets and propagandists have been tempted by the mystical vision of the Cross restored to St Sophia. As late as 1917, the Russian Soul was pictured as yearning towards Constantinople, the city whence Christianity came to Russia. And in 1878, during the Russo-Turkish war, Longfellow evoked the spirit of the White Tsar—Peter the Great—and hailed him as presiding over the attack on Constantinople and proclaiming:

The Bosphorus shall be free.
It shall make room for me,
And the gates of its water streets
Be unbarred before my fleets.
I say it: the White Tsar
Batyushka, Gosudar!
And the Christian shall no more

Be crushed as heretofore
Beneath thine iron rule,
O Sultan of Istamboul.
I swear it, I the Tsar,
Batyushka, Gosudar!

How Hill would have envied Longfellow's flourish of Russian words!

Walter Savage Landor did not share the admiration expressed by Longfellow and Hill for Peter the Great. In one of his *Imaginary Conversations*, written a little more than a century after Hill's poem, he takes up the relationship between Peter and the unfortunate Tsarevich Alexis. Peter rehearses all the strong measures he had taken to develop courage in Alexis from childhood, such as feeding him gunpowder in his grog, making him witness hangings, look at severed heads, and so forth. Peter accuses Alexis of not rejoicing at the victories over the Swedes and Poles: 'Didst thou get drunk at home or abroad, or praise the Lord of Hosts or St Nicholas? Wert thou not silent and civil and low-spirited?' But Alexis laments the loss of life and the destruction of civilized men. Then Peter accuses him of praising the primitive simplicity of Scythians, and preferring a vagabond life to a civilized one, a cart to a city, a Scythian to a Muscovite, and having views that strike at the root of politeness and sound government: 'Have I not shaved my people and breeched them? Have I not formed them into regular armies, with bands of music and haversacks?' Alexis appeals to his father not to harm him, lest Peter be accused and the throne be shaken. But the appeal is in vain. Alexis is led off to be judged, and the chancellor soon returns to report his death, apparently from shock, when the accusations of treason were read to him. Whereupon Peter calls for brandy, bacon, sturgeon and good strong cheese. The editor of the 1901 edition of Landor's *Imaginary Conversations* calls this a somewhat harsh picture of Peter. It is a portrait that would have rendered Mr Hill speechless—if anything could.

Landor's conception of Catherine the Great is still more colourful. He introduces the Empress and her friend the Princess Dashkoff listening outside the bedroom door while the murder of Catherine's husband, Peter III, is taking place within. There is much business of dripping blood. 'What bubbling and gurgling,' whispers Catherine. 'He groaned but once. . . . Listen, his blood is busier now than it ever was before. I should not have thought it could have splashed so loud upon the floor, although our bed, indeed, is rather of the highest. . . . The drops are now like lead. . . . How now—which of these fools has brought his dog with him? What tramping and lapping! The creature will carry the marks all about the palace with his feet and muzzle.'

As the dialogue continues—the murder being over—Dashkoff waxes a little sentimental: surely Peter must have once loved Catherine and, like other parents, they must have rejoiced over their infant. Catherine is merely amused at these pale-faced reflections of some epithalamiast from Livonia or Bessarabia. So Dashkoff turns to the question of how this murder will affect Catherine's reputation in Europe. Catherine is not worried. If she should ever be found out as having countenanced the conspiracy, Europe could be persuaded that its own repose made the step necessary. A sovereign may cover a throne with blood more safely than a subject can pluck a feather out of the cushion: 'Kings poison and stab one another in pure legitimacy.' As for her reputation, 'I can purchase all the best writers in Europe with a snuff-box. . . . Not a gentleman of the Academy but is enchanted with a toothpick if I deign to send it to him.' Voltaire will make her the Joan of Arc of Russia, but Dashkoff reminds her that Voltaire treated La Pucelle rather scandalously, and so that is not a very happy thought. Voltaire, says Catherine, amuses her and buoys her up. Where will you find another who writes so pointedly? Who cares for truth anyway? Then, realizing that they will have to put on a good act when the murder is discovered, she asks Dashkoff to sing something in French. The next victim will be Ivan the heir, but that affair will have to be postponed—'two such scenes together and without some interlude would perplex people. Sing, sing!'

Landor explains in a note that it is not necessary to inform the generality of readers that Catherine was not present at the murder of her husband, 'nor is it easy to believe that Clytemnestra was at the murder of hers; our business is with character'. The editor of the 1901 edition of the *Imaginary Conversations* is at pains to state that the scene described is 'unhistorical'; that Peter III was a man of brutal passions and debased intellect, and Catherine a woman of superior intellect, even if of inferior character, who had suffered from her husband's brutalities sufficiently to explain her conduct, which Landor has made 'needlessly black'. Thus neither character nor circumstance in Landor's little drama can be considered historical. But the drama is likely to be remembered rather than the historical facts.[3] The scene helps to build up that popular notion of the bloody Romanoffs which is extravagantly expressed in Landor's note at the end of the Conversation: 'Can we wonder that a set of despots who have in unbroken succession murdered or instigated the murder of sons, wives, husbands, fathers, should feel the necessity of reducing the world to slavery and ignorance, of abolishing the use of letters, of extinguishing the enthusiasm of poetry, of hoodwinking the glances of fiction, of shutting up the records of history, and of laying one vast iron hand upon the human mouth, covering the lips and nostrils of aggregated nations, fastened and waxed together for that purpose, like the reeds of Pan's pipe?'

The other conversations composed by Landor, in which Russians participate, stress diplomacy rather than murder. The royal speakers are Alexander I, Nicholas I and his brother Michael. They discuss foreign policy with their ministers, specially in relation to Turkey and Greece, and the talk is more subtle (as Landor notes) than such talks ever are, but his purpose is to heighten effects in order to strengthen his warning: Remember now and forever, Russia alone can play deep at every table and stake nothing. Landor would surely be welcomed in the chorus of present-day Western political commentators.

But let us return to Catherine the Great, whose reputation had been building up for many decades before Landor celebrated her deeds. Even during her seventeen years as grand duchess, the *Ency-*

clopedia Britannica remarks, 'the scandalous chronicle of her life was the commonplace of all Europe'. Horace Walpole, in a letter of June 9, 1766, rather casually wishes for her violent death. 'We have a Russian Garrick here,' he writes, 'the head of their theatre, and, like Shakespeare, both actor and author. He has translated *Hamlet*, and it has been acted at Petersburg. I could wish the parallel were carried still farther, and that after this play acted before the Empress *Gertrude*, the assassin of her husband, she were to end like Hamlet's mother.' Rather obscure, but apparently it was better to be discreet even in a letter. The reference to the visiting Russian Garrick is evidence of the progress of the arts in Russia. He was Alexander Sumarokov, who adapted *Hamlet*, making it end happily with the marriage of Hamlet and Ophelia, and produced it in 1750. (The first performance of Shakespeare's *Hamlet* on the Russian stage was in 1810.)

However scandalous the chronicle, Catherine's main interests were intellectual and political, and her love affairs were subsidiary. Later in the year of Horace Walpole's letter (1766), Catherine, after long study, had issued instructions to a commission called to formulate a new code of laws. This *Nakaz*, with her permission, was published in an English rendering by Michael Tatischeff in London in 1768.[4] Catherine, influenced at that time by French ideas, includes among her proposals some that suggest a Welfare State or a New Deal. No. 346, for instance: 'Alms bestowed upon a Beggar in the Street can never acquit the State of the obligation it lies under of affording all its Citizens a certain support during Life; such as wholesome Food, proper Cloathing, and a Way of Life not prejudicial to Health in general.'

Concerned as we are with both fact and fancy in the growth of popular notions about Russia, let us call in Jeremy Bentham to balance Landor. Bentham thought that Russia under Catherine 'had shown its willingness to be informed and led by the philosophic legislator', and in Catherine's tentative proposals for legislation she had recognized *the principle of utility*. Jeremy's brother Samuel, a master shipwright, trained in science and mathematics, had gone to Russia and been welcomed at court. But he got into trouble by falling in love with a maid of honour, instead of with Catherine, as was customary. He left the court, but joined Potemkin, who had plans for a Black Sea fleet and for a colony organized as a complete industrial unit. Needing two women as dairymaids and a man as supervisor, Samuel wrote to Jeremy about the colony, and Jeremy proposed coming to Russia, bringing the three at his own expense. The very chaos and barbarism of Russia seemed promising to Jeremy Bentham, who at that time was disappointed in England: 'At least Russia had nothing to unlearn; there was no pretence that her constitution and organization were the best possible.' An account of Bentham's stay in Russia from 1785 to 1788 is a fascinating chapter in C. W. Everett's *The Education of Jeremy Bentham*, 1931 (chapter viii, 'The Age of Catherine'). In January 1785 he arrived at Potemkin's headquarters at Kremenschug in the Ukraine. He found a mixture of wealth and barbarism—wedgwood ware, silver dish covers, along with dirty iron knives and forks. The model colony became little better than a madhouse, with its assortment of English, Welsh, and German experts in dairying and gardening, and with much laziness, thieving and drinking. Bentham had studied Russian enough to ask for what he wanted, but like many another later visitor, not enough to understand the answers: 'I know just as much of Russ as I know of the language of cats.' Yet he stayed on for two years, lodged comfortably enough at Zadobras near Crichoff. He translated, reflected, wrote. He planned to meet the Empress and to prepare a comprehensive code to govern Russia, but postponed this till he had completed his translation of the English penal code, and he did not even meet the Empress when, in 1787, she passed through Crichoff.

It is too bad that Landor did not exercise his talent upon an imaginary conversation between Catherine and Bentham, on the subject of 'the greatest happiness of the greatest number'. Perhaps Bentham communicated an interest in things Russian to his friend and pupil, Sir John Bowring, linguist and political economist, whose study of the Russian literature and language produced one of the first important translations into English: *Specimens of the*

Russian Poets, 1821–1823. But an earlier translation should not go unnoticed here, though one wonders how many people noticed it. It is one of the first—if not the first—piece of *imaginative* literature translated into English from the Russian: *Ivan Czarowitz: or the Rose without the prickles that stings not. A Moral Tale by Catherine the Great*, 1793.

Catherine as the author of moral tales remains uncelebrated in English letters. The feminine Bluebeard who had murdered her own husband inspired Landor, and the mistress of three hundred lovers, more or less, inspired Byron. The process of restoring the woman and the empress hidden beneath the legends has been likened by Katharine Anthony (whose biography in 1925 contributed to the restoration) to the scraping off of the gilt and varnish that concealed the original ikons in the Uspensky cathedral in the Kremlin—a process Miss Anthony watched in 1923. The Catherine of history has been largely restored—with her diplomacy, campaigns and conquests, her plans of liberal reform, her correspondence with Grimm and Voltaire, and her method of educating her favourite grandson Alexander—a method carefully omitting the matter of the reproductive process, even in botany. But when Bernard Shaw wrote his apology for his play *Great Catherine* in 1913, he probably expressed correctly the nature of the enduring interest in Catherine: 'Catherine's diplomacy and her conquests do not interest me. . . . But Catherine as a woman, with plenty of character and (as we should say) no morals, still fascinates and amuses us as she fascinated and amused her contemporaries. They were great sentimental comedians, these Peters, Elizabeths and Catherines who played their Tsarships as eccentric character parts, and produced scene after scene of furious harlequinade with the monarch as clown, and of tragic relief in the torture chamber with the monarch as pantomime demon committing real atrocities, not forgetting the indispensable love interest on an enormous and utterly indecorous scale. . . . If Byron leaves you with an impressions that he said very little about Catherine, and that little not what was best worth saying, I beg to correct your impression by assuring you that what Byron said was all there really is to say that is worth saying. His Catherine is my Catherine and everybody's Catherine.'

Byron's Catherine plays her part in Canto ix of *Don Juan*, when the young hero is sent to St Petersburg—'that pleasant capital of painted snows'—with a despatch from the front of the current war. The empress smiled at the blushing and beardless youth, though she usually preferred nervous six-foot fellows for her favourites. But she sometimes liked a boy—'And had just buried the fair-faced Lanskoi.'

> . . . the sovereign was smitten,
> Juan much flattered by her love or lust;
> I cannot stop to alter words once written,
> And the two are so mixed with human dust,
> That he who names one, both perchance may hit on:
> But in such matters Russia's mighty empress
> Behaved no better than a common semptress.
>
> An order from her majesty consigned
> Our young lieutenant to the genial care
> Of those in office; all the world looked kind,
> (As it will sometimes look with the first stare,
> Which youth would not act ill to keep in mind.)
> As also did Miss Protasoff then there,
> Named from her mystic office 'l'Eprouveuse',
> A term inexplicable to the Muse.

With these advantages, Juan grew to be a very polished Russian:

> Damsels and dances, revels, ready money,
> Made ice seem paradise, and winter sunny.

Don Juan's mother in Madrid is most pleased with her son's good fortune:

> She could not too much give her approbation
> Unto an empress, who preferred young men;
> Whose age, and what was better still, whose nation

And climate, stopped all scandal (now and then):
At home it might have given her some vexation;
But where thermometers sunk down to ten,
Or five, or one, or zero, she could never
Believe that virtue thawed before the river.

But Juan, falling ill—some said he had been poisoned by Potemkin—is urged by the physicians to travel, for the climate was too cold for him, meridian-born, to bloom in; and though this opinion made the chaste Catherine look a little grim, she had to yield.

So much did Juan's setting-off distress her,
She could not find at first a fit successor.

Byron's description of even a middle-aged Catherine is engaging:

Though somewhat large, exuberant, and truculent,
When *wroth*—while *pleased*, she was as fine a figure
As those who like things rosy, ripe and succulent,
Would wish to look on, while they are in vigour.

iv

Other Poets Play with a Few Russian Themes

THOMAS MOORE felt about Russian rulers much, apparently, as Landor did, at the time of the Holy Alliance, but wrote about them in a very different mood—lightly satirical. His *Fables for the Holy Alliance*, dedicated to Byron (1823), characterizes two of them:

When Catherine ere she crushed the Poles
Appealed to the benign Divinity,
Then cut them up in protocols
Made fractions of their very souls
All in the name of the blessed Trinity;
Or when her grandson Alexander
That mighty Northern salamander
Whose icy touch, felt all about
Puts every fire of freedom out . . . etc.

In a romantic mood, in one of his ballads, he presents The Russian Lover:

> Fleetly o'er the moonlight snows
>   Speed we to my lady's bower . . .

(A chilly place, but)

> Lovers lulled in sunny bowers
>   Sleeping out their dream of time
> Know not half the bliss that's ours
>   In this snowy icy clime. . . .

A point of view about love among the snows at quite the opposite pole from that of Don Juan's mother.

Wordsworth contributed *The Russian Fugitive* (1830), based on a story he had heard early in life, which interested him and which he thought would make a pleasant subject for an opera or musical drama. He made of it a jingling poem in four parts and forty-seven stanzas, which runs along thus: A beauty, of Gallic parentage sprung, flees the Tsar's unhallowed pursuit of her virtue, escapes through Moscow's gates to the forest hut of her foster parents, and is there sheltered until a secret refuge on an island in the midst of a swamp can be fixed up for her by a Woodman. She remains for a year in this retreat, communing with Nature and a picture of the Virgin until a Hunter in pursuit of a deer discovers her. He promises to intercede for her at court, is successful, the Tsar relents, and she is married to the Hunter. A few references to the Haughty Towers of the Kremlin create the Russian atmosphere. One stanza will probably satisfy the reader:

> From Moscow to the wilderness
>   It was my choice to come,
> Lest virtue should be harbourless
> And Honour want a home.
> And happy were I, if the Tsar
>   Retain his lawless will,
> To end life here like this poor deer,
>   Or a lamb on a green hill.

More rewarding to the reader is a poem by Robert Browning,

based like Wordsworth's, on a story he had heard years before—perhaps when he was in Russia in 1833. It was told by 'my friend the Russ', Browning says of *Ivan Ivanovitch*, which appeared in *Dramatic Idyls*, 1879.

The young Robert Browning accompanied the Russian Consul-General in England, Benckhausen, to Russia as a nominal secretary. Unfortunately Browning's letters to his sister were destroyed, and so we have only a few scattered reminiscences of this experience. He was 'strangely' impressed by the endless monotony of snow-covered pine forests through which they drove for days and nights, at the speed of six post-horses, without seeming to move from one spot. He heard many songs during this journey, and H. L. Hovelaque (*La Jeunesse de Robert Browning*, 1932) says that his ear was so good that he remembered the melodies and could hum them fifty years later, when he was in Venice, to the old prince Gagarin. In St Petersburg he saw the traditional ceremony carried out when the ice in the Neva breaks up, and the Tsar takes a glass of water from the river. In his *Letters* there is a reference to a play he wrote, of which there is no trace, entitled *Oxlya, Player-Girl*; 'it was Russian and about a fair on the Neva, and booths, and droshkies, and fish-pies and so forth, with palaces in the background'. (*Life and Letters*, ed. Mrs Sutherland Orr, 1908, note on page 61.) We have not the play, but we have the poem, based on a famous incident supposed to have occurred, according to Browning's friend, the Russ, in the time of Peter, 'when hearts were great, not small, Germanized, Frenchified'. Ivan Ivanovitch was a famous carpenter in a village on the great road from Neva's mouth to Moscow's gates of gold, who was at work one winter morning on a huge shipmast trunk, when a horse stumbled into the hamlet dragging a sledge that held a woman and a frozen corpse. The woman was the wife of Dmitri who, called to do some work in another village, had stayed behind to fight a fire, and sent his wife and three babies in the sledge. The old horse knew the way, and at night the woman lighted a twist of pitch. But the torch dwindled, and there came a terrifying sound of padding feet.

'Tis the regular pad of the wolves in pursuit of the life in the sledge!
An army they are; close-packed they press like the thrust of a wedge:
They increase as they hunt: for I see through the pine trunks ranged each side,
Slip forth new fiend and fiend, make wider and still more wide
The four-footed steady advance.

The woman is telling her story. And she is extremely articulate, explaining in detail how she tried to keep her little boys quiet, but Stepan screamed as the Satan-faced first of the band lolled out the length of his tongue and laughed and let gleam his white teeth and pried with his paws among the rugs. Then the second boy shrieks. She lets the first go: he was a weakling, and

If one must go, 'tis men
The Tsar needs, so we hear, not ailing boys! Perhaps
My hands relaxed their grasp, got tangled in the wraps:
God, he was gone! I looked: there tumbled the cursed crew,
Each fighting for a share: too busy to pursue.

But the pursuit starts up again and through the woman's attempt at justification, it is clear that she lets the wolf pluck the second boy from her grasp. She falls back upon witchcraft to excuse her cowardice:

Who knows but old bad Marpha—she always owed me spite
And envied me my births—skulks out of doors at night
And turns into a wolf and joins the sisterhood,
And laps the youthful life, then slinks from out the wood,
Squats down at door by dawn, spins there demure as erst.

The baby, though covered with her body, is frozen to death. The wise Ivan Ivanovitch is not deceived by this well-decorated tale. As she kneels before him, he strikes off her head, saying 'God it was bade—Act for me,' wipes the blood off his axe, and goes into his hut. The people clean up the mess, put head and body together in seemly fashion, and then all gather—even the Jews and some passing gypsies—into a sort of village court, waiting for the village elder and the priest, Starosta and Pope, and the landlord, the pomeshchík (Browning's accents are a little off) to come to judge the case. The landlord is rather on the side of the mother, and goes so far as to say that though his serfs are supposed to give their lives for him, they might, under certain circumstances, save themselves first. But that is far from the opinion of the old Pope, who discourses with Browningesque subtlety about motherhood. Among what monstrous things should a mother be classed, who drops her child into the jaws of the wolf?

> Because of motherhood each male
> Yields to his partner place, sinks proudly in the scale:
> His strength owned weakness, wit-folly, and courage-fear,
> Beside the female proved male's mistress—only here.

(Masculine supremacy is saved by that 'only here'). He considers Ivan Ivanovitch has acted as God's servant in executing judgment, the crowd acquiesces, the amiable landlord defers to their collective verdict. Several men, despatched to tell Ivan that he is free, find him kneeling on the floor putting the finishing touches to a model of the Kremlin, which he amuses himself carving on winter nights. His wife is baking bread, his old mother is spinning—clearly a family that takes things as they come.

> They told him he was free
> As air to walk abroad. 'How otherwise?' asked he.

It is quite a story that Browning made, after forty years, of Russian wolves and peasants. *The Englishwoman in Russia*, an interesting 1855 travel volume, tells the same story, without moral decorations.

V

Nineteenth Century Travellers: George Borrow and Lewis Carroll

THE NINETEENTH century found many travellers recording their experiences in a Russia that no longer afforded the surprising adventures celebrated so zestfully by the Elizabethans. Among them, just as an example of a typical sentimental variety, we might mention Captain Frankland, of the Royal Navy, who visited the courts of Russia and Sweden in 1830 and 1832 and published his

Narrative in 1832. He rather distinguished himself by his knowledge of Alexander 'Pouschkin', 'the Russian Byron', upon whom he called, and whose opinion on the political and social state of Russia he confusingly mingles with his own. One cannot tell whether it is he or Pushkin who considered the Russian serfs not yet in a condition either to desire or to deserve emancipation from bondage; were they freed from the yoke, the greater number would willingly return to it; 'the protection of the seigneur is like the wing of the mother extended over her helpless offspring'. One suspects the captain of this amiable figure of speech. He is delighted with his own sensitiveness to the sublime and beautiful; he all but wept with pleasure when he first gazed upon the Kremlin; and with sadness when at Tsarskoe Selo he visited the tomb of Alexander I and bent over his empty bed and deserted toilet table. (He had seen Alexander in England in 1814.)

A very different sort of visitor was in Russia from August 20, 1833, until September, 1835. This was George Borrow, who had been sent by the Bible Society of London to St Petersburg, to superintend the publication of a translation of the New Testament into Manchu. A Russian Bible Society, founded in 1813, had been suppressed in 1826. Writing from St Petersburg, October 18, 1833, to the London Bible Society, Borrow laments the state of the country in respect to religion, in what one feels to be the conventionally correct phrases: 'Without the Scriptures men can never be brought to a true sense of their fallen and miserable state and of the proper means to be employed to free themselves from the thraldom of Satan.' Only a few days before, the last remaining copies of the New Testament in Russian had been distributed. The people pursue on the Sabbath their everyday affairs and are prone to theft, being deterred only by law, not by conscience. But later on, he calls the Russians the 'best-natured, kindest people in the world' . . . 'If you go amongst them and speak their language, however badly, they would go through fire and water to do you a kindness.' And Borrow did know Russian. He found it surprising 'that so much goodness is to be found in their nature as is the case, for they are mild, polite and obliging, and in most of their faces is an expression of great kindness and benignity'.

Borrow's imagination was fired by the harmonious meeting of East and West in St Petersburg; for example, 'the Oriental cultivation of a twelve-inch beard among the middle and lower classes placed them in marked contrast with the moustached or clean-shaven patricians or foreigners'. There were new types, 'curious blendings of nationalities, unthought-of and strange to him', comments Herbert Jenkins in his *Life of George Borrow*, 1912, 'a mine of wealth to a man whose studies were never books except when they helped him the better to understand men'. St Petersburg he called 'the finest city in the world' with its palaces and the noble Neva flowing majestically through the Queen of Cities; and years later in his *Wild Wales*, 1862, Borrow wrote, 'If I had my choice of all the cities of the world to live in, I would choose St Petersburg.'

In 1835 he paid a hurried visit to Moscow—'by far the most remarkable city it has been my fortune to see'. He wished particularly to see some of the several thousand gipsies there and to hear their famous choirs, said by the Russians to be unrivalled. Some of the gipsies lived luxurious lives and married into the nobility; others lived profligately and sang in taverns. On a visit to a garden where some of the lower-class gipsies went, he stood up in his carriage and addressed them in the language of the English gipsies. A shout of wonder arose; 'greetings were poured forth in torrents of musical Romany, amongst which, however, the most pronounced cry was *ah kak mi toute karmuma*—oh how we love you'. They took him for one of their brothers from across the sea. On another occasion, he talked to them of Christ and they listened attentively. (Jenkins: *Life*.)

But when his Manchu Bibles were ready and Borrow wished to go into China with them, the Russian Government, solicitous about its good relations with China, would not grant a passport across Siberia, except on condition that he leave his Bibles behind—his only reason for going. So ended his Russian experience. But it had one significant result: the publication in St Petersburg in 1835, in an edition of 100 copies, of *Talisman: from the Russian of Alexander Pushkin. With Other Pieces*. It contained four short poems by Pushkin and three 'ancient Russian songs'. The translator was Borrow. Before this date, there had been only some *Specimens of Pushkin*, with a notice, in the *Foreign Review* in 1827; in 1832 an article in the *Foreign Quarterly Review* on Pushkin, with a few passages translated from *Poltava* and from *The Fountain of Baktchisarai*; and *Poetical Translations from the Russian Language*, W. H. Saunders, London, 1826. John Hasfeld, a Danish friend of Borrow's, presented the book to Pushkin, who expressed gratitude and regret at not having met the translateor.

This same John Hasfeld sent a letter from St Petersburg to the *Athenaeum*, published March 5, 1836, speaking of Borrow's work on the Manchu Bible and his translations of Pushkin, and adding some pungent remarks on the general ignorance about Russia, that are worth quoting. 'One would suppose,' he writes, 'after reading the *Athenaeum* for the last twelve months that St Petersburg was the veritable Ultima Thule or some few leagues beyond it. Here your journal is found in every well-furnished library, and yet not a passing word do you bestow upon us.' To repair this omission, he gives a short view of the literary scene in St Petersburg, describes the active and enterprising Russian press, and the first four volumes of a Russian *Encyclopaedia*, to be completed in twenty-four volumes, with 7,000 subscribers, and comments on the silly stuff that appears in England on the subject of Russia. 'It is quite ludicrous to read the ignorant nonsense that is poured out upon you in the way of Tours, Travels, etc., by people who have spent perhaps a month or a summer at the utmost on the banks of the Neva, and made a hurried visit to Moscow, Kieff, and some other half-dozen cities as rapidly as post-horses could carry them, under the protection and tutorship of a *valet de place*. Believe me, these valets are your only oracles; they relate and create in proportion to the gold they extract from the well-filled pockets of Englishmen; down goes absurdity after absurdity into the journals of their hungry pupils, and out they issue from Paternoster Row, to the astonishment of the untravelled and to our infinite amusement. However, as the joke is now somewhat stale, do entreat the publishers to send us a deaf and dumb man; he could only describe what he saw and might therefore stand a chance of being original by not being absurd.'

That year, at least, 1836, the *Athenaeum* seems to have been moved by Hasfeld's criticism or by some other urge, to offer a sheaf of statistics about the number of volumes in the Library of St Petersburg, called third among the libraries of Europe, with 396,155 printed volumes, 16,944 manuscripts, and the finest collection of Oriental works in the world. Other libraries have been established at Archangel, Vladimir, Vologda, and eighteen other cities. In 1835 there were imported into Russia 300,000 volumes in foreign languages. 584 original works were issued from the Russian press. 440 of the 1,682 establishments for instruction had been founded since the accession of Nicholas I (1825). Several reviews during that year of books of travel bear out Hasfeld's criticism. One (August 13) is *Travelling Opinions and Sketches in Russia and Poland*, by a felicitously named gentleman—Rayford Ramble, Esq., who, says the reviewer, 'informs the reader that he travelled in 1819, though he first communicates to the public his opinions and sketches in the present year of grace'. The reviewer ungratefully wishes that Mr Ramble had allowed not merely seventeen years, but one hundred and seventy or seventeen hundred to elapse; 'his book is utterly worthless'. Obviously the close ties of the present day between reviews and book advertising in the Press had not in 1836 been formed. A review (December 24) of the Reverend R. B. Paul's *Tour to Moscow* is gentler, calling it an unpretentious narrative, and expressing unwillingness to give the writer pain—'but why publish it? What could any man glean worth submitting to the public, in an eight-weeks' run from London to Moscow and back again? The account of the Russian baths, though not new, is the best specimen we can offer.'

Perhaps, as in our own day, observations that should have been published were not published, and those that should have not been published were published. Rayford Ramble published, Lewis Carroll did not. The author of *Alice in Wonderland* made a tour to Russia in 1867. He kept a journal, but not until 1935 was his *Russian Journal and Other Selections* published.[5] This is 'the only record of the only foreign travel by its author'. He must have talked about his journey to his friends; so we may assume a little Lewis Carroll influence upon the notions about Russia. One cannot help wishing there had been hundreds of George Borrows and Lewis Carrolls reporting about Russia. No apologies are offered for concluding a chapter that begins with *Love's Labour's Lost* with *Alice Through the Looking-glass.*

Lewis Carroll arrived in St Petersburg July 27, 1867, straightway procured a dictionary and began to make progress in the language. He transliterated an interesting Russian word meaning 'of persons defending themselves' thus: zashtsheeshtshayoushtsheekhsya—and not at all a bad job. Towards the end of his stay, he tried to make a maidservant understand something, but succeeded only by drawing pictures. His interest centred naturally in churches and monasteries, and in St Isaac's at St Petersburg and St Basil's at Moscow he was impressed by the wonderful effect of the unaccompanied chanting voices—a deacon had the most magnificent bass voice he had ever heard. The effect of the women's voices at the Strasnoi Nunnery in Moscow he found singularly beautiful. He visited Nizhni-Novgorod and found the market wonderful with the people of different races and religions, Chinese, Persian, Mohammedan. At the theatre there he saw a burlesque of 'Aladdin and the Wonderful Lamp', with first-rate acting and very fair dancing and singing. His comment on the acting suggests a detail similar to the future Stanislavsky method. 'I have never seen actors who attended more thoroughly to the drama and the other actors, and looked less at the audience.'[6]

He sketches a little scene at the hotel, where the food was very good and everything else was very bad; 'as we sat at dinner we furnished a subject of the liveliest interest to six or seven waiters, all dressed in white tunics belted at the waist, and white trousers, who ranged themselves in a row and gazed in a quite absorbed way at the collection of strange animals that were feeding before them'.

Back in Moscow, he describes 'this wonderful city, a city of white and green roofs, of conical towers that rise one out of another like a foreshortened telescope; of bulging gilded domes, in which you see *as in a looking-glass*[7] (italics mine) distorted pictures of the city; of churches which look, outside, like bunches of variegated cactus (some branches crowned with green prickly buds, others with blue and others with red and white), and which inside are hung all round with ikons and lamps, and lined with illuminated pictures up to the very roof; and, finally, of pavement that goes up and down like a ploughed field'. Passing one night through the Kremlin, he had the 'last impression of that most beautiful range of buildings in perhaps the most beautiful aspect of which it is capable—a flood of cold, clear moonlight, bringing out the pure white of the walls and towers, and the glittering points of light on the gilded domes'.

Travelling back from Russia to Prussia, he is struck with the different aspects of the soldiers—the Prussians fierce and coarse-looking, the Russians more gentle and intelligent. And he concludes with a generalization already familiar about the Russian peasant: 'with his gentle, fine, often noble-looking face (he) always suggests to me a submissive animal, long used to bearing in silence harshness and injustice, rather than a man able and willing to defend himself'. He should have remembered that long Russian word—'of people defending themselves'.

So we begin and end with travellers' tales. The poets have shed the somewhat dubious light of their imaginations upon the Russians, rulers and peasants alike. Leaving aside Lewis Carroll's looking-glass—which we may consider out-of-time, we have reached the 1830's, and are still barely on the threshold of the era when the English had a chance, through translations, to learn of the Russians from their own literature.

[1] The Russia Company, alarmed at the freedom of Fletcher's book, had it suppressed, but it appeared in abridged form in Hakluyt's *Principal Navigations*, *Voyages*, *etc.*, 1598; in *Purchas His Pilgrimes*, 1625 ed.; and as *History of Russia* in 1643 and 1657; it was edited in full for the Hakluyt Society in 1856.

[2] According to E. A. Bond, editor of the 1856 Hakluyt Society edition.

[3] According to the *Encyclopaedia Britannica*, Peter III died in the course of a scuffle during dinner. Alexis Orloff could not remember what happened.

[4] This was apparently the second translation from the Russian to appear in

England, not counting grammars. The first (1767) was a *Chronological Abridgement of Russian History* by Lomonosov—whose grammar was published in 1755.

[5] A private edition of sixty-six copies was printed several years before by the owner of the MS. notebooks, Morris L. Parrish, Dormer House, Pine Valley, N.J.

[6] Stark Young, *New Republic*, February 28, 1923, review of acting of Moscow Art Theatre, and of their method 'which professes the intention of ignoring the spectators and of producing an effect of life, as life would be seen going on if the fourth wall of a room were removed'.

[7] Alice did not go through the looking-glass until 1871.

CHAPTER II

ADVANCEMENT OF LEARNING ABOUT RUSSIA

i

In the United States up to the Civil War

IT IS usual and in the main correct to date the beginning of a really informed concern with Russian letters in England from the outbreak of the Crimean War (1854). A similarly serious interest in the United States began in the Civil War period. From then on in both countries, translations from the Russian—usually at first from German and French versions—appear with increasing frequency, until by 1887 Matthew Arnold could write that the novel of a country 'new to literature, or at any rate unregarded till lately by the general public of readers', the novel of Russia, had inherited the vogue lost by the French novel.

But for at least twenty years before the Crimean War, there had been a Russian literature worthy of attention beyond its own borders. The contrast is striking between what was being written in Russia and what was known about it in England and the United States. All the work of Lermontov, Pushkin, and Gogol had been completed. Pushkin had died in 1837; yet Carlyle in his 1840 lecture, 'The Hero as Poet', called Russia 'mute', having no voice of genius. And Arnold wrote in 1887, 'the Russians have not yet had a great poet'. By 1855 the early and brilliant work of Turgenev, Tolstoy, and Dostoevsky had been published: Turgenev's *Sportsman's Sketches*, his play *A Month in the Country*, Dostoevsky's *Poor Folk*, Tolstoy's *Childhood* and *Boyhood*, and some of his stories of the Caucasus. Russian drama had to its credit two of the great satiric comedies of nineteenth-century European literature —Griboyedov's *Woe from Wit* and Gogol's *Inspector General.* Russian modern literary criticism had made an impressive beginning with Belinsky, who died in 1848, having in his short career become 'the moving spirit of the progressive Westernizers and the herald of a new literature', as D. S. Mirsky states in his *History of Russian Literature.*

To gain some notion of what cultivated English and American readers were learning about Russian culture, one turns naturally to the periodicals that claimed to survey in articles and reviews the world of letters and politics. In the United States the *North American Review* began its long career in 1815; in England the first number of the *Westminster Review* appeared in January, 1824, the *Foreign Quarterly Review* started in 1827, and the *Athenaeum* in 1828. Out of much turning over the pages and running a finger down the indexes of some of these magazines, one can sample what they have to offer. A Philadelphia magazine, the *National Gazette and Literary Register*, has a disputed claim to have discovered Russian poetry for the English-speaking world on the basis of the publication in 1821 of a few stanzas of poetry translated by W. D. Lewis from the Russian of Neledinski-Meletski—a minor writer of sentimental pseudo-folk songs. The claim cannot stand up against the rival merits of Sir John Bowring's *Specimens of the Russian Poets*, 1821, which included translations from an impressive list of poets—Derzhavin, Karamzin, Lomonosov, Zhukovsky, Krilov, Dmitriev, Bogdanovich, Davidov, etc.[1]

In 1827 the *North American Review* (volume xxiv) reviews *Russian Tales*, from the French of Count Xavier de Maistre (published in Philadelphia, 1826). The review is ascribed to Edward Everett by Royal Gettman, who has explored the field in his dissertation on Turgenev's reputation. The tales are taken quite seriously by a serious writer in a serious magazine, as 'a faithful description of Russian manners'—by a retired French general in the Russian service. One of the tales, *Prisoners of the Caucasus*, is praised for its geographical range from the wastes of Siberia to the mountains of the Caucasus, bringing a fresh air of novelty to readers of fiction, glad to 'escape from Portman Square and Bromley Park; from the banks of the Garonne and the passes of the Apennines and all the rest of the traditional geography. . . . Something of Oriental adventure attaches itself to whatever is Russian; while the "fairy frostwork" of the North is superadded with its glittering and brilliant imagery'. It is from these mountain fastnesses that the 'whole proud family of *homo sapiens Europaeus*' comes, and there 'the most perfect models of female beauty are still supposed to be found'.

In quite another realm of discourse are political articles (having to do with Alaska and the whole west coast problem), indexed in a manner that makes us wonder if the date is 1822 or a half century or a century later, or today:

Russia:

—— danger of, to Europe. . .
to the cause of liberty . . .
—— real objects of, . . . etc.

The reader of the *North American Review* in October, 1826, could have had the refreshing experience of finding out what a Russian who had travelled in the United States and resided there for several years thought about the republican experiment.[2] The reviewer calls it a modest and sensible book and hopes it will be read to see 'with what candour and discretion the subject of a despotic prince can speak of a republic and its institutions'. The Russian's strictures are mild; he notes a certain lack of cleanliness, chiefly in taverns and inns, more noticeable in the south than in the north; for 'wherever the law sanctions or even tolerates slavery, uncleanliness is in some measure incurable, because it is the inevitable result of that social disease'. The Russian finds—with a certain regret for its cause, slavery—a higher level of cultivation and refinement among Southern planters than elsewhere. He regrets the absence of a well-organized police, and criticizes the relative weakness of executive power, and the small financial incentive to able men to enter public employment; but reminds himself that the experiment is only forty years old. The reviewer comments with old-fashioned courtesy: 'It is true that the experiment of our policy is not yet complete and conclusive; but if its defects are not at all yet brought to light, so neither are its virtues; time, as we doubt not, shall expose the principles which tend to dissolution or decay; it will also, we hope, elicit others, which are, so to speak, preservative and curative.'

The American reader was thus made aware that Russians might be gentlemanly critics. In the July, 1836, number of the *North American Review*,[3] Mrs Robinson reviews very competently a collection of *Slavic Popular Poetry*, Serbian, Polish and Russian, by Wenceslaus Olesky. The Russians, she says, have very few ballads of high antiquity in their present form, but she suspects many now current are far older than they seem. She refers to the 'heroic prose tales which make the delight of the Russian nursery'. Her generalizations are of the agreeable sort: 'the Russians have ever been a singing race'. A postillion's song is 'eminently characteristic of the cheerful, childlike, caressing disposition of the nation'. She comments on the prevalence in the language of caressing epithets and diminutives; and finds recognizable in their poetry a national trait—their almost Oriental veneration for their Tsar.

Books about Russia, chiefly from the French, are reviewed through the 'thirties and 'forties. By 1856 it was possible for the *North American Review* to list seven books for a long composite review—books all concerned with Russia—and to state that in the past ten years there had been so many publications on Russia 'that it seems difficult to say anything new with regard to that Empire'. Already, he regrets to say, 'not a few of these books seem to have been expressly written for the purpose of defaming Russia, and thus flattering the present irritation of the English and French against their enemies'. On this ground he disposes quickly of four of his items, two by French authors and two by British: 'a mere succession of invectives', for one; for the others, 'gossipy', a repetition of other people's tales, entertaining and untrustworthy gossip, etc. But *Studien über Russland* by von Haxthunsen (mistake for Haxthausen) and *Russia as It Is* by Count de Gurowski receive qualified praise, and lead the reviewer on to a discussion of serfdom in Russia. 'We knew', he writes, 'that the Russian peasantry and the working people in general were more or less enslaved; but we learn from various allusions scattered through these more modern publications, that they have not always been so, that early history knew them as a free people, and that the chains which bind them now have been gradually wound around them. No writer, however, gives us the history of this process'. The reviewer attempts to outline the history. Comparisons with Negro slavery are inevitable. The familiar argument in defence of Negro slavery—that the slaves themselves, being fed and clothed and relatively happy, do not wish to be free—he considers the strongest argument against slavery, proving as it does the human degradation of slavery. Whatever validity it might have for Negroes, it has none for the Russian serf, of the same race as his lord. He notes the distinction between crown peasants and privately owned peasants, the crown serfs living in almost free communes; comments on the serf orchestras and theatre companies, kept by wealthy landowners, and on the unsurpassed mimic talent of the Russian people. And then he gives his readers something new: a long extract from one of Turgenev's *Sportsman's Sketches*, translated from the German *Aus dem Tagebuche eines Jägers*. Turgenev's name appears in one of its many spellings —Tourgueneff. The sketch is *Lgov*, where a long conversation with a serf brings out many of the practices and results of serfdom, as they affect a typical individual. Turgenev's sketches, says the reviewer who is also familiar with some of the work, in French, of Turgenev's uncle Nicholas, are drawn 'with a masterly hand and bear the stamp of truth'; he 'unrolls a series of pictures of Russian country life of an incomparably graphic genuineness'. Since both Turgenevs are warm friends of their country, he regards their charges against the serf system as those of 'unexceptionable witnesses'. This was a nice beginning. But not till 1885 did an American translation of the *Sportsman's Sketches* appear.

Sympathy in the North was with England, not Russia, in the Crimean War—a sympathy with liberal institutions, religious freedom, popular enlightenment, as against arbitrary power, barbarism, intolerance. But this preference for England was not shared necessarily by the South. Andrew D. White, who was attaché at St Petersburg (1854–1855) to our ministry, tells us in his *Autobiography* (p. 455, 1922 ed.), that some of the visitors to the ministry were from the Southern States, and wanted to help Russia in the war with arms, their sympathy arising from what they felt was a tie between their part of the country and Russia: 'while the American Republic was blessed with slavery, the Russian Empire was enjoying the advantages of the serf system'.

Generally speaking, until the Civil War, the American reader would have derived only the sketchiest ideas about the cultural life of Russia from his magazines. In 1842 (July) he might have found in *The Dial* among serious articles on religion, theology, German philosophy and so on, a notice about 'Entertainments of the Past Winter' and a quotation from the *Revue de Paris* of December, 1839 (not the freshest of news), of a letter from St Petersburg: a glowing description of L'Ombre, a ballet at the Imperial Theatre, in which Mlle Taglioni so delighted the Emperor that he sent her a magnificent set of diamonds and turquoises —and a fine ring to M. Taglioni. The sober *Dial* readers learned that the dilettanti of St Petersburg know 'where they shall pass the greater number of their evenings this winter'.

Gleason's Pictorial Drawing-Room Companion, 'a record of the beautiful and useful in Art', and 'a weekly literary *mélange* of notable events of the day', published in Boston, gave its readers in 1854, along with Bullfinch's Greek myths and Horatio Alger's stories, seven or eight articles on Russia by a certain Professor D. Etienne de Lara, who had lived for two years in St Petersburg. According to the editor this 'excellent series of papers' contains a fund of original anecdote and weighty and valuable information about the vast Russian empire. Much of the general information seems accurate enough. But the cold and the wolves have the traditionally undue emphasis; travellers are pursued by large packs, and the unnatural mother once more throws her children to the wolves, and goes insane, instead of being decapitated.

ii

In England up to the Crimean War

THE ENGLISH reader during the thirty years before the Crimean War was in the way to be far better informed than the American. In the first number of the *Westminster Review* (1824), of which John Bowring was editor, a twenty-two page article, entitled 'Politics and Literature of Russia', presents an alarming picture of Russia as a political threat to Europe and the champion of barbarism; but finds hope for the future in the increasing number of Russian poets and historians. This part of the article is based upon material in *The Polar Star*, a Russian miscellany edited by two writers who are Anglicized as A. Bestujev and C. Rilevim—a mistake for Ryleyev, the Decembrist, executed in 1826. After the 'warlike and anonymous fragment' of the twelfth century, the hymn used in the campaign of Igor, there is nothing, says the article, until the time of Peter the Great. But then comes a succession of writers: Kantemir, Lomonosov, Sumarokov, Fonvizin; and Catherine the Great, also, who 'in the midst of her follies and crimes' had a passion for literature and could 'abstract herself from sensual indulgences to write Russian verses'. Later come Derzhavin, Dmitriev, Karamzin (whose 'history is entitled to the highest praise as a specimen of style'), Oserov ('most admired dramatist'), Krilov ('highest praise as a fabulist'), Zhukovsky, Batinshkov (evidently intended for Batyushkov), and finally Pushkin ('very original'). The achievements in the field of poetry of two ladies, Anna Bunin and Anna Volkov, are praised: 'In the Russian periodicals which lie before us we have been much struck with the lively productions of some female pens. A good hope is built on the intellectual improvement and cultivation of the mind of woman in Russia, whose influence may gradually lower the tone of despotism.' The article ends on a note of pride in 'our list' of authors—such a number of civilizing elements in a country just escaped from absolute barbarism; 'the preparation for important changes in favour of human happiness is silently going on'.

The *Foreign Quarterly Review* published long reviews of foreign books, especially French and German. The second number takes up the *Anthologie Russe*, by P. J. Emile Dupré de Saint Maure, which appeared in 1823, and the reviewer does a very thorough job, making comparisons with Bowring's *Specimens* whenever the same selections are found in both books. He does even more: both anthologies have versions of Zhukovsky's *Svetlana*, and the reviewer has a Russian friend furnish a literal English translation, to be compared with both French and English versions. The French collection contained between thirty and forty extracts from sixteen Russian authors; the French verse forms were based on literal translations from the Russian. The reviewer, continuing to be a most diligent fellow (it may have been Sir John Bowring himself, for according to Miss Muchnic he did some reviews for the *Foreign Quarterly*), then draws upon a Balbii's *Atlas Ethnographique* (1826) for an account of the language, of Church Slavonic, of literary history going back to the Expedition of Prince Igor, of folk-songs, and of the activities of the 'Northern Nero', Ivan the Terrible, in establishing schools and introducing printing. He continues with information about Lomonosov and Sumarokov and Derzhavin, whose poems (Derzhavin's) have great originality—'no small recommendation in a literature so completely one of imitation'. This reproach of imitativeness remains a standard one for some years. He praises the easy, harmonious and mellifluous versification of a very young lyric poet, Poushkin, whose *Ludmila* and *Captive of Caucasus* were included in the *Anthologie*; and mentions an original play by Griboyedov (*Woe from Wit*, evidently) not yet acted. It waited thirty years to be translated into English. Krilov the fabulist is praised, though he sometimes sins 'from excess of moral refinement'—something the Russians were not usually accused of.

The French translation of Karamzin's[4] *History of the Russian Empire* is reviewed in September, 1828—not too favourably, Karamzin being called an industrious compiler, without much judgment or taste. The earlier portion of Russian history is hitherto almost entirely unknown to the English public, continues the reviewer, who then rehearses some of Ivan IV's unparalleled cruelties until he becomes too disgusted to go on—thereby showing himself to have a much more queasy stomach than such lusty Elizabethans as Jerome Horsey.

At the end of this volume (January, 1829) the publication in Russia is listed of Pushkin's *Eugenius Oneguin.* This must have been the first seven chapters; the date of the first complete edition was 1833; as for an English translation, there was none till 1881. There is a pathetically hopeful note in an advertisement: 'A young Russian teacher who has been some time resident in London intends, if he can meet with encouragement, to publish a volume of select pieces from the best prose writers and poets, with faithful English translations.' Evidently he did not meet with encouragement. But in St Petersburg, so we learn from some foreign notes, English poetry enjoys high favour, and versifying is all the rage among the young men with and without talent—facts that clearly indicate to the commentator 'the mental fermentation that exists and which is slowly but gradually spreading over the whole extent of the vast Russian empire'.

Altogether one might feel hopeful about the prospects of English discovery of Russian literature and Russian culture. But political notes sounded at the same period, usually in connection with reviews of German and French books, have a dismal resemblance to political comment of a much later date. In September, 1828, for instance, there is a review of a French translation of a German book by a German baron formerly in the service of the Tsar: *La Dernière Heure des Turcs.* The book itself is dismissed with this comment: as contemptible as its author. But it affords the reviewer a chance to have his say about Russia, Turkey, and Greece, in a pro-Turk and anti-Russian spirit. With very little emendation, his remarks could be published in a 1953 newspaper. For example: 'The Greek revolution unquestionably owes its origin to the intrigues and influence of Russia. . . . Let Greece be really emancipated, let her be dependent neither on the Russian nor the Turk, and the wishes of all good men will be accomplished. . . . But that independence will be no more than a mockery, if Russia is permitted to have any share in protecting her. That high trust must rest in two of the most powerful and most honourable Christian States—England and France.'

There is comparatively little to be gleaned during the next few years from the *Foreign Quarterly Review*. In July, 1831, disparaging remarks about the paucity of works of *belles lettres* in Russia include a comment on the rather 'scrappy and sketchy' work of Pushkin, who 'prefers exhibiting his versatility and indolence' instead of concentrating his talents in some undertaking of at least tolerable magnitude. (He was then completing *Evgeny Onegin.*) But then we should not expect books up to the standard of the best of *our* novelists; and at least three Russian productions have begun to attract the attention of foreigners, and 'will assist in breaking down the barriers of prejudice and pave the way to an acquaintance with the literature of a country which has hitherto held out nothing sufficiently promising to entice us to encounter the labour of acquiring its language'—that 'famoust and most copius language in the world' as Queen Elizabeth had called it. In this same volume, however, is a literary notice that does more justice to Pushkin: whose 'long and eagerly expected new dramatic poem of Boris Godunov has at length appeared and for the beauty of its language and the rich vein of poetry that pervades it is generally allowed to be superior to any of his former productions'.

Less than a year later (May, 1832) there is an article on Pushkin with special attention to *Poltava*, and we are told that Pushkin is known in Europe, his name not strange to English ears, and his productions have been cursorily noticed from time to time by more than one periodical. Interesting in this article are comparisons with Byron: *Onegin* is considered inferior to *Beppo* and *Don Juan*. A chance to compare *Poltava* and Byron's *Mazeppa* (Mazeppa being a character in both) is given by the translation of three and a half pages from the dialogue between Mazeppa and Maria. A thirty-three-line passage, rendered in rhymed couplets, is given from the *Fountain of Baktchisarai*. *Ruslan and Ludmila* is called a charming legendary romance.

Some inferior Russian romances and tales are reviewed in 1838; they are not what the English reader might like to have out of Russia, imitating as they do the worst of German horrors and Parisian boudoir scenes when they might have given us realistic and interesting pictures of Russian daily life; a Russian *Vicar of Wakefield*, for instance, or something in the line of Jane Austen, or 'even' Miss Mitford, or something finely touched like Miss Edgeworth's work. It is pertinent to note here that Turgenev, then twenty years old, might very well have been reading Miss Edgeworth. 'It is possible, nay probable,' he is quoted as saying (*A Book of Sybils*, by Anne Thackeray Ritchie, p. 140) 'if Maria Edgeworth had not written about the poor Irish of the County Longford and the squires and squirees, it would not have occurred to me to give a literary form to my impressions about the classes parallel to them in Russia. My brother used, in pointing out the beauties of her unambitious works, to call attention to their extreme simplicity and to the distinction with which she treated the simple ones of the earth.' One hopes that the reviewer lived long enough to read some of the *Sportsman's Sketches* and to recognize the realization of his wish. He would have had to wait sixteen years for a few samples in English in *Fraser's Magazine*.

In 1839, 1841 and 1842 factual information of considerable extent about Russian books and authors of the eighteenth and nineteenth centuries became available. The *Foreign Quarterly Review* furnished a Table in October, 1842 ,of authors and artists living and dead, that included Pushkin, Krilov, Griboyedov, Karamzin, Derzhavin, etc., omitted Lermontov, and gave Gogol the name of Ivan instead of Nicholas. In July, 1841, the *Westminster Review* examined two Russian reference works on literature and offered a tolerably complete general sketch of Russian literature in its various departments. And in 1839 a history of Russian literature, with a lexicon of Russian authors, by Dr Friedrich Otto, was translated from the German by George Cox, Fellow of New College, Oxford. The translator's preface is very interesting. Written in 1837, it expresses the hope of putting into execution a long-since projected journey to Russia—not carried out, for he died before the book was published. He starts out by referring to the 'constant theme of declamation among a numerous and influential party in this country'—the risk of the kingdoms of Europe being subjugated 'by the barbarism of Russia'. He thinks, however, that it is not the barbarism of Russia which is to be dreaded, but her civilization; and goes on to speak of the extensive efforts of the government to spread the knowledge of the Russian language through out the empire; so that it promises to become the vernacular as well as the medium of literary composition to a population of sixty millions. This should interest Europe, and particularly England, the great political rival of Russia; it might be worth her while to acquaint herself with the progress that has been made in intelligence and refinement by a nation she vainly affects to despise as rude and uncivilized, when in fact she has little real knowledge upon the subject. He is surprised and disappointed that no one followed in the footsteps of Dr Bowring, whose translations from the Russian poets were beautiful enough to incite others; it is deplorable that hardly half a dozen persons in Great Britain understand perfectly the language spoken and written in the largest and most politically important country in Europe. He has done this translation to stimulate a desire to be acquainted with a language in which so many excellent works have been written—and so much *original* work: 'much of Russia's poetry is not less new or less beautiful than her music. There is the same sweetness, the same richness, and the same plaintive melancholy about them both'. It comes as a bit of a shock that the late George Cox considers that the one great and important end of the study of languages, as of all other scientific pursuits, is and ought to be the endeavour to throw additional light upon the truth of Revelation. We realize suddenly that we are back in the years before Darwin. But the concluding sentence strikes a familiar contemporary note: he disclaims responsibility for the political bias (if any be discoverable) which may exist in this book.[5]

The curious reader, looking over the list of authors, will be inclined to regret that the Germans were first in the field and established their system of transliteration; so that we meet Schtscherbatoff and Tatischtscheff and Wsewoloschskj ('see Chmelnizkj') and Dawüdoff (Deniss Wassiljewitsch) and Krüloff (Iwan Andrejewitsch). Some of these versions persist for many decades. As late as 1874, Henry James writes Iwan Turgenew if he is reviewing a German translation, or Tourguénieff, if it is a French one. Interest in the problem of transliteration resulted in 1867 in some very whimsical exchanges in the *Athenaeum* between the Russian language and the English. 'There is one letter of the Russian alphabet which the Germans can render only by heaping seven of theirs together. Written according to the fashion of Cyril, it wears a graceful and intelligible air. In its Teutonic dress it offers the uncouth appearance of SCHTSCH.'

iii

Travel Books

TRAVELLERS' TALES, whether the traveller were French, German, or English; whether a linguistically competent reviewer reported upon them after reading the original French or German or a translation; and whether the traveller laid claim to a grounding in history or politics or not: these bulk much larger as sources of information about Russia than such books and articles as have been singled out for notice in the preceding pages. 'Few readers', remarks the *Foreign Quarterly Review* in 1843, 'have not rambled through Russia very lately under the guidance of the amiable, the sharp-sighted, and plain-spoken Kohl.' J. G. Kohl was one of the German travellers. A French one (accompanied by his wife) was Xavier Hommaire de Hell, whose *Les Steppes de la Mer Caspienne, le Caucase, la Crimée, et la Russie Méridionale, Voyage Pittoresque, Historique et Scientifique* (Paris, 1843–1846) was reviewed in July, 1846. The reviewer is convinced that till recently most erroneous notions prevailed in England on almost everything about the internal condition of the Russian Empire. It was remote and vast, its armies numerically great, its princes and nobles who travelled in the West left an impression of lavish wealth, it had struck down the Napoleonic eagles, cowed Turkey, and 'aspired to wrest the empire of India from the grasp of Great Britain'. But that is all false, and Hommaire, de Custine, Lacroix and others are correcting the falsifications. 'To seem the thing it is not *is* the grand problem of Russian existence—personal, social and political.' The impression produced is the result of elaborate and successful cultivation of all the arts of imposture: 'barren of invention, the Muscovites are quick imitators, and the mendacious spirit that characterizes their government pervades likewise every phase and product of their spurious civilization'. The reviewer is rather sentimental, waxing eloquent over the charm of a part of the narrative contributed by Mme Hommaire, and saying much about wedded bliss that seems as irrelevant to the correction of falsifications about Russia as many a later digression from the same subject.

The *Athenaeum* from the beginning of its career in January, 1828, paid a good deal of attention to travel books, quoting extensively. The tone of the reviews was likely to be sceptical. The author of a travel journal, Dr A. B. Granville, is called a bit simple-hearted; he was, however, complex-titled—M.D., F.R.S., F.L.S., M.R.I., F.G.S. and M.R.A.S. He had been in St Petersburg in 1801, and was therefore able on this second visit in 1827 to take note of changes in Russian society. There were now not merely the classes of nobles and serfs, but functionaries, heads of institutions, minor nobility, etc. They seemed to the doctor like similar groups in the first capitals of Europe, in their elegance and ease of manners, though a foreigner could only judge of them as they appeared among their friends and guests; 'what they may be with their inferiors I know not'. Their hospitality to 'persons well recommended and properly introduced, be they Russians or foreigners, is unbounded'. The ladies are accomplished, often speaking French, German and English; informed about the literature and history of Europe; and they display in easy conversation 'exquisite *finesses d'esprit*'. Dr Granville liked the food; but the reviewer recalls that a Dr Clarke, author of a book on Russia, had hated it; and he reflects that similar reports might be made about

English food, if one traveller had dined with the Duke of Devonshire and another with 'a decayed gentleman or a rising attorney'. Dr Granville he considered over-enthusiastic about the emperor; 'for when we have simply mentioned that he combines the characters of Titus, the Antonines, Trajan, Justinian, Alfred and Henri Quatre, with a great many spick and span excellencies of his own, and that he has positively no vice—our readers will probably be satisfied without our going into details, that he has no intention of reaching Constantinople this season'.

There was fear of Russian intentions in that direction. Colonel George de Lacy Evans wrote a pamphlet in 1828, *On the Designs of Russia*, which 'stated the case against Russia in the fullest term and remained as an authority to be cited frequently by later alarmists'.[6] A 'non-alarmist' composed a reasoned refutation of Colonel Evans's pamphlet, and this was favourably reviewed in the *Athenaeum*.[7]

The June, 1830, number finds amusing and instructive a book by Edward North, *Travels in Russia*, intended by the author 'to give some account of Russia as it is and not as it is represented to be'. A *History of Russia*, in the Cabinet Cyclopaedia series, proved very disappointing to the reviewer (September, 1836), who called the author 'wholly unqualified', 'ignorant of the very elements of the subject he here professes to treat and unable, we suspect, even to read the language of the earlier records in which that history is written'. A rather surprising note is sounded in a review (October, 1837) of a French compilation of official documents on education in Russia: there actually is a system of national education in Russia, and there isn't any in England—may the new reign see one established! That Russia should be ahead of England is a humiliating thought. The Reverend R. Lister Venables, M.A., author of *Domestic Scenes in Russia in a Series of Letters describing a year's residence in that country, chiefly in the Interior*, is worthy of notice because he did reside in the 'interior'—so little known. There are long quotations, and the verdict: 'we have shown him to be unaffected and reasonably amusing, and now part from him in good humour'. (February, 1839.)

The Marquis de Custine had written a book about Russia, *Russia in* 1839. This has very recently been retranslated into English, provided with an introduction by a general who is also an ex-ambassador from the United States to the Soviet Union, and published in 1951, as part of the evidence that the Kremlin was 'brooding' over a century ago. (See the review in the New York *Times* book section, April 1, 1951.)[8] *The Athenaeum* reviewed this book when it was first published. In March, 1844 (things moved at a leisurely pace in those days), it reviewed *A Russian's Reply to the Marquis de Custine's Russia in* 1839. *The Athenaeum* was not surprised to discover that the Marquis was not an impartial reporter. '*The Athenaeum* always laughed at the Russophobia, and our countrymen appear at last to be ashamed of it, so that they may now be content to hear Russia vindicated. Whoever, therefore, has read the Marquis de Custine's work, let him read also the present Reply—which by turns is jocose, sarcastic, reflective, indignant, recriminative, argumentative, illustrative, stout in denial, fertile in repartee, but not sufficiently abundant in documentary and matter of fact evidence.' The quotations from the Russian's reply are singularly appropriate to the mid-twentieth century: 'It would appear that we Russians are endowed with a most remarkable spirit of ubiquity, and most profound views. Russia is at the bottom of every commotion and manifested in a thousand places. Is there a disturbance in Paris or a rising in Ireland? If Russia is not the cause, she has her allotted share in it.' There follow examples of her intervention. To the Chinese, 'she sent cannon on the backs of hippogriffs'—an early name for a new projectile, perhaps. 'Like a polypus with a thousand feet, she everywhere extends the snares of her political espionage.'

In September of 1844 *Revelations of Russia: or the Emperor Nicholas and His Empire in* 1844. *By one who has seen and describes.* is reviewed in the *Athenaeum.* The reviewer mentions the abundant books on Russia of late—in number out of proportion to the amount of knowledge imparted. The particular revelations, with all their air of authenticity, could not possibly have been gathered together except by report. There is undisguised partisanship, devoted to proving everything rotten. The field, the reviewer sums up, has been left largely to tourists, whose sketches are graphic, lively, *outward*, gossipy, biased. The Marquis de Custine, for example, carried his theory with him and visited Russia for confirmation. The result: 'Russia still lies a huge, dark, uncomfortable secret on the frontiers of Europe'. The date—a necessary reminder—is September 28, 1844.

A few other examples from this period, taken from *Athenaeum* reviews of books, will further illustrate both the confusing and contradictory pictures brought back by the travellers, and the parallels with similar modern confusions and contradictions. Perhaps a digression here may be permitted: that while a 'cold war' is on in the years following World War II, adverse comments are welcomed, and revived from these records of over a century ago; but an equally impressive list of favourable comments could be culled from these records. In the next chapter we shall see how the Crimean War led the English to seek the facts and impressions that would discredit their enemy; whereas during the Civil War the Americans sought for material that threw an amiable light on their friend. Since perfected methods of communication and propaganda did not exist in those days, as they do in our advanced era of international goodwill, lots of things slipped through into print that were inconsistent with the respective attitudes of hostility and of friendship.

To return to the illustrations. Anthony C. Sterling, author of *Russia under the Autocrat Nicholas I* (reviewed in the *Athenaeum* March, 1846), declared the whip to be the type of Russian civilization; and in a chapter on Russian literature, he helped promote cultural amity by remarking that the names of Russian authors are 'for the most part unknown in Western Europe and lead us to wish with Voltaire that the Russians had more sense and fewer consonants'. Sterlings 'systematic account' had been 'selected and translated' from an article in the *Conversations Lexicon der Gegenwart* by I. G. Golovine. Robert Bremner made a visit to Russia in 1836, and in 1839 published a book called *Excursion in the Interior of Russia, including Sketches of the Character and Policy of the*

Emperor Nicholas, etc. He supports his claim to be believed in a way familiar to us of the present day: His talks with Russians, he tells us, were held 'under circumstances which enabled them to throw off the mask which in their own country few of them can dare to dispense with. To all who know what Russia really is, it is unnecessary to say that it is not *in Russia* that the true state of opinion among the higher classes of that country can best be learned'; therefore he relies on contact with Russians outside of Russia, and claims to be free of bias.

The Russophobia at which the *Athenaeum* declared it had always laughed (March, 1844) has been made the subject of a special study, in a Harvard University Press publication, 1950, by J.H. Gleason, entitled, *The Genesis of Russophobia in Great Britain: A Study of the Interaction of Policy and Opinion*. The period under examination is 1815 to 1841; influencing both policy and opinion were such events as the Greek and Polish revolutions, and Near-East, Middle-East and Persian-Afghanistan crises. Mr Gleason concludes that during much of the period in question, Great Britain's policy was, in the main, more provocative than Russia's. 'British nationals laboured in the Balkans, in the Caucasus, in Afghanistan and Persia, as well as in Constantinople, Syria and Egypt, far more efficaciously than did their Russian counterparts, and it was the British, not the Russian, sphere of influence which advanced. British statesmen insisted that their aims were defensive, but had the Russians appealed to the criterion of deeds rather than words, which their British contemporaries applied against them, an impartial judge must probably have rendered a verdict in their favour.' (Page 3.) After the crushing of the Polish revolt, Nicholas I, kindly regarded at the advent of his reign, was depicted as a monster in human form, and 'the new stereotype took the public imagination.... An estimate of Nicholas and his ambitions became a conventional element in the travel literature on Russia'. (Page 134.) Retroactively, Alexander and Catherine suffered revisions in their reputations. Although fervent Russophobes were probably a small minority of the nation, the articulate sentiment in English magazines and newspapers was firmly anti-Russian during the period Mr Gleason studied. After an adjustment of differences that had threatened war over the Near Eastern question, achieved in the Straits Convention, anti-Russian propaganda died down for a few years. 'Yet the stereotyped estimate of Russian character and purpose persisted, hibernating till a new crisis developed in 1853.' (Page 274.) Then the sentiments of the Thirties were refurbished for the new situation. And 'the solidification of a hostile stereotype with regard to Russia occurred in 1853 as rapidly as it did only because its mould had been well fashioned two decades before'. (Page 276.)

Mr Gleason finds the roots of the Russophobia in private interests, domestic partisan politics, the character of the information available about Russia, personalities (such as the inflammatory David Urquhart, who did wonders with the seizure of the British ship *Vixen* in the Black Sea), propaganda, the accident of events and social and political philosophies. Paradoxically enough, increasing knowledge about Russia in the travel books, the accounts of exploration in Central Asia, and the official reports of Russian naval and military strength, 'tended to make her threat seem more concrete and more imminent, but was not sufficient in most quarters to demonstrate her weakness. It contributed notably to the developing stereotype'. (Pages 284 ff.) A study such as this of Mr Gleason's is a guide and a warning to anyone attempting to estimate the role of literature in promoting understanding between nations. One's first reaction is a despairing question—what chance has a Pushkin in so complex a pattern of influences? But Pushkin was at least soon to be given a chance.

iv

A Link Between English and Russian Culture: Thomas Budge Shaw

A COMMENT on Russian literature in the *Athenaeum*, April, 1846, suggests a continuing state of ignorance, in spite of the few translations that have been noted. And this comment appears *after* three important articles by Thomas Budge Shaw (1845), devoted to Pushkin's life and works, had been published by Blackwood's *Edinburgh Magazine*. The comment occurs in the course of a review of what is called one of the best Russian periodicals, published in St Petersburg, 'The Library for Reading', or Biblioteka dlya Tcheniya,—'an outlandish title'. Although English literature goes by steam packet to St Petersburg, 'of Russian literature the merest glimmering, a few faint rays, have as yet reached this country; the reason for which, it will probably be said, is that it is so dull and lustreless as to have scarcely any rays at all'. The magazine is then criticized as having too little material on national themes; 'even Russian readers themselves must desiderate more literary produce of genuine home growth, as they must be nearly surfeited with translations from foreign works of fiction'. Probably the criticism of the magazine was deserved. But the general comment on Russian literature—in view of its achievements by this time—is funny: to expect a Russian Fielding would be too much; perhaps one might hope for a Russian Scott, would be content with an Edgeworth or Bremer.[9] The writer was evidently not content with a Pushkin and a Gogol, or perhaps knew nothing about them.

In Blackwood's *Edinburgh Magazine*, July–August, 1845, appeared three articles on Pushkin's *Life and Works*, by Thomas Budge Shaw. Shaw is called by Carl Lefevre (*Gogol's First Century in England and America*, 1841–1941, University of Minnesota doctoral dissertation) one of the first important links between English and Russian culture in the nineteenth century, indicating 'the outline of a pattern that we shall see again: that of a man who has a personal and circumstantial interest in Russia and Russian literature, interpreting it to the Western European nations'. Shaw, born in 1813, was a B.A. of Cambridge University, who visited Russia in 1840, settled in St Petersburg and from 1842 was adjunct professor of English literature at the Imperial Alexander Lyceum and, after 1853, tutor and professor of English to the grand dukes till his death in 1862. The Blackwood's articles, with copious translations from Pushkin's lyric poetry, were written in St Petersburg. In 1847 (October), again in Blackwood's, he published the first English translation of Gogol's story *The Portrait*. (Reprinted in the American *Living Age*, 1847.) Shaw's account of Pushkin—'undeniably and essentially the great national poet of Russia'—is in what one might call an 'elevated' style, with much about the laws of nature and of destiny that regulated the march of Pushkin's career. Noting that Pushkin's grandfather was an African—Annibal, the Tsar's 'sable protégé' (his great-grandfather was an Abyssinian)—he comments: 'the cold blood of the north, transmitted to his veins from the rude warrior of Germany, was thus mingled with that liquid lightning which circles through the fervid bosom of the children of the desert'. There is a careful account of his education and of his main works, and his last hours are described in a letter quoted from Zhukovsky to Pushkin's father: 'it is generally known, even in England, that Pushkin was mortally wounded in a duel'. Nothing is said of Pushkin's political views, but that is not surprising, as Shaw acknowledges help from the rector of the Imperial University of St Petersburg, who was also editor of the periodical, *The Contemporary*, from which Shaw quotes.

The second and third articles contain a number of translations: *Feast of Peter the First*, *Lay of the Wise Oleg*, *André Chenier*, *The Mob*, *The Black Shawl*, *Napoleon*, *The General*. If there is enough interest, concludes Shaw, he might continue with extracts from the narrative poems. But apparently there was not. It is worth noting that resemblances between Pushkin and Byron are not labelled 'imitations'.

Commenting on *Evgeny Onegin*, Shaw finds it the fullest embodiment in Russian literature of the nationality of the country—an expression of 'those apparently discordant elements the union of which composes that hard riddle, the Russian character'. Though he finds it a riddle, as many before and since have persisted in finding it, he was at least sitting down in St Petersburg with the riddle, and trying to solve it in one of the most promising places—the work of a great national poet. When he turns to English attitudes towards Russia, he becomes rather excited. Pushkin's poem, *To the Slanderers of Russia*, which he translates, is a reply to 'the hackneyed calumnies against his country, repeated with such nauseating uniformity, and through so long a period of time, in wretched verse, or more wretched prose, in the leading articles of obscure provincial newspapers and on the scaffolding of obscure provincial hustings'. Whatever the merits or demerits of the role played by Russia in the events referred to by Pushkin—relating to Poland—Shaw thinks the tirades come with poor grace from England and France. He goes on: 'there is a very excellent and venerable proverb which expressed the imprudence of the practice of throwing stones, when indulged in by the inhabitant of an abode composed of a vitreous substance, not to mention a still more grey-bearded and not less wise saw, specifying, in terms rather forcible than dignified, the impolicy of the pot alluding in an opprobious manner to the blackness which characterizes the sitting part of its fellow utensil, the kettle'. And he thinks Pushkin justified in asking whether England and France had the clean hands and clear conscience to justify them in their 'incessant and insolent attempt to sit in judgment on their European sister'. 'We certainly think that the recollection of the Afghan War, the bombardment of Copenhagen, of the splendid exploits of Whig policy and Whig non-intervention in Spain, might make England a little more modest and a little less inclined to declaim against the wickedness of other nations.' It did not—then or later. Mr Shaw was asking too much of any nation.

This survey suggests that up to about 1855, as since, it was possible, but not easy, to find reliable information about Russian life and literature. Public interest was in a languishing state until in England, the Crimean War, and in the United States, the emancipation of the Russian serfs and our own Civil War, stimulated deep political interest in Russia.

[1] Bowring had planned a history of Russian literature, but decided to publish first 'a few translations of the poetry of a people, the political influence of whose government on the rest of Europe has been long moving with gigantic strides, and will soon be more sensibly felt'. From Bowring's Introduction.

[2] Review of 'A Sketch of the Internal Condition of the U.S.A. and of Their Political Relations with Europe'. By a Russian. Translated from the French, by an equally anonymous American.

[3] Talvi, wife of Dr Edward Robinson, published in the Biblical Repository of Andover, Mass., in 1834, 'Historical View of the Languages and Literatures of the Slavic Nations'. Republished in book form, enlarged, in New York, 1850. Called a remarkable work of scholarship by Leo Wiener (*Anthology of Russian Literature*).

[4] Karamzin's *Tales from the Russian* had been translated and published in London, 1804.

[5] Wiener (*Anthology*) says of Cox's translation of Otto's *History*—'adds a number of its own inaccuracies to the blunders of the German original'.

[6] J. H. Gleason, *Russophobia in Great Britain*, page 102.

[7] *A Few Words on our Relations with Russia: including some remarks on a recent publication by Col De Lacy Evans entitled 'Designs of Russia'*. By a Non-alarmist, 1828.

[8] The 1951 translation, under the title *Journey for Our Time*, is by Phyllis Penn Kohler. There have been several English translations of Custine's Journals, including one published in the United States in 1854; this was abridged, but at that, is twice the length of the 1951 version, according to the New York *Nation*, September 29, 1951. The 1844 *Athenaeum* reviewer is brief and brisk in disposing of the marquis as an impartial reporter. Its contemporary, the *Quarterly Review*, in the same month of March, 1844, devoted fifty pages to a scathing exposure of Custine's glaring inaccuracies and misrepresentations, with precise quotations, French and English, and documentation from other, reliable sources, that gave the marquis the lie direct. Custine appears, in his less than three months' stay, to have taken from the gossip of others, or invented for himself, a vast deal of nonsense. The *Quarterly* reviewer has a field day with his contradictions. Abridgments no doubt eliminate many of them, and make the story more plausible, and more effective as propaganda. Custine, says the *Quarterly* reviewer, saw a spy in every acquaintance, never thought of the emperor but as the head jailer of an immense prison; nevet got into his carriage without vivid apprehension that the Muscovite on the box might turn out an *Agent de Police*, and the drive find its termination in Siberia. As late as 1861, Sutherland Edwards, author of a surprisingly good book, *The Russians at Home*, was indignant over the 'monstrous misrepresentations' of Custine, who, as made clear by the *Quarterly Review*, pretended to have seen and heard things he did not see and did not hear.

[9] Frederika Bremer's *Tales* were translated from the Swedish in 1846.

CHAPTER III

THE CRIMEAN WAR AND THE CIVIL WAR: HOSTILITY AND FRIENDSHIP AND THEIR EFFECT IN PROMOTING KNOWLEDGE OF RUSSIA AND HER CULTURE

i

Crimean War in England

IN MARCH, 1854, France and Great Britain allied themselves against Russia; in July invasion of the Crimea was decided upon; in September the combined forces landed at Eupatoria and began to advance towards Sevastopol; bombardment commenced October 17, continuing through a winter terrible to both Allied and Russian forces; the final assault was delivered September 8, 1855. Meanwhile Nicholas I had died. Florence Nightingale had come upon the scene and established her hospital work. Leo Tolstoy had fought in one of the hottest spots—the famous Fourth Bastion. Before the Treaty of Paris was signed in February, 1856, Tolstoy had published his three sketches—*Sevastopol in December*, *in May* and *in October*. The Treaty of Paris had (to quote the *Encyclopedia Britannica*) 'as sole tangible result the exclusion of Russian warships from the Black Sea—and even this endured only for fifteen years'.

The Crimean war awakened curiosity in England about the enemy, and there was a demand for details about Russian life and manners. It was supplied in part by garbled versions of some of the work of Lermontov, Gogol, and Turgenev—sometimes without acknowledgment to the authors. *Sketches of Life in the Caucasus* (1853) gave no credit to Lermontov's *A Hero of Our Times*, but the first complete and acknowledged version of that famous novel, translated by David Bogue, appeared in 1854, and another version, *Hero of Our Days*, translated by Theresa Pulszky, came out as No. 112 of the Parlour Library that same year. Gogol's fortunes were even more mixed. *Home Life in Russia* (1854), 'by a Russian noble', 'revised by the editor of *Revelations of Siberia*', appeared in two volumes. The material was largely stolen from Gogol's *Dead Souls*, by this editor who was a Pole. Carl Lefevre, who has thoroughly explored Gogol's fortunes in England, remarks: 'We shall see other Poles and other instances of a Polish bias in connection with comments on Russian literature and on Gogol, early in the twentieth century'. The preface was full of 'blatant falsehoods' (see *English Bookman*, October, 1932, v. 83: 66–70). There is a statement, that falls familiarly upon our modern ears, that the author's name cannot be divulged, because he is still anxious to return to his native country and is aware that avowal of his handiwork and such a display of his satirical powers might serve as a passport to 'the innermost regions of the Siberian wilds'. The editor adds another now long-familiar touch: the work requires no verification, its genuineness being avouched by almost every line. The *Athenaeum* (December 2, 1854, page 1154) promptly exposed the fraud in a review, noting that for a dozen years *Dead Souls* had been one of the most popular books in Russia. The reviewer was relying on Prosper Mérimée, who in his *Nouvelles* (Paris 1852) had a long critique of *Dead Souls*.

This exposure did not stop the *British Quarterly Review*, in the spring of 1855 (vol. 21, January–April), from publishing an anonymous article entitled 'Russians at Home, Past and Present', based upon the steal from Gogol. Lefevre comments: the anonymous author was 'definitely seeking information which he could use in denouncing and reviling the enemy'; for he says that 'everything relating to home life or intimate history of our bitter enemy—and we may add the enemy of liberty and the enemy of humanity—is at this moment deeply and painfully interesting'. He seeks in his discussion of *Home Life in Russia* to provoke disgust, to stir hatred of the entire Russian people as a nationality or race. Yet he claims to be without malice in saying: 'The time has come when a stand must be made against a false and faithless Tsar and a nation proved by ancient and modern authorities to be of a nation of liars, drunkards, plunderers and slaves. In conclusion we say that, if the Russians be not vanquished and driven back now, seventy millions of slaves may at no distant day be prompt and apt instruments in imposing a bondage like their own on the civilized world.' Mr Lefevre ways that this is the only article he found that attacks the whole Russian people—not just the Tsar, or the Government, or the ruling class. The only article, of course, in the Crimean War period. Many even more terrifying vilifications can be found later, and we have seen examples of earlier ones. The most melancholy thought is that one would not be surprised any day to find it resurrected as an example of how even in 1855 the truth was known about the Russians. And all this was based on an 'arrogant literary forgery'.

Dublin came to the rescue of Gogol. In the *Dublin University Magazine* (September, 1855, vol. 46, pp. 298–308), appeared a translation of Gogol's charming story, *Old World Landowners*, along with an understanding and humane discussion, as Mr Lefevre calls it, of the questions of despotism and censorship in Russia and their effects upon writers; and of Gogol as a social critic. His early life in Little Russia is described, and there is the first English comment, good though brief, on his famous drama, *The Inspector General*.

Turgenev is the third Russian—and this time it is a living author, not yet very far along in his career—from whose work information was sought concerning the enemy. The August 1854 number of *Fraser's Magazine for Town and Country* published 'Photographs from Russian Life', and these photographs turn out to be by M. Ivan 'Tourghenieff', selected from a French translation, *Mémoires d'un Seigneur Russe*, by Ernest Charrière (Paris, 1854).[1] The article offers lengthy and readable selections from some of the best of Turgenev's *Sportsman's Sketches*: 'Khor and Kalinych'; a passage from the scene of the singing contest in the tavern ('The Singers'); and another from the sketch of the landowner who beat time to the blows being inflicted on his butler

('Two Country Gentlemen'); another from 'Radilov and His Wife'; and another from the sketch of Arkady Pavlovich Pyenotchkin, the Frenchified gentleman with the vicious bailiff ('The Agent'). Other stories are referred to—'The Village Doctor', 'The Village Lovers', 'The Russian Hamlet'; and special mention is made of the beautiful 'Byezhin Meadow': 'There is a chapter in which some boys, watching horses, recount around a night fire in the steppes the various superstitions of the country, that is full of poetry and racy with nationality'. Turgenev himself is described as a nobleman singularly exempt from prejudice; not a professed writer, and no seeker after effects, but with a fine perception of the beauties of scenery and of the peculiarities of human character; 'none the less an artist because a practised eye will detect the absence or even the want of art'. This is perhaps the first definition of the quality of Russian realism. As for the picture of the serf system, those who seek the artificial stimulus of horrors or 'who desire that the simpler pictures of slave life shall be set in a connected narrative of refined cruelty and pain, as in the work of Mrs Stowe', will not care for the passages quoted. Both bright and dark sides are given, but the final impression is 'a profound conviction of the iniquity of serfdom as an institution and of its degrading effects on the subject as well as on the master. The book is a Russian *Uncle Tom's Cabin* without its blood and gunpowder.'

The sketches inspired in the reviewer some general reflections about Russia, interesting as generalization about an enemy in a war climate of opinion. After all the travel books, one is surprised to be told: 'it might be said, without much exaggeration, that we know as little of the interior life of Russia as that of Dahomey or Timbuctoo'. For this situation, blame rests in part on the jealousy of the Russian Government, in part on the fact that the country is not tempting to travellers. And then the travellers are not always the best judges or the keenest observers; the English especially are often slaves of egoism and national prejudice; whereas the Germans, though more liberal, are 'less locomotive', and often too preoccupied with some theory or other to perceive faithfully what they philosophize about. And the language is an almost unsurmountable barrier. Then, the books professing to give an account of the people are almost without exception 'tinged with political feeling'. The Russians are nevertheless worth studying, being, 'like all semi-civilized nations', full of character: the nobles, with their original barbarism and recent artificial polish; the middle class, struggling to maintain a false and difficult position; the serfs and peasants, a mixture of simplicity and cunning, but with a 'peculiar goodness of heart which not even the detestable institutions under which they live have succeeded in stifling or corrupting'. But they must be studied outside of the cities.

Household Words (conducted by Charles Dickens) published in 1855 (March 3, March 31, April 21 and November 24), under the titles 'The Children of the Tsar', 'More Children of the Tsar', 'Nothing like Russia Leather', and 'A Singing Match', some summaries and quotations based on *Mémoires d'un Seigneur Russe*—by this time translated into English. All but the fourth are duly credited to 'M. Tourghenief'. Reading them had aroused the 'irresistible temptation to scatter broadcast by means of our columns a few of the sketches which it gives of Russian life. Some of these are touching groups, making us conscious, after all, of the bond of common brotherhood which urges us individually to fraternize with individual members even of a hostile nation'. In the third number 'we will again call on M. Tourghenief to illustrate the social condition of Russia'. Some of the scenes are 'astounding', and the whole series 'confirms the accounts previously current of the barbaric civilization, the feudal tyranny, and the many instances of personal merit', under the control of the 'world's arch-enemy, the emperor Nicholas'. (March 3, 1855.)

What else did the reader of *Fraser's Magazine* find in that volume No. 50, July–December, 1854, which contained Turgenev's sketches? There are, of course, political and military articles. Statistics and tables concerning Russian garrisons are enlivened by such political comments as this: Peter the Great was admirable, but the House of Romanoff is smitten with the curse of madness, and history will gibbet this most sanctimonious Vandal—Nicholas I.

Regret is expressed that the English had not given the people of Odessa a week to get out and then bombarded the city 'without intermission till nothing remained to mark the site of the southern capital but a heap of hot ashes'. 'Russian Defeats and Their Effect on Europe' is an historical survey with the theme of justified distrust of Russia ever since the peace of 1815, all shades of political opinion in England agreeing, at least, upon mistrust, if not apprehension, of Russia. Lord Castlereagh, in the 1815–1822 period, yielded too much to Russia; 'the noble Lord did not use language sufficiently English or sufficiently anti-Russian'. There is much about the integrity and independence of Turkey; about the spread of the empire under Peter and Catherine; about sinister designs on British possessions in India, and the Russian effort to acquire an influence over Persia. In brief, the Russian government is one 'whose progress from the earliest ages has been marked by treachery, by fraud and by the most insidious corruption'. The article takes from the Tsar and the Russian people any credit for the victory of 1812, and gives it to the early and unprecedented winter. An ill-natured little footnote states that there is no word signifying 'gentleman' in Russian, and it is therefore not surprising that the Emperor knows so little of what becomes a gentleman.

It must have come as a surprise to the reader of *Fraser's*, in view of the general barbarism of the Russians from the ungentlemanly Tsar on down, to find that some English prisoners captured by the Russians had such a pleasant time. He would have discovered this in a review of *The English Prisoners in Russia: a Personal Narrative of the First Lieutenant of H.M.S. 'Tiger'*, by Alfred Royer, Lieut R.N., 1854. The lieutenant fell in a big way for the Russian officers and the court ladies, and enjoyed himself as a gentleman among other gentlemen. The reviewer is disgusted at the way he was taken in by the smiles, teapots, sealing-wax, sherry and so on of the generals and grand dukes. On one thing only he agrees with the lieutenant of the *Tiger*—the superiority of the tea-machine, called a samovar, to 'the whole tribe of urns, bright kettles, spirit-cauldrons and such-like barbaric items of ironmongery'. It was on his journey across the desert that the lieutenant of the *Tiger* 'fell in with a samovar', and the reviewer quotes a passage about it and its operation—in a sarcastic mood, one fears.

Agreeably, in this same volume, music enters into the Eastern Question, in the form of a serious appraisal of opera, ballet and concerts in St Petersburg. 'Phases of Music in Russia' is peppered with political sneers, but seems to be well-informed and appreciative. 'Political accidents and the astonishing ignorance which everywhere prevails in England with reference to everything connected with Russia, have made many persons fancy the Russian to be the type of everything that is brutal and ferocious and that the instinctive tendency of serfs and Cossacks is to plunder,' and this, the article asserts, is an error. A bouquet is presented to the mujiks: with their real musical gifts, they have, in contrast with the pugnacious and violent lower classes of most European countries, 'the suavity, gentle demeanour, polished manners and cajoling softness of a courtier'. It certainly looks as if some mujiks had put a good deal over on this gentleman. Performances of the opera are described in detail; so are the opera-goers, whose taste isn't any worse than that of fashionable opera-goers anywhere; the toilettes of the ladies come in for praise, but not their looks; the ballet shows skill in grouping and taste in costuming. But some of the concerts were the worst the gentleman had ever heard —'always excepting the Cambridge University concerts'.

On the whole, the reader of *Fraser's* in this war year would have learned that there was some culture in Russia, that peasants had good hearts and musical gifts, and that Russians liked tea so much that they had a most ingenious machine for making it; and he would also have learned that the Russian government was not to be trusted, that the ruling house was insane and that the Russian language did not contain the word 'gentleman'. He might, too, have been made aware of the existence of a fine writer and looked up the French version of Turgenev's *Sportsman's Sketches*.

A reporter with an unusual fund of Russian experience was an Englishwoman who left Russia at the beginning of the Crimean War, after a residence of ten years, and whose *Impressions of the*

Society and Manners of the Russians at Home appeared in 1855 in New York and London (Scribner's and J. Murray). Her intention was modest: a simple account of the manners, customs and '*genre de vie chez eux*' of a people whose domestic habits were comparatively little known to the English nation; and to whose amiable and social excellences she tried to do full justice. Accepting the phrase of the French describing the Russians—as a '*nation de barbares polis*'—she allows the Russians the good as well as the bad qualities of barbarians. To some extent she anticipates such later interpreters of the Russian character as Maurice Baring (who divided Russians into the two types of Lucifer and Ivan the Fool), by splitting the individual into two characters, with diametrically opposed traits, and public and the private. Her illustrations are of the contradiction between their politeness to equals and their brutal manners towards serfs and servants. Some of her stories recall material in Turgenev's sketches, and one wonders whether she knew his work, but she does not mention his name, nor that of Gogol, although she describes appreciatively a performance in St Petersburg of his *Inspector General*—'*Reviseur*', as she calls it. These '*barbares polis*' had an excellent French theatre in St Petersburg, and she saw a well-done performance of *Hamlet* at Tver. She is scornful of the travellers who visit only St Petersburg and Moscow, for she did a good deal of travelling under often primitive conditions, and can tell about it in very amusing detail. Her descriptions are effective—as for instance a view of St Petersburg on a 'white night', from one of the bridges—the long line of palaces fading away in the distance, the quays, the river, fabrics of a vision erected on the enchanting shores of a lake of silver. The Russian language evokes even more admiration from her than from Jerome Horsey: one of the richest and most beautiful in the world, soft and agreeable in sound, not, like the Italian, too effeminate, and all ready for a Slavonic Milton or Shakespeare, but having so far produced only a Pushkin, a Karamzin, a Krilov. (She seems to know nothing of Lermontov, Turgenev and the early work of Dostoevsky and Tolstoy.) She blames the censorship for hampering literary production.

Of some writer who spoke of 'the sties of the Russian nobility' she remarks that he had never obviously entered the house of a nobleman. Some of the poorest nobility, it was true, lived in a pretty sordid way behind the front they presented to the world, but others lived well both in town and country, and she gives interesting and explicit descriptions and considers it unfair to speak falsely of a people merely because one's nation is at war with them.

It is when she talks of the peasants and speculates about the future that she is most interesting. In many ways she admires them; their festivals, their summer dress, their grace. She was reminded of Greek chariot races, immortalized on vases or in friezes, when she watched two peasants, standing up in their carts, racing their horses. She apologizes for comparing the half-civilized boors of Russia with the productions of Phidias, but nevertheless the comparison came to mind. For the besetting sins of the Russian serf—lying, drinking, cunning—she considers slavery mainly responsible. The possibility of a future revolution occurs to her as she describes peasants in a tea-house in St Petersburg, sucking up their tea through the piece of sugar: 'They seem happy and contented enough as we see them now, but doubtless each could tell of some act of oppression and violence which weighs heavily on his heart and which will inevitably be avenged some day or other by him or his children's children.' After an account of a charming rural scene during a celebration of some saint's day, she voices foreboding of the time when the peasants will awaken to their true condition; and she looks at the axes worn in their belts—she has elsewhere described their skill with the axe —and shudders. Though she quotes a Russian gentleman to the effect that Russians look forward to a revolution that will make the French tragedy seem a game of play, she thinks it a long way off when she notes the servility bred by the system. Seeing a serf thanking his master for a beating, she says, 'it will certainly take . . . centuries for such a people to be in a condition to appreciate the blessings of freedom and *perhaps they are too Asiatic ever properly to do so* . . .' (italics mine). But after relating some anecdotes of official corruption, she reflects that a Russian friend of hers is perhaps right—nothing but the hurricane of revolution could clear the social atmosphere.

There was a famous Russian exile living in London at this time, Alexander Herzen, who in 1852 had written a pamphlet on Russian serfdom, in English for the British public, and had protested in it against the undue attention paid to the issue of American slave emancipation in relation to the burning question of the liberation of the Russian serfs. Carlyle found Herzen's account of the development of revolutionary ideas in Russia[2] interesting enough to write to him in 1855; if it were not true, he reflected, that sometimes a burning crisis may be considered beneficent, he himself would prefer Tsarism or Grand-Turkism to the sheer anarchy which is got by Parliamentary eloquence, Free Press, and the counting of heads; 'in your vast country, which I have always respected as a huge dark "Birth of Providence", the meanings of which are not yet known, there is evident down to this time one talent in which it has pre-eminence, giving it potency beyond any other nation . . . : *the talent of obeying*'.[3] It must have been disconcerting to Herzen to have his countrymen praised for a talent that was an obstacle to the spread of the ideas he was advocating in his exile. But Carlyle was simply discovering in the Russians the opposite of what he disliked most in the English at the moment. In this he foreshadowed what became a fairly typical English pattern; for much of the rich material in English literature on the theme of the Russian soul suggests that it was something the English needed or fancied they needed, and as their needs varied through the years, the soul assumed new and contradictory shapes.

The possibility of literary relations developing on a personal basis has hitherto scarcely appeared. But in 1858 a handsome bearded stranger called upon Thackeray in London, announcing himself as a Russian admirer of his books. The stranger was Turgenev. They took a liking to each other, and 'before long Turgenev was regaling Thackeray with a Russian folksong that made him shake his sides with laughter'. Mrs Carlyle had already met Turgenev when she wrote to her husband (July 11, 1858) about a Russian visitor named Botkin, who had translated into Russian *Heroes and Hero Worship*, and who said, 'Mr Carlyle is the man for Russia'. She found him quite a different type from Turgenev: 'he does not possess himself like Tourgueneff, but bends and gesticulates like a Frenchman'. She hoped he read English better than he spoke it—else he must have produced an inconceivable translation; 'he was all in a perspiration when he went away and so was I'.

Translations now began to multiply. In 1860 *Cossack Tales* appeared in London:—English versions of Gogol's *Taras Bulba* and *Night of Christmas Eve*, translated by George Tolstoy. The first translation of a book by Leo Tolstoy was *Childhood and Youth*, London, 1862, and the translator was Malwida von Meysenbug, the friend of famous writers, musicians, and leaders of European thought—Wagner and Liszt, Nietzsche and Ibsen, and in her old age the inspirer of Romain Rolland. Pushkin's *Queen of Spades*—'anon'—was published in Chambers's *Papers for the People* (No. 38, October, 1850) and was reprinted in 1854 in the annual, *Gift of Friendship*. A badly printed version of Pushkin's prose novel, *The Captain's Daughter*, was published in 1859 (F. Hollinger, Soho). In 1857 Griboyedov's famous comedy *Gore ot Ouma* came out in a translation by Benardaky. That isn't very impressive, so far. But a few years later, 1867, a hopeful interest in the Russian language is expressed in those amusing letters (referred to in the preceding chapter) supposed to be exchanged between the English and the Russian languages, published in the *Athenaeum* (May 4, May 11, June 15). The first letter, from St Petersburg, notes how familiar to readers there, were the leading English novels, in Russian translations, and how English philosophers, historians, and travellers spoke to thousands 'in my voice', i.e. Russian. By contrast, how few Russian books there are even listed at book auctions in London, and how grotesquely titles and authors are distorted! For example, a St Petersburg society, Lovers of the Russian Word, published Readings that took place at their meetings. Out of the transliterated names of the society and the title of the book (Lyubiteli Russkago Slova,

Chtenie, v besyedye) the catalogue of the auction printed: Ytehie be Becbab, by A. P. Caoba. Little wonder that the Russian language (June 15) hopes that 'a rent will take place in the dense curtain of ignorance . . . which is now interposed between Slavonic studies and English eyes. I dream, I trust not foolishly, of a time when there will be Slavonic chairs endowed in your universities, when professors whose eyes have grown dim with poring over Cyrillic or Glagolitic characters will link together the learning of the East and West of Europe, and the banks of the Isis and the Cam will echo to sighs inspired by the regrets of a Pushkin or a Koltsof, and the gentle laughter provoked by the raillery of a Gogol or an Ostrovsky'.

Twenty years later, 1887, part of the dream came true, with the admission into the curriculum of Oxford University of the Lithu-Slavonic languages. And only a year later, 1868, an article in the *Edinburgh Review*, by W. R. Ralston[4] (July, vol. 128) on 'Modern Russian Drama' gave English readers their first glimpse of Ostrovsky. The article was based on a review of Ostrovsky's works in four volumes, published in St Petersburg 1859–1867, and translates long passages from the plays.

In 1859 a young Englishman named Charles Turner went to Russia, and in 1864 was appointed Lector of the English language at the Imperial University in St Petersburg, holding the office for forty years, until his death. Turner's long career as an interpreter of English literature to Russians and Russian literature to Englishmen is so important and interesting that it will be sketched later, along with the careers of several other English and American promoters of cultural relations. Now let us turn to the United States, and see what a friendly rather than a hostile interest in Russia at the time of our Civil War did to promote knowledge of Russians and their culture.

ii

Civil War Period. U.S.A.

UNTIL THE Civil War, as we have seen in previous pages, the American reader could have had only the sketchiest ideas, largely erroneous, about the Russians and their literature. There were, of course, American travellers in Russia, as there were English, French and German. But it is unnecessary to comment upon them here except in the briefest fashion, for on this subject we have one of those green oases of information surveyed for us by graduate study. Dr Anna M. Babey published in 1938 *Americans in Russia 1776–1917: A Study of the American Travellers in Russia from the American Revolution to the Russian Revolution.* One of Dr Babey's generalizations about American travellers is certainly applicable with suitable qualifications to those of other nationalities: 'In books and articles, American travellers to Russia reflected much of what characterized their background, local and national, their interests, predilections and prejudices. A trip abroad served as the occasion for the expression of themselves. . . . The presence of certain factors in our American development—such as the elements involved in our westward expansion'—(which made Siberia and its enormous possibilities particularly interesting to Americans from the West, with frontier transformations in mind) —'the steady trend towards democratic rule, the development of popular education, the emancipation of women, and the shifting trends in capitalistic and labour organization—seemed to urge many Americans to look for the presence or absence of such factors in Russia'. Dr Babey notes throughout her study the relationship between American developments and the kind of opinions expressed by American travellers. Examples are the curiosity about the Russian peasant, aroused by the almost contemporaneous emancipation of slave and serf in the United States and Russia; about the status of Russian women and Russian education, stimulated by the American movements for emancipation of women and for popular education; about the Russian Orthodox Church, which Protestant American travellers tended to praise because of their opposition to the Roman Catholic Church. The optimism characteristic of the earlier American point of view led many to take a cheerful view of the future of Russia—especially if she turned away from 'government paternalism' and entered 'upon the path of rugged individualism'.

Looking back for a moment to earlier official relations between the two countries, we find that the same Princess Dashkoff, whom Landor pictured listening with Catherine the Great to the blood dripping from the murdered Peter, met Benjamin Franklin in Paris in 1780 at the Abbé Reynal's. Franklin nominated her to membership in the Philadelphia Philosophical Society, and she was elected; in return, she secured his election in 1789 to membership in the St Petersburg Academy of Sciences. In 1781–1783, John Quincy Adams went as companion, interpreter and secretary with Francis Dana to Russia, on the unsuccessful mission to persuade Catherine to recognize the new American State. A little later, mutual interests brought the two countries into formal diplomatic relations, Thomas Jefferson being responsible for opening up such relations during the Napoleonic wars, in 1806, when he was seeking some counterweight to British sea-power. John Quincy Adams went again to Russia in 1808, spent five years there, and even struggled with the Russian language. But as French was the language at court, he did not really need to win the struggle. He was a success at St Petersburg, and often took walks with Alexander I. 'One day,' as Samuel Flagg Bemis relates in the *Virginia Quarterly Review* (autumn number 1945), in his article—'John Quincy Adams and Russia'—'on one of their many promenade meetings, the Tsar asked the minister about West Florida, which the United States had just annexed rather summarily. Adams explained it as best he could without blushing. The Emperor smiled and bowed. "We keep on growing, bit by bit, in this world", he remarked. (*On s'agrandit un peu dans ce monde.*) He who had just annexed Finland could understand Florida easily enough.'

The possibility of Russia's growing bit by bit on the west coast of the United States had just been eclipsed by the death of Rezanov (1807), who had secured, in the interest of a fur trust, the signature of the Emperor Paul (Alexander's predecessor) to a twenty-year grant to the Russian-American Company of dominion over the north-west coast of North America, from latitude 55 degrees northward. The story of Rezanov's success with the Governor of New Spain in California, his love affair with the daughter of the *commandante* of San Francisco, his diplomatic skill in winning the clergy to his cause—has been told in an effectively romantic novel by Gertrude Atherton (*Rezanov*, 1906). In more sober terms, in her article in the *Encyclopaedia Britannica*, Mrs Atherton sums up: 'His correspondence with the company betrays a clearly defined purpose to annex to Russia the western coast of North America, and encourage immediate emigration from the parent company on a large scale. Had he lived he might have accomplished his object. The treaty (with Spain) was never signed, the reforms of Rezanov (in Alaska) died of discouragement, the fortunes of the colonies gradually collapsed, the Spanish girl who had loved Rezanov became a nun, and one of the ablest and most ambitious men of his time was forgotten in the cemetery of a poor Siberian town.'

The emancipation of the Russian serfs (1861) inspired, at least in the North, a very friendly curiosity about the whole system. Probably a writer in the *Atlantic Monthly* (C. C. Hazewell, July, 1861) was not alone in reflecting, 'That freedom should come to a people from a despot's throne was almost as hard to understand as that the rankest kind of despotism should rise up from among a people the most boastful of their liberty that ever existed'. He takes note of what was evidently a common argument in the slavery controversy—that the Tsar was hostile only to the enslavement of white people, and would never have freed black men; 'this faithlessness of Russia to the cause of human oppression' was a sore subject with 'our pro-slavery people'. Andrew D. White's article in the *Atlantic Monthly*, November, 1862, entitled, 'Development and Overthrow of the Russian Serf System', is very enthusiastic, the long history dramatized by the recurring refrain of disappointed hopes—'and the serfs waited'. White was a university professor by this date, but he had been attaché to the American Embassy in St Petersburg in 1854–1855, and as an eye-witness he writes of Russian conditions with some authority. He pays a glowing tribute to 'Alexander the Earnest'.

By the time our own slaves were emancipated and the Civil

War ended, there is a retrospective air about the still interesting comparisons between serfdom and slavery, but there is as well a concern about the future that both countries faced in adjusting to a great social change. Reviews of important English, French and German books on serfdom and emancipation are made the occasion for reflections and prophecies. One such extensive review, based on several foreign books, in the *North American Review* (July, 1867), is particularly interesting for its mixture of accuracy and misconception, and for its generalizations. It is accurate about the Crown peasants, the artels and the communal land system. When, however, it is stated that there were no ruins of an ancient culture, and that Russia had nothing to do with Greece or Rome, or the Roman Church, we realize how undeveloped as yet were historical and archaeological studies of the early periods. The reviewer notes that the accounts of the actual conditions of the serfs differ as greatly as the Northern and Southern view of Negro slavery; some use strong lights, others the darkest shades. Also, 'the same virtues and vices on which such stress was laid by Southern slaveholders as peculiar to the Negro and justifying his servitude are put forward with almost equal prominence by the champions of Russian serfdom. "Sheep-like docility", "an incomparable sweetness of temper", affection for superiors, strong family and religious feeling, hospitality, are allowed them; but frivolity, carelessness and indolence are their special traits.' The writer looks forward to the growth of a middle class and of a country gentry more like farmers, and he sees a promise of safe and steady progress in the Russian tendency to combine with his fellows —a tendency he thinks may be an 'inborn propensity' of the Russian peasant. In the artels he sees workingmen's associations suggestively like our own. But the great obstacle to this safe and steady progress is the absence of a public opinion in the Western sense.

There is a popular notion that the Russian Government was friendly to the cause of the North, and a persistent legend that units of the Russian fleet were sent to New York and San Francisco to bolster the morale of the North in 1863–1864. In 1915, Dr Frank Golder questioned the legend on the basis of research in the Russian archives in St Petersburg; this research seemed to prove that Russia very much needed a friend at that time, for she feared Anglo-French intervention in support of the Polish insurrection; and she also wanted her fleet where it could not be bottled up, and where it could do some damage, if necessary, to British and French commerce.[5]

For whatever reason, the Russian fleet did visit New York, and two young Americans (both born in 1840) met some of the officers and liked them. Eugene Schuyler and Jeremiah Curtin had long and distinguished diplomatic and literary careers that appear to have started off with this visit to the fleet and acquaintance with the Russian officers. Schuyler promptly began the study of Russian, translated Turgenev's *Fathers and Sons* (published in 1867), and was appointed consul at Moscow, arriving in the fall of 1867, meeting Turgenev on the way, at Baden, and receiving from him letters to friends in Russia, among them Leo Tolstoy. As for Curtin, he accepted an invitation to go to Russia, and worked as a translator in St Petersburg before entering on diplomatic duties as assistant-secretary to the U.S. Legation, holding this and other positions till 1870. He travelled extensively in Eastern Europe and Asia, studied the Mongol language and customs in southern Siberia, collected myths and folk-tales of Russians, Magyars and Western Slavs, published translations from Polish and Russian. Dr Babey states that these were the only two among American diplomats who had an interest in Russian life before they entered on their diplomatic duties. Those Russian officers must have been very engaging and perhaps visiting fleets should be encouraged.

Visiting Anarchists, too, perhaps. In that Age of Innocence hospitality was not narrowly circumscribed. Michael Bakunin came to Boston in 1861, by way of Siberia and San Francisco, bringing letters of introduction to a number of respectable Bostonians, such as Samuel Longfellow, brother of the poet, Governor Andrew, George Snelling (a sympathizer with the Polish insurrection of 1831), and others. Martin Kennard, a businessman of Brooklyn, wrote an account of the visit twenty years later; the MS preserved in the Harvard College Library was first published in the *New England Quarterly*, March, 1942. Kennard describes Bakunin as large, well proportioned, 'in bearing noble, in personage genial and attractive, and well-nigh entirely enveloped in a rubber mackintosh'. To Kennard's comment on the inclement weather, Bakunin replied, 'To one who has been confined eight years in prison and in chains and spent five years in Siberia, this is beautiful'. Bakunin told how he had escaped, and Kennard looked upon the stranger 'with a wondering interest and perhaps I may venture to say with amazement'. But the poet Longfellow's small daughter, 'laughing Allegra', thought he was an ogre, when he came to dinner, on November 27, 1861. She came into the dining-room, to find him sitting in *her* place at papa's right hand —'this big creature with a big head, wild bushy hair, big eyes, big mouth, a big voice and still bigger laugh.... No entreaties or persuasion could induce me to cross the threshold of that door. I stood petrified and while I resented his having my place at table, what was dinner to me as long as he didn't make his dinner off me? So I vanished dinnerless.' (*New England Quarterly*, June, 1946, article by David Hecht.) Her father described his guest (who came for lunch and stayed till midnight) as a Russian gentleman of education and ability, who spoke English with fair facility, having begun to study it in prison in 1849. But he called himself the 'Russian Bear'. Though he spent only a week in Boston, he duly recorded his primary declaration of his intention to become a citizen. He left soon after, to rejoin his wife in London and resume his revolutionary activities, along with the group Mr E. H. Carr has written about in *The Romantic Exiles*.[6]

The Innocents Abroad liked Tsars and grand dukes as much as those at home liked officers and anarchists. Mark Twain and the other 'Quaker City' Pilgrims were entertained at Yalta, by both Emperor and Grand Duke, in 1867. Mark Twain liked Alexander II as much as later he detested Nicholas II. 'Any man could see that there was an intention to show that Russia's friendship for America was so genuine as to render even her private citizens objects worthy of kindly attentions.' Mark Twain believed in the sincerity of the polite speeches of the Emperor. 'There is character in them—Russian character—which is politeness itself and the genuine article. Not the ceremonious politeness of the French. A Russian imbues his polite things with a heartiness, both of phrase and expression, that compels belief in their sincerity.' 'The Empress said the Americans were favourites in Russia, and she hoped the Russians were similarly regarded in America.' Everybody talked English. The unostentatious costume of the Emperor is described. 'A determined looking man, though a very pleasant looking one. . . . It is easy to see that he is kind and affectionate. There is something very noble in his expression when his cap is off. There is none of that cunning in his eye that all of us noticed in Louis Napoleon's.' Mark Twain found the 14-year-old Grand Duchess Marie so charming and simple that he indulged in a flight of innocent fancy, of the young girl pleading with the Autocrat of Russia for some supplicating wretch condemned to misery in the wastes of Siberia. 'Many and many a time she might rule the Autocrat of Russia, whose lightest word is law to seventy millions of human beings.' He thinks of the terrible power of this unassuming man; it seemed preposterous—if he were ill, all the nations would know it before the sun rose again—if he dropped lifeless, his fall might shake the thrones of half a world. And then he adds, with a characteristic wisecrack—'If I could have stolen his coat, I would have done it. When I meet a man like that, I want something to remember him by.' The Grand Duke Michael, third brother of the Emperor, taller than the Tsar, straight as an Indian, must, says Mark, have been so desirous of proving that Americans were welcome guests in the imperial palaces of Russia, that he rode all the way to Yalta and escorted our procession to the Emperor's. The Innocents didn't know who he was then, and were all the more appreciative when they found out, and were entertained at *his* palace, where they had a picnic. 'When it was time to go, we bade our distinguished hosts good-bye, and they retired happy and contented to their apartments to count their spoons.' The pilgrims had been cheerful and comfortable for half a day in the home of royalty—'I would as soon have thought of being cheerful in Abraham's bosom as in the palace of an Emperor'.

And they all behaved very well, realizing that they represented the American people, not the American Government. They had taken care to suppress their poet; he had to swear not to issue a line of poetry while in the Tsar's dominions, or else remain on the ship under guard. Later, when the Innocents met a few admirals and the Chief Inspector of the railroads, Mark Twain felt this latter gentleman was laying it on a bit thick in describing his success in employing ten thousand convicts on railroad work—all quiet and peaceable. Mark Twain spoke up for America: 'I said we had eighty thousand convicts employed on the railways in America—all of them under sentence of death for murder in the first degree. That closed *him* out.'

On the theme of Russian-American friendship, Oliver Wendell Holmes contributed three occasional poems. One, *America to Russia*, was read on August 5, 1866, by the Honourable G. V. Fox, at a dinner given in St Petersburg to a mission from the United States. A warship, says the poet, is bearing our greetings to Russia, but warship or not,

> . . . lightly as the sea-bird swings,
> She floats the depths above,
> A breath of flame to lend her wings,
> Her freight a people's love.
> When darkness hid the starry skies,
> In war's long winter night,
> One ray still cheered our straining eyes,
> The far-off Northern light

The poem concludes:

> A Nation's love in tears and smiles,
> We bear across the sea.
> O Neva of the banded isles,
> We moor our hearts in thee!

The other poems commemorated a visit to our shores of the Grand Duke Nicholas: one of welcome at a reception in Boston, December 6, 1871, and the other for the banquet on December 9. Public school children sang the first, to the Russian national air:

> Bleak are our shores with the blasts of December,

Fettered and chill is the rivulet's flow.
Throbbing and warm are the hearts that remember
Who was our friend when the world was our foe.

It concludes:

God bless the Empire that loves the Great Union!
Strength to her people, long life to the Tsar!

In the banquet poem, Russia is urged to leave the Grand Duke with us

. . . till the summer is green.
Both shores are his home, though the waves roll between.
And then we'll return him, with thanks for the same,
As fresh and as smiling and tall as he came.

One wonders if we were in the habit of shortening, perhaps by a head, our foreign guests? But one doesn't wonder why the Pilgrims suppressed their poet.

Here was a friendly soil and a friendly climate of opinion, but not very much as yet planted. The most promising seed was the 1867 translation by Eugene Schuyler of Turgenev's 1861 novel, his greatest, *Fathers and Children*—the first English translation of a major work by a major Russian novelist. And it was translated 'with the approval of the author'. It was reviewed in the July 1867 number of the *North American Review* by Charles Eliot Norton, then editor of the magazine. In certain important respects the emphasis of his review is that characteristic of American as distinguished from English criticism of Russian literature in the early period; an emphasis on artistic values rather than on political and social implications. Norton is disturbed by the danger to a work of art of the author's yielding to the temptation of making his characters typical of classes, rather than true portrayals of individuals. Turgenev has made his characters exhibit the various features of the older and younger generation of living Russians, and has thus created an interest superior to that of a mere novel of incident, but has exposed his novel to failure as a work of art. He has not altogether avoided this danger, but the most jaded novel reader—and it is funny to think of novel readers as being 'jaded' in 1867—will find entertainment in this good novel, full of character and incident closely studied from Nature. 'The author possesses a sentiment of the beauty of Nature and is a careful observer of her various displays.' Norton does not give a summary of the story, because 'the story is itself intended as a vehicle of ideas'. But what these ideas are, how related to the social order which Turgenev is interpreting, why Turgenev, the artist, felt moved to use a story as a vehicle of ideas—all that comes in for no consideration whatever.

At all events, Turgenev was launched in the United States. Within the next six years (1867–1873), sixteen translations appear, of which six were books—among them *Smoke* (1872), and *Rudin* (1873). *Lippincott's*, a popular magazine, published a number of short items, including the moving short story of the deaf and dumb serf *Mumu*; and other short pieces or extracts from Pushkin, Griboyedov and Tolstoy. During the same years in England, there were only a half-dozen translations of Turgenev's work, three of them the novels *Smoke*, *Liza* and *On the Eve*. The critical articles on Turgenev for which the *Atlantic Monthly* became noteworthy in the seventies—especially those by Henry James, T. S. Perry and W. D. Howells—were, as often as not, based on the reading of French and German translations. Though the United States was ahead at the start, it was in England that the complete translation of Turgenev's novels appeared first: the translation by Constance Garnett, 1894–1899. The American translation of the novels and stories, by Isabel Hapgood, was completed in 1903–1904.

What was the picture of Russians, seen through their literature, that the reader of the popular magazines would get, in 1871, just at the outset of the *Atlantic Monthly* period of really informed criticism? A long article by A. C. Dillman was published in *Lippincott's Magazine* in May, 1871 (pp. 494–502). Dillman is making an ambitious survey; he is delimiting the proper realm of art; he is generalizing and relating, very sketchily, the literary history to the political history; he is drawing upon the opinions of foreign critics. He obviously does not know the Russian language, and his spelling of Russian words and names reveals the contemporary chaos of transliteration. There is Toorgenef, and Schtschedrin, and Goutscharof (a vague adumbration of Goncharov), and Lemonossof. Little could be done to disguise Gogol, but Gogol's minor Russian officials, the *tchinovniks*, appear as 'thievish Tscinowinks'—as if tiddlywinks had invaded their ranks. As for generalizations, there is one that from now on is popular: Russian works of art are melancholy, sombre, pessimistic and that is a serious defect. Dillman is puzzled and disappointed that the removal of serfdom—the principal 'odium' that had attached to the Empire—has not also removed the melancholy. And yet, as he surveys Russian history going back to Peter the Great and even earlier, and notes the absence of pulpit, rostrum or popular tribunal; the choice facing the nobility of either abnegating self-respect in the service of the State, or dreaming away an aimless existence on remote estates; the yoke of servitude pressing on the masses—he does not find it surprising that writers should have adopted the role of accusers. Pushkin's 'Byronic misanthropy' bears a 'specific Russian character'. Lermontov's despair was even blacker. He does grant gifts of comedy, satire and humour to Gogol and Griboyedov. Though he finds some contemporary Russian realists very coarse—he does not name them—he admits they may be discharging the duties of a moral and sanitary police. Turgenev is an idealist; there is not the faintest trace of a polemical tendency in his work; no intent 'which imperils the originality of the poetical impression', in his *Diary of a Hunter*, or his *Noble Nest*. The admittedly far-reaching effect of the *Diary* (in promoting the abolition of serfdom), he lays to the fact that Turgenev had simply truly related what he had seen. The mission of art, for Dillman, is to represent the beautiful, and the duty of the artist is to view life harmoniously and reconcile its contradictions through faith in the ideal destiny of mankind. But he regretfully concedes that when things are as bad as they are in Russia, an ideal representation of life is not to be thought of, until the general misery is relieved, and the poet has to accuse, and cannot avoid pessimism. And Dillman thinks things are really pretty bad; he is apprehensive of the immediate future, because of the revolutionists with their leagues of 'crazy iconoclasts and conspirators against the old order of things'. Turgenev in his *Fathers and Children* administered a scathing rebuke to the self-conceited Russian youth who represented the so-called 'nihilism' and enunciated detestable doctrines. He quotes, from some 'vision' by Turgenev, a passage about the devil conveying the author through the air and looking down in the clear moonlight upon a young female, reclining at an open window, 'reading by the glow of her paper cigarette a cynical effusion of the latest literature, while a party of drunken bloods riot through the streets'.

But in all this, there is no real explanation of the part played in Turgenev's novels, and with Turgenev's intention, by the social developments and political events of the day. This indifference to an important aspect of Turgenev's art is carried on for some time in the American criticism of Russian literature, especially in the *Atlantic Monthly*—with a kind of finesse achieved by just ignoring the problem.

[1] This French translation was criticized by Turgenev himself as '*une véritable mystification littéraire—c'est à ne pas s'y reconnaître*'. In 1885, under the title *Russian Life in the Interior*, this bad French version of the *Sportsman's Sketches* was translated into English.

[2] Pamphlet in French 'On the Development of Revolutionary Ideas in Russia', published in London.

[3] E. H. Carr: *The Romantic Exiles*. Appendix.

[4] See also Ralston, 1866, *Fortnightly Review*, 'A Russian Poet' (Koltsov) and 1876, *Contemporary Review*, xxvii, 'Poems of Nekrassov'.

[5] See Harold H. Fisher, *America and Russia in the World Community*, Claremont, Calif., 1946, p. 35. Also Thomas A. Bailey, *America Faces Russia: Russian-American Relations from Early Times to Our Day*. Cornell University Press, 1950.

[6] For an interesting account of Bakunin's essays on American life, which are marked by some very shrewd and penetrating judgments, see David Hecht, *Russian Radicals Look to America 1825–1894*, Harvard University Press, 1947.

CHAPTER IV

ART AND POLITICS

i

The 'Atlantic Monthly' and the Art of Fiction

THE ATLANTIC MONTHLY was interested in the art of fiction. It performed a signal service to its readers under the editorship of William Dean Howells—from 1866, when he became assistant editor, until 1881—in making them aware of foreign novelists—Stendhal, the Goncourts, Flaubert, Zola, Bourget, Björnson, and others; and especially Turgenev. For some years all the reviews and notices of foreign books were written by Thomas Sergeant Perry—described by Mr Van Wyck Brooks as 'all but universally curious', with a feeling for modern fiction that was 'clairvoyant'. Howells and Perry, says Mr Brooks, kept the *Atlantic* 'well abreast of all the new developments in the world of letters'. Perry was the close friend of both the James brothers, and, again according to Brooks, he introduced the work of Turgenev to Henry James and Howells.[1] Dr Royal Gettman has made a thorough study of the reputation of Turgenev's novels in the United States, and he ascribes to Perry about a dozen essays on Turgenev between 1871 and 1877, most of them in the *Atlantic*.

Perry and Howells, reminiscing in the *North American Review*, many years later (1912), recall that they began their reading of Russian fiction with Turgenev, and that Perry had translated *Rudin* from the French; they wonder whether they had read Gogol first in German or in French? It was fortunate that an influential magazine like the *Atlantic* had such linguistically competent editors and reviewers. The first long article that Henry James wrote on Turgenev, which was published in the *North American Review* (1874), comments upon the excellent German version in course of publication. Perry translated *Virgin Soil*, 1877, from French and German versions; it was not until 1888 that he began to study Russian, and not until 1908 that he visited Russia, to see the Moscow Art Theatre. None of the others in this early group went to Russia or studied the language. But the elder and the younger Henry James both came to know Turgenev. After the younger James published the essay in 1874, the elder wrote to Turgenev at Carlsbad, inviting him to come to Cambridge, where his novels were read, and where he was often the subject of conversation, 'in the evening, on the piazza, facing the sunset' (Brooks, *New England: Indian Summer*). If he came, he could tell them, 'between the fumes of his pipe', what he saw, of promise or of menace in their civilization. 'Turgenev, who was touched, replied that, though he did not smoke, he would enjoy a quiet evening with them.' But he never crossed the ocean. The next year the younger Henry in Paris became his close friend.

Proficient in French and German though Perry, Howells and James were, they were getting very imperfect renderings of the original. When a little later translators like Isabel Hapgood and Nathan Haskell Dole began to work on the Russian novelists, the deficiencies were pointed out with vigour. Miss Hapgood heads an article in the *Nation* (1886) 'cobbling extraordinary', noting that Turgenev, however, suffers less from the French translation than does Tolstoy—whose *War and Peace* in the American version is no more true to the French than the French to the Russian. A trickle of good English translations of Turgenev was coming through, however, even in the '70's: Charles Turner's of *On the Eve* (1871) was in 1873 reviewed in the *Atlantic*; so also was W. R. S. Ralston's *Liza* (1869) (the translation of Turgenev's *Noblemen's Nest*); and his *Songs* (1872), illustrative of Slavonic mythology and Russian social life, were interesting to the *Atlantic* reviewer because they helped to make much in Turgenev more clear.

Turgenev was being read and discussed. He was also being taken as the interpreter of his people, of Russia, but taken in an odd detachment from the political, social and even literary background of that people. The detachment was due partly to sheer ignorance. But it was also justified by the viewpoint of *art for art*, or *art for morality*, not less definite because not explicitly formulated. This aesthetic and moral interpretation was quite expert—no one could deny that James and Howells were as good as any American writers could be for this service. Royal Gettman has analysed, on the basis of the many reviews and essays concerned with Turgenev, appearing during these years, his influence on the development among American critics of the idea of the Novel as an art form, on the conception of the moral issue in Realism; and on certain matters of technique, such as the point of view, and 'the disappearance of the author' from his work. By this phrase was meant objectivity in fiction, in the interest of dramatic effect. Dr Gettman concludes: 'There was in this country a reasoned and usable body of opinion on the method, scope and purpose of fiction.... Turgenev played an important part in the development and application of this criticism'. When one reflects upon all the things that alarm us nowadays, it is restful to come upon this question in G. P. Lathrop's article on the novel in the *Atlantic* (1874): he has been criticizing Dickens: 'Is it not alarming, to say the least, that the eminent novelist should take sides, as he does, with the characters in his stories?' Turgenev does not do this; perhaps 'his self-exclusion is almost too rigid'; but Lathrop is all for a resolute 'act of self-renunciation on the part of the author'.

Turgenev is admired by his various critics for many things: for revealing the innermost secrets of character; for artistic impartiality; for moral earnestness—'One feels the presence not only of a great genius, but a clear conscience', writes Howells of *Liza*, which 'is life, nothing more, nothing less'. But in the long review (1873) he says nothing of the political and social background, the differing points of view of those intellectuals who were Westernizers and those who were Slavophiles. And Henry James (*North American Review*, 1874) emphasizes that Turgenev's object is always the same—to find 'an incident, a person, a situation, *morally* interesting'. (Italics mine.) Turgenev believes in 'the intrinsic value of "subject" in art'. Having found his subject, he presents a view of human life 'more general, more impartial and more unreservedly intelligent than that of any novelist we know'. James also emphasizes his taste: 'he is particularly a favourite with people of a cultivated taste; and nothing, in our opinion, cultivates the taste more than to read him'. Both Howells and James at this time stress Turgenev's realism, but Howells has some reservations: his determined realism sometimes carries him too far 'in the description of passages which will hardly bear such treatment, however pure the artist's motive, without becoming a little more acceptable to the vicious than the virtuous'. (Which passages these are, in *On the Eve*, we leave the vicious reader to discover.) James calls his merit of form of the first order and illustrates by a comparison of *Uncle Tom's Cabin* with *A Sportsman's Sketches*, which is less 'a passionate *pièce de circonstance* than a disinterested work of art'. He says nothing whatever of the political conditions that imposed 'disinterestedness' on Turgenev, if he were to be published at all. In commenting upon *Fathers and Children*, he gives the hero his label of 'so-called Nihilist', of 'red-handed Radical, fresh from the shambles of criticism, with Büchner's *Kraft und Stoff* as a text-book', and notes the theme of conflict between the generations; but has virtually nothing specific to say of that situation, which separated fathers and sons in thoughts and habits, so brilliantly interpreted by Turgenev that this novel is in the stream of Russian history.

But James knows as little about Turgenev at this early date as about Russian history, though he speculates a little about both. Turgenev may have a charming combination of an aristocratic temperament with a democratic intellect, he thinks. How does he feel about life? That is the great question about a writer. James fears he is morbid, pessimistic; his stories are full of failures. James does not object to a sad story, and in truth it is adversity failure—especially failure that comes from a flaw in character—that often gives moral interest to a person or a situation; but he is afraid that Turgenev is often 'wantonly melancholy'. Perhaps he is disappointed about Russia, and James generalizes about Russia in terms that suggest he is thinking along the same lines about his own country: 'the fermentation of social change has thrown to the surface in Russia a deluge of hollow pretensions and vicious presumptions, amid which the love either of old virtues or of new achievements finds very little gratification'.

Turgenev's melancholy bothers T. S. Perry, too—a melancholy natural enough in tales of the peasants; but 'in all there is a dreary picture of superstition, affectation, pretence, half-civilized polish and idleness; they give us a very black picture of Russian life, which has apparently all the outward forms of civilization, distinctions of caste more marked by observance than by intrinsic difference, with a dreary formality wholly unrelieved by humour. In this respect there is a marked resemblance to the Southern States and especially to them as they were before the war.'[2] The next year (June, 1875)—this time in a review of a German version of the same book, probably also by Perry—the sadness is again explained as the result of living in a country 'which has acquired all the outside show of civilization, *thinly covering the fury of untamed half-savage natures*'. This last phrase is typical of one extreme of the generalizing that goes on through the years; the other extreme is some variation of Asiatic or Oriental submissiveness and apathy.

But Perry has an unexpected flash of insight into Turgenev's melancholy, his black moods, when he suggests that there might be some personal cause—not just the general state of Russia. It was not until our own Freudian era that this personal cause was convincingly analysed in Yarmolinsky's biography of Turgenev.

The sadness and melancholy, as characteristic of Turgenev, becomes accepted criticism, however explained, and one of the more amusing illustrations of its widespread acceptance is to be found in Howells's novel *April Hopes* (1888). There is a scene of ladies, old and young, gossiping in a quite highbrow way about their reading, as they sit on the porch of a summer hotel. One of them is reading *Fumée* by a terribly pessimistic writer called Tourguenieff. Another declares that he gave her a very bad quarter-hour with his *Liza*; whereupon the *Fumée* reader—with the snobbishness of a woman who reads her Turgenev in French—remarks, 'That is the same as the *Nichée des Gentilshommes*, isn't it?' Not to be outdone in literary competence—even if she does read her Turgenev in English—the other replies, 'I don't build my ships to cross the sea in, as Emerson says; I take those I find built'. The *Fumée* reader, Mrs Pasmer, says she was already on the other side, and adds that she must get hold of *Liza*, for she likes a good heart-break. 'Heart-break? heart-crush!' says the other. 'Where Lavretsky comes back old to the scene of his love for Liza, and strikes that chord on the piano—well, I simply wonder that I'm alive to recommend the book to you.' One of the other ladies now offers a suggestion not too cordially received by Mrs Pasmer, that Mrs Pasmer's daughter reminds her of Liza. But the reader of *Liza* demurs: 'Oh, I doubt if you will see more than a mere likeness of temperament. All the conditions are so different. There couldn't be an American Liza. That's the charm of these Russian tragedies. You feel that they're so perfectly true there, and so perfectly impossible here. Lavretsky would simply have got himself divorced from Varvara Pavlovna, and no clergyman could have objected to marrying him to Liza.' Then they discuss the proper uses of despair—in fiction; and the fact that marriage at the end means happiness—in a book; and so on to speculation on the question why there are so many divorces. It is all a pleasant glimpse of those more smiling aspects of life that Howells considered the more American.

ii

Marianna and Her Virtue

HOWELLS ESTABLISHED, in 1877, a department in the *Atlantic* called the Contributors Club, where the youngest generation aired its problems (according to Van Wyck Brooks), and where the art of fiction was one of the chief preoccupations. And the art of fiction was all involved with morality. Was Henry James's *Daisy Miller* a loyal service to American girlhood? One of Turgenev's later heroines, Marianna of *Virgin Soil*, was generally considered a very dubious service to Russian girlhood.

At the outset, when the Contributors are just getting into their stride, we find a lively questioning of the authority of the James-Howells-Perry group, so far as the praise of Turgenev is concerned, but the very questioning is evidence of the interest his work had excited. 'Speaking of cults and Turgenef (I adopt the simplest permissible spelling), the people I know who follow Turgenef as a cult are of the best taste.' (May, 1877.) But he should not be put at the head of modern fiction, for he is unequal, as well as brilliant, his plots are loose-jointed, creating the effect of an unfinished frieze; his women figures are charming, but his satire on Russia is savage and unrelieved; and the end of *Smoke* is annoying—if everything is smoke, why bother? Here is the typical disregard of Turgenev's subject, as related to the Russian situation. There is no inkling of the relation of the mood of *Smoke* to the deep disappointments of liberal hopes in the later 1860's and thus, the main purpose ignored, Turgenev's novel is considered saved only by some exquisite details and touches of insight. But the political situation in Russia was beginning to catch up with the critics, both professional and amateur. It could not be ignored in *Terres Vierges*. This French translation (by Durand-Greville, Paris, 1877) of the novel we know in English as *Virgin Soil*, raised questions of virginity that had little to do with the soil, but a lot to do with the morals of Russian Socialists—Nihilists—Revolutionaries—all very loosely defined; and, surprisingly, with some disturbing movements among women in the United States. In the comments upon Turgenev's Marianna, the name of Mrs Woodhull crops up.

Victoria Woodhull was one of the most famous of our own 'new women'; along with her sister Tennessee Claflin, she published *Woodhull and Claflin's Weekly*, which was supposed to advocate free love, and which, earlier in the midst of the Beecher-Tilton case, had printed accusations of adultery against Henry Ward Beecher. The two sisters had been jailed for sending obscene matter through the mails, but the charge had not been pressed. (*Crusader in Crinoline*, by Forrest Wilson.) Victoria

Woodhull also had other interests, being President of the American Association of Spiritualists.

Henry James reviewed *Terres Vierges* in the *Nation*, April 26, 1877. Either James or Perry (Perry according to the Index, but Gettman says James) reviewed it in the *Atlantic* in July. James had to recognize the political theme. And it is especially interesting that this is the novel that is supposed to have influenced his own *Princess Casamassima* a few years later, with its revolutionary group, and its frustrated young hero who has a close resemblance in many important points with Turgenev's defeated hero, Nezhdanov. One looks in vain for any clear account, in James's review, of the Narodnik movement—'to the people'—in which Marianna and Nezhdanov were involved. It is, he says, a clandestine movement, and Turgenev's wisdom is shown in his perception of the fact that such a movement is fertile in revelations of character and contains the seeds of an interesting psychological drama. 'The opposition of different natures convoked together by a common ideal, this ideal being one which appeals with peculiar force to youthful generosity, accompanied by a due share of that 'little knowledge' which is a dangerous thing—such, roughly speaking, is the subject of *Terres Vierges*.' He goes on to say that the novel gives a picture of a portion of the young generation in Russia, of which we had a glimpse in *Fathers and Sons*, and of which the Nihilist Bazarov was so robust an exponent—'the young people of liberal instincts who find no legitimate channel of expression and who expend their ardour in aimless machinations, compounded in equal parts of puerility and heroism'. He notes again Turgenev's predilection for failures, which has made failures almost the Russian type *par excellence*, and has perhaps made failures more interesting than they really are. But James—developing his own predilection for a certain type—finds their interest to lie in their 'exquisite consciousness' of their shortcomings, which comes from the fine and subtle intelligence, the 'subjective tendency', with which Turegnev endows all his Russians who are not positive fools and grotesques.

James does not raise any question about the virtue of Marianne:

'There is something very beautiful and very characteristic of Turgenef in the idea of the mutual purity of these two young people. They have started on a wild goose chase and would be quite at a loss to say what they propose to do and how they propose to do it; but the delicacy of their enthusiasm is such that they do not even desire to possess each other, and in their moments of tenderest *épanchement*, they only shake hands affectionately like plighted comrades.'

Though James is not interested in the wild goose chase of the 'movement', he has a perceptive moment when he finds both Marianna and Solomin types of one of the 'latent forces of the future, in a country in which these will probably let themselves loose on a great scale'.

But the review in the *Atlantic* in July has a very different opinion about Marianna, and has a great deal more to say about the 'movement', and about the 'present curiosity about Russia' and about the 'secret societies of that country which have so widespread and vague a reputation'. The book is recognized as both contemporary history and novel, and not quite satisfying as either. 'The fruitless and wholly superfluous conspiracy' swamps at times the proper romantic interest of the novel; two uncongenial horses have been harnessed together—information and entertainment. The efforts at revolt against despotism are called aimless, misdirected and fantastic; yet there is some attempt to explain the going to the peasants and trying to be like the peasants. But Marianna goes farther than to the peasants; and 'it is assuredly a stain upon the book that she even proposes that last step of Socialism for supporting which Mrs Victoria Woodhull has become notorious in this country. This repels the reader and fills him with disgust for a heroine who with many unattractive qualities yet comes near being a very fine character.'

The Contributors were quite busy for some months over Marianna and her virtue, and she has some staunch defenders, one of whom (October, 1877) thinks the 'stain' implied in taking the 'last step of Socialism' was created by the reviewer's imagination. For there is not a word in the French text to confirm it, and

Marianna is too fine to be assigned without some evidence to the 'alliance of Mrs Woodhull'. But another Contributor in the same number—a new reader of Turgenev and a disappointed one, who finds nothing but talk, talk, talk, pamphlets distributed in a fog, and a Russian atmosphere consisting of the samovar and a bewildering variety of names—calls Marianna a bold, unpleasant girl, cold-hearted, insolent and sullen, who cuts off her hair, and has 'views' and is willing to become Nezhdanov's mistress 'from principle only'. And in November comes another opinion about Marianna's leanings towards the Nihilistic doctrine of free love, 'which is in Russia very much what Mrs Woodhull's notions are in this country'. Possibly the author's meaning has been perverted; but Contributor gives chapter and verse from the quarto edition, not having the duodecimo at hand—and being evidently a very scholarly person—and comes to the reluctant conclusion that Marianna is lining up with Mrs Woodhull. And not only Marianna. Turgenev, he thinks, is portraying actual conditions, and the London *Times* and the *Pall Mall Gazette* are called on as evidence. An 'old resident', quoted in the latter paper, gives a lurid picture: Russia is infested with Nihilism, especially the whole female population immediately above the peasantry; 'the widest possible definition of women's rights is acquired at the institutions of noble young ladies as well as at the humblest boarding and day schools, and the enjoyment of those rights after marriage is encouraged by the immorality of the men and the facility with which auricular confession to a debased and servile priesthood condones every offence against the laws of God and man'. The old resident's gun shoots down nearly everything in sight, but the Contributor adds his bit about the conduct of many Russian female students at Zurich, which has brought disgrace upon the cause of education for women.

By March, 1878, Turgenev's heroines are examined as a group, and enough instances are cited to prove it scarcely worth while to accuse Marianna of greater enormities than her sisters. And this very enlightened Contributor puts Marianna safely in the moated grange of Art: 'Turgenev is supreme in his skill as an artist and his young girls love with a naïveté, an intensity, a directness, which is admirable in art. If one wants to moralize over the pictures he draws, one may readily declare that all these young girls suffer in proportion to their love. The question is whether one may sensibly moralize upon a work of art.'

The Contributors who frowned upon Marianna must have been puzzled or affronted by Henry James's characterization of Turgenev's young girls—'the faintly acrid perfume of the New England temperament' which he detected in them—'the hint of Puritan angularity'.

iii

The Problem of Nihilism

ADMIRABLE FROM an aesthetic point of view as was the effort of the best American criticism in the '70's to establish canons of art for the novel, and to exclude extraneous considerations of time, place, and circumstance—morals were not extraneous—Russia was making it difficult to keep politics out. 'Nihilism' was not merely immoral, it was political. Marianna was not merely immoral—if she was; she was also in a 'movement'. And her creator, Turgenev, as Henry James was to acknowledge a few years later, in his beautiful tribute to Turgenev in *Partial Portraits* (1884), was not only an artist. He had something in reserve, and that was Russia, 'in a large measure'. 'His genius for us is the Slav genius, his voice the voice of those vaguely-imagined multitudes whom we think of more and more today as waiting their turn, in the arena of civilization, in the grey expanses of the North.' There was a 'matter which filled his existence a good deal more than the consideration of how a story should be written—his hopes and fears on behalf of his native land. He wrote fictions and dramas, but the great drama of his life was the struggle for a better state of things in Russia.' It is not fanciful to find in *The Princess Casamassima* (1886), the one major novel by James that tackles the matter of social revolution, an echo of these thoughts in the phrase of the hero Hyacinth that he is 'a mere particle in the grey immensity of the people'.

At the very end of the '70's (December, 1879), the *Atlantic* published an article by Clara Barnes Martin entitled, 'The Greatest Novelist's Work for Freedom', which draws upon Turgenev's own reminiscences, and which quotes from a German source that 'to have made known to contemporaries and to posterity what serfdom means is the position of Ivan Turgenev in history'. The writer even thinks that he influenced history, for he showed so clearly the baneful effects of serfdom on the landowners as to arouse in them the instinct of self-preservation and make them ready to yield to reform from above. She is at pains to give Bazarov another label—he is a realist, not a Nihilist, bearing no likeness to the 'red-handed agitator of today'; for she shares the usual confusion between Nihilism and the terrorist movements, and 'under the decent veil of French' quotes a statement that Nihilism spits on the soul and on God. She also protests against the inference that since all despotism is bad, all resistance to it must be good.

And this was apparently a widespread inference. The *North American Review* (January, 1879) had let 'a Russian Nihilist' have his say in an article entitled 'The Empire of the Discontented'. All that is wrong with Russia is the Tsardom; all Russian Tsars have been more or less maniacs; there is a rotten glittering aristocracy, a spy system, a bribe-corrupted officialdom, miserable masses; the opposition is not one party or secret society, but many groups and individuals—nobles, professional men, government officials, school teachers, army officers. It is true that with so many reports, from so many different angles, from observers with so many different experiences, Russia looks like a modern Sphinx, 'a puzzle for all mankind, *an unravelled incomprehensible mystery*'. (Italics in the text.)

But the magazine balanced the budget in the June, 1880, number with 'Popular Fallacies about Russia', by E. W. Stoughton, who applied a dazzling coat of whitewash to the Russian Government, past and present. Catherine was the 'greatest and wisest female ruler who ever lived', Alexander II was a humane and Christian monarch, who—he knows on the highest authority—intends to grant his people such political advantages and liberal institutions as they are able to appreciate; and the Nihilists are merely assassins, few in number, with no theory except to destroy and live without labour on the plunder of others, bent on destroying God and Right and then snapping the chains of science, civilization, property, marriage, justice and morality. In some remarks concerning a 'loathsome missionary' he appears to be talking about Bakunin—the Russian Bear who frightened Longfellow's little girl. The peasants, says Stoughton, abhor the Nihilists, but they attract to their cause some half-educated excitable students and even some women, 'paraded as belonging to respectable families and even to the nobility', but usually of a class 'to whom the doors of decent houses are never opened'. These disreputable people have convinced the British Press—and through that, our own—that the Government of Russia is despotic, cruel and irresponsible; and this of a Government 'whose rule at home and influence abroad have long been marked by wise and honourable statesmanship, and generally by an enlarged benevolence, especially towards the oppressed Christian populations of Europe'. A government which thus cares for oppressed Christians in Turkey would of course manifest the utmost solicitude for the welfare of its own people, and it is cheap and cowardly to ascribe to it interested motives; people who do that are themselves devoid of generosity and benevolence. The Tsar is wise, humane, brave and beloved by his people. Mr Stoughton is clearly of the pure to whom all things are pure.

Stoughton did not convince T. S. Perry, who reviewed an Italian book on Nihilism a few months later in the *Atlantic* (October, 1880): 'That Russia is abominably governed, not even Mr Gladstone will deny.' As witness that the official world is foul with corruption, he calls upon Gogol and all subsequent books on Russia; 'our own' William Tweed is a clumsy apprentice in comparison with some of the descendants of Rurik. And when he reads of the unwisdom of the Government, he wants to buy a bottle of petroleum and join the Nihilists himself.

A rather startling picture, that of T. S. Perry of the *Atlantic*, among the 'Nihilists'. But a much more startling picture presented itself to a Harvard audience gathered to hear Wendell Phillips deliver the Phi Beta Kappa address in 1881, soon after the assassination of Alexander II. His topic was 'The Scholar in a Republic', and the address has been called, by James Freeman Clarke, one of the epoch-making Phi Beta Kappa Cambridge orations. Others were those by Everett in 1824 and Emerson in 1837. His thesis was the timidity and selfishness of scholars in the face of their republican duty, when they allow others to lead in agitating the 'great social questions which stir and educate the age', such as the emancipation of women, temperance, Irish freedom, and the revolutionary cause in Russia. After disposing of the others, Phillips comes to the Russian Nihilists, whom he sees as the living representatives of Sam Adams, John Brown and George Washington. 'Nihilism is the righteous and honourable resistance of a people crushed under an iron rule. Nihilism is evidence of life . . . the last weapon of victims choked and manacled beyond all other resistance. . . . God means that unjust power shall be insecure; and every move of the giant prostrate in chains, whether it be to lift a single dagger or stir a city's revolt, is a lesson in justice.' For every single reason our fathers had for rebellion, Russia counts a hundred, and 'of all the cants that are canted in this canting world, though the cant of piety may be the worst, the cant of Americans bewailing Russian Nihilism is the most disgusting'. Noting the absence of a free Press, debate and discussion in Russia, he asks where there is any ground for peaceful change. 'In such a land dynamite and the dagger are the necessary and proper substitutes for Faneuil Hall and *The Daily Advertiser*,' said Phillips, leaning gracefully upon the desk and talking for one hour and fifty minutes as if extemporizing—though Bliss Perry (*And Gladly Teach*) says the galley proof had already been set up, and not a word in the spoken speech was different. T. W. Higginson, who was present, has recorded: 'He held an unwilling audience spellbound, while bating absolutely nothing of his radicalism.

Many a respectable lawyer and divine felt his blood run cold the next day, when he found the fascinating orator whom he had applauded to the echo had really made the assassination of an emperor seem as trivial as the doom of a mosquito.'

iv

Narka and Vera—Nihilist Heroines

A CERTAIN approval of Nihilists reached down from a Phi Beta Kappa orator to writers of popular fiction, as we may infer from a long advertisement printed at the back of W. D. Howells's *April Hopes* of a novel by KathleenO'Meara, published by Harper and Brothers, 1888. *Narka the Nihilist* sounds like a fascinating work; the scenes and incidents are 'purely Russian', and the time the present—of which Tolstoy treats. (Tolstoy had been moving in on the American scene for several years now.) These scenes suggest 'the marvellously realistic pictures of the author of *Anna Karenina*', though it would be unjust, the advertisement admits, to the younger novelist to compare her work with his. *Narka* portrays an involved and ingenious complication of events. 'Tolstoy's stories even when he has a story to tell are simply the intuitive outgrowth of the thoughts and actions of the real men and women he draws. His *dramatis personae* make his plots, while Miss O'Meara's plots . . . make her men and women'. Here is the plot: Narka Larik, a low-born Russian Jewess, is a peculiar product of Russian soil and of autocratic Russian rule; possessed of a beautiful person, a glorious voice and a strong moral and mental constitution; suspicious, as all Muscovites are, a thorough and consistent hater, a devoted friend, truthful to a degree. (Apparently a low degree, for she swears on the holy image of the blessed St Nicholas to an utter falsehood in order to screen her lover and aid his cause.) 'The scenes are laid among that curious mixture of Oriental magnificence and barbaric discomfort, of lavish expenditure and shabby makeshift, to be found in a Russian castle, with its splendid vastness, the immensity of its grounds, the immensity of the forests on all sides of it, and the general scale of immensity on which everything about it and within it, is invariably conducted.' A pretty immense place Russia! Even Henry James spoke of 'grey immensity'. 'Add to these, Russian prisons, Paris salons, French convents, the lyric stage at Milan, Socialists, Nihilists, priests, patriots, and vivisectionists [*sic*], and it will readily be seen how strong and effective a story can be made by a woman so gifted in the telling of stories, the weaving of plots, and the study of character as Miss O'Meara has already proved herself to be. Narka Larik is a better woman morally than Anna Karenina, intellectually she is the superior of Katia, and she is quite worthy to stand by the side of these two illustrious countrywomen of hers as the exponent of all that is true and womanly in modern Russian life.'

Narka lives on in library catalogues, though Miss O'Meara's fame seems to have been quite eclipsed by Tolstoy's. But another Nihilist heroine was created, in 1881, by a writer who did become famous—Oscar Wilde. Vera belongs with Narka. *Vera: or The Nihilists*, a drama with a prologue, suggests, if nothing else, the extraordinary notions of the period. The prologue takes place in 1795, the play proper in 1800; and we learn that the Nihilists are already peopling the snowy landscape, and the serfs had been emanicipated sometime prior to 1795. The Tsar (unnamed) is a cruel tyrant, but his son (whom he tortures) loves the people. Somehow or other, this son escapes often enough from surveillance to join the secret society of Nihilists, disguised as a student of medicine. Vera, daughter of an innkeeper, is a member of the group—and—you have guessed it—she and the disguised Tsarevich fall in love. A nightingale is introduced from the south to sing to them in the bleak north. The Nihilists meet in a large garret, lighted by oil lamps; masked men stand about silent; one in a scarlet mask writes at a table; a man in yellow, with drawn sword guards the door; other figures in masks and cloaks enter, with the password—*Per crucem ad lucem*—answered by *Per sanguinem ad libertatem*. The meeting opens with the president's saying—What is our mission? Answer in chorus—To give freedom. Our creed? To annihilate. Our duty? To obey. The oath is hair-raising: To strangle whatever nature is in us; neither to love nor to be loved, neither to pity nor to be pitied, neither to marry nor to be given in marriage till the end is come; to stab secretly by night; to drop poison in the glass; to set father against son and husband against wife; without fear, without hope, without future, to suffer, to annihilate, to revenge. Vera, who manages to go to court balls, has acquired a reputation by her activities that makes even the Tsar afraid of her; he orders that she be hunted down with bloodhounds; 'and when she is taken I shall hew her limb from limb; I shall stretch her on the rack till her pale white body is twisted and curled like paper in the fire'. There are scenes between the Tsar and his son where the son pleads for the people.

> Tsar: Why do you beard me thus to my face?
> Tsarevich: Because I am a Nihilist.
> (Dead silence for a few minutes.)

At the end of act ii, the Tsar steps out on the balcony and is shot. Later the Nihilists suspect that the medical student is a spy, and the plot thickens; but at the end, after the nightingale sings, Vera foils, at the expense of her own life, the effort to kill the new Tsar. Even without the vivisectionists—whose role intrigues us in Miss O'Meara's novel—the action is overwhelming. And the misinformation staggering.

It is, I hope, pardonable to introduce Narka and Vera to the reader, instead of offering the more tiresome documentation of absurdities on the subject of Nihilism that could easily be gathered from the periodicals. There were importations from the French, such as *A Nihilist Princess*, by L. Gagneur, reviewed in the *Atlantic* (October, 1881) by someone accustomed, 'as most of us are, to meet Russians and their notions and customs in M. Tourgueneff's books', and hence disappointed to find the same topics touched by less delicate hands. But 'Nihilism is so terrible and tremendous a fact in these days' that any novel about it is interesting—and this one is 'breathless and melodramatic'.

[1] But note that the *Revue des deux mondes* was 'the educational staple' of the James boys in their 1855-8 stay in Europe and Turgenev published frequently there. See Daniel Lerner, *Influence of Turgenev on Henry James*.

[2] *Atlantic Monthly*, May 1874, article based on a French version of *Sportsman's Sketches*, for which Turgenev wrote to Perry, thanking him, and adding that he felt a 'great sympathy and admiration for your native land'.

CHAPTER V

AMERICAN ATTITUDES TOWARDS RUSSIAN LITERATURE AND CULTURE, 1880–1905

i

The 'Russian Craze'

RUSSIANS WERE interesting to Americans. They were not yet considered threatening—as they were intermittently so considered by the English, when the rivalries of power politics produced crises. From about 1885, and continuing rather acutely for fifteen years or so, there was what Royal Gettman, with his attention focused upon Turgenev and his reputation, has called a Russian craze in the United States. It is proved by the records of circulating libraries; the marked increase in the number of translations of books about Russia (such as Rambaud's *Histoire de la Russie*) and from Russian writers; and the popularity of lectures, such as those by Nathan Haskell Dole in Philadelphia and other cities; by Serge Wolkonsky, who gave one of the Lowell lectures in Boston, and spoke at clubs, universities and churches in Chicago, New York, St Louis and Washington—his lectures appearing in book form in 1897, as *Pictures of Russian History and Russian Literature*; and by Ivan Panin, whose *Lectures on Russian Literature* given in the United States, were published in 1889. Dr J. Allan Smith (*Tolstoy's Fiction in England and America*—unpublished dissertation, 1939) notes that by 1889, in the United States, there were twenty-seven editions of Tolstoy's novels and tales, representing sixteen different titles and twenty-one distinct translations. Before 1885, only one novel, *The Cossacks* (in a translation by Eugene Schuyler), had appeared (1878). One must remember that some of Tolstoy's social and religious writings—notable *My Religion*—were known to English and American readers before the great novels. Summing up his survey, Dr Smith says (page 29): 'Unless the temper of the times underwent a change, unless the public interest were focused once more on the Sleeping Giant of the North, unless promise of widespread popular support were unexpectedly to appear, there was little reason to suppose in 1882 or 1883 or 1884 that publishers and public alike would soon turn to Tolstoy or that the vogue of the Russian would soon reach a magnitude out of all proportion to the interest aroused in the past.' Among the causes helping to stimulate this interest, about 1886, were the preparatory knowledge of Turgenev; Tolstoy's religious views, at a time when science had shaken the basis of Christian faith; the availability of good historical studies of Russia (like Rambaud's); the studies of Russian novelists by the two Frenchmen, de Vogüé and Dupuy—of whom more later; a war scare in Afghanistan; and—perhaps not least—the fact that until 1891, Tolstoy's works were not protected in the United States by international copyright. By 1890, says Dr Smith, the main lines of criticism of Tolstoy were laid down; and Tolstoy was fortunate in having for interpreters de Vogüé in France, Arnold in England, and Howells in the United States—all discerning, enthusiastic and influential. In 1899 a twenty volume International Edition of Tolstoy's works was issued by Charles Scribner's Sons.[1] Up to about 1890, Dr Smith finds, the critical tendency was to keep artist and ethical teacher apart; those who admired the artist deplored his increasing moral attitudes. Stephen Crane, for instance, was asserting about 1890 that Count Tolstoy was the world's foremost writer, finding *Anna Karenina* too long, however, 'because he has to stop and preach, but it's a bully book'. Howells was an exception, praising both message and fiction for their power in setting forth the moral basis of life.

And then there was Dostoevsky. Just as the literate—including ladies like those at the summer resorts in Howells's novels—were getting used to Turgenev and even enjoying his melancholy, Dostoevsky appeared to present a more difficult challenge to comprehension. In the year of his death, the *Atlantic* (September, 1881) noted that only one of his novels existed in an English translation—*Buried Alive, or Ten Years of Penal Servitude* (New York, Henry Holt). The article recounts some of the facts of his life, including the reading of *Poor Folk* by Belinsky, and his enthusiasm, the Petrachevsky 'plot', the arrest and condemnation to death, the exile, the epilepsy (attributed to forced labour in the mines), and so on. There is a charming, if sentimental, picture of Dostoevsky as the 'Great-Heart of the weak and oppressed', calm, noble, consistent, firm in battling against revolutionary propaganda. Dostoevsky did not 'catch on' at this time, and no other translations appeared until 1886. But people who knew French were discovering him. Leaving the Atlantic seaboard for the moment, we find Lafcadio Hearn writing in the New Orleans *Times-Democrat* (between 1882 and 1887) about, among other things, the popularity of Russian literature abroad, especially in France. French literature may really be purified and reanimated by an invasion of foreign idealism and the thinking of a race that is 'if you will, half civilized, yet full of faith in man and in God and in truth, full also of youth and hope'. An article entitled 'A Terrible Novel' is devoted to *Crime and Punishment*, 'the most frightful and powerful romance conceived by any modern writer'. The plot, oddly enough, for it is usually recognized as intricately wrought, Hearn calls 'thin', but the book has the power of ghastly mesmerism. The Russians he finds unrivalled in psychological work, and he introduces—I think for the first time in American criticism—the Russian Soul, 'struggling for utterance under a mountain weight of oppression' and 'everywhere manifesting symptoms strangely akin to madness. Mysticism, reverie, hopeless ambition, vain rage, mark the psychology of the time'.

In 1886 and 1887 appeared *Crime and Punishment*, *Injury and Insult*, *The Idiot*, *The Friend of the Family* and *The Gambler*, all in English translations. This spurt of interest was due in large measure to the work of two French critics: Ernest Dupuy, author of *Les Grands Maîtres de la Littérature Russe au dix-neuvième siècle* (Trans. 1886) and Melchior de Vogüé, whose *Le Roman Russe* (1886)[2] is considered by D. S. Mirsky, an authority, to be 'the main landmark of the penetration of Russian literature into

Western Europe'. Edmund Gosse, looking back from the vantage-point of 1908, described it as 'one of the most powerfully influential products of literary criticism in the nineteenth century . . . a revelation of the most blazing order', in which Comte de Vogüé presented to Western Europe that 'mysterious soul of Russia'. Articles by de Vogüé had appeared in 1885 in the *Revue des deux Mondes* on Dostoevsky, and the reviewers had seized upon them. *The Nation* (January 21, 1886) declares that the new writer had not delighted his readers as had Tolstoy, but 'he has been read with surprise and emotion and the sensation he has produced has been powerful if not always pleasant; . . . the charm of strangeness and remoteness is intensified; the race is a different one from our own, more primitive, with ways of living and thinking and feeling often very far from anything in our experience, sometimes opposed to our most cherished opinions and beliefs. . . . The vagueness of our knowledge of all that belongs to Russia gives a corresponding poetic colouring to what we read and adds to its charm. As we become familiar with these strange writers, what impresses us most strongly in all of them, unlike as they are to each other, is a certain simplicity and grandeur of soul, a tenderness of nature, an inclination towards unbounded self-sacrifice, which is all as new to us as it is attractive'. It is in Dostoevsky especially that all these characteristics are to be found—in the 'chaos of a tender pitiful heart'. De Vogüé's study helped to attach the Russian Soul rather specially to Dostoevsky—'most Russian of the Russians', in whom cruelty and tenderness, love of the actual and love of the abstract, were blended into a kind of mystic realism. De Vogüé's phrase, 'the religion of suffering', became Dostoevsky's label.

A lively account of how sensitive readers were affected by the spell of the Russian writers is to be found in an article in the *Atlantic* for August, 1887, by Harriet Waters Preston, a New England essayist on Provençal poets and a translator from the Latin and French. It was *Le Roman Russe* that inspired her outburst of enthusiasm, which mixes information and misinformation in a manner that is fairly typical of the period. De Vogüé's criticism she declares to be the best since Sainte-Beuve. He not only knows Russian, but is married to a Russian—'one of those marvellous Russian women who dazzle and reduce to despair all the rest of the feminine world'. Most of us are now consumed with a passion for German opera or Russian romance, both appealing to 'the same dark and disillusioned yet restless and expectant temper in the modern mind'. These tremendous works of the imagination from beyond the Carpathians exercise a special fascination over Americans—for reasons she never makes clear. 'No one reads the Russian novel with gusto who does not read also French with ease.' She does, of course, and her article is peppered with the French titles. But the greatest of the novels in dramatic and analytic power—*Guerre et Paix*, *Anna Karénine* and Turgenev's masterpieces—have long since been translated into English, and are found everywhere, in circulating libraries, on private shelves, on Paris *quais*. It is less-known books through which she sets out to track the Russian style and ethics: *Ames Mortes*; *Souvenirs des Morts*; *Récits d'un Chasseur*, etc. She tells how Dostoevsky was introduced to 'Pouchkine' sometime in the '40's as a new Gogol; and 'before the old man was halfway through Dostoevsky's first book, he was paying a tearful homage to the author of *Les Pauvres Gens*'. The 'old man' had died in 1837 at the age of 38, and *Poor Folk* was published in 1846; so it is quite a story. *Taras Bulba* (an historical novel in prose) is referred to as 'a powerful tragedy in verse'. What she has to say of Tolstoy has more relation to fact, but she gives the impression that after writing *My Religion* he had 'disappeared from the scene of his immense achievements and the company of his intellectual and social peers' and gone to live with the peasants and practise a humble handicraft. Convinced that his work of destruction and denial is done, she sees him ready to inaugurate a new worship, adumbrate a new art, and prophesy a new morality. His simple tales breathe, not—as de Vogüé puts it—*un souffle du cimetière*, but rather the dews of Paradise; and nothing can compare with *Les Deux Vieillards* and *Ce qui fait vivre les Hommes* except 'that softly sparkling mosaic of the Good Shepherd and his flock in the church of SS.

Nazario e Celso at Ravenna'. The Russian is prone to a mystical and exalted kind of piety, indicating 'the deep and steadfast Oriental element that underlies the seeming versatility and receptivity of his nature'.

ii

Contrasting Opinions: Whitman, Dillon, Brandes

THE INTEREST Russians had for Americans had earlier had the friendly tinge due to the perception of likenesses. Both countries had at almost the same time done away with their slave systems, although the problems each faced in readjustment differed in significant ways, of which the race question in the United States was of course the most striking. The Russian *mir* was still sometimes compared with the New England town-meeting, but that American institution was becoming obsolete. Both countries still resembled each other in having a vast undeveloped territory, a frontier, though that of the American West was rapidly contracting. Talk about the affinity between Russia and the United States drew a warning from T. S. Perry in the *Atlantic* (October, 1880): 'the only resemblance is that both enter late into the company of civilized nations, but from diametrically opposed quarters—they struggling against despotism and we against excessive license'. And what he had called 'the spirit of the Slavs' (in an earlier article, June, 1877, *Atlantic*) was characterized by adjectives no one, American or European, would have applied to the American spirit: patient, enduring, unenterprising. *Oriental* was one of the favourite epithets.

A relatively late, and perhaps the most eloquent expression of the earlier friendly feeling of likeness between the two countries, is the preface which Walt Whitman wrote for the first Russian edition of *Leaves of Grass* in 1880. It is addressed 'To the Russian People':

> You Russians and we Americans! Our countries so distant, so unlike at first glance—such a difference in social and political conditions—and our respective methods of moral and practical

development the last hundred years—and yet in certain features, and vastest ones, so resembling each other. The variety of stock-elements and tongues, to be resolutely fused in a common identity and union at all hazards—the idea, perennial through the ages, that they both have their historic and divine mission—the fervent element of manly friendship throughout the whole people, surpassed by no other races—the grand expanse of territorial limits and boundaries—the unformed and nebulous state of many things, not yet permanently settled, but agreed on all hands to be the preparations of an infinitely greater future—the fact that both Peoples have their independent and leading positions to hold, keep, and if necessary to fight for, against the rest of the world—the deathless aspirations at the inmost centre of each great community, so vehement, so mysterious, so abysmic—are certainly features you Russians and we Americans possess in common. As my dearest dream is for an internationality of poems and poets, binding the lands of the earth closer than all treaties and diplomacy, as the purpose beneath the rest in my book is such hearty comradeship, for individuals to begin with, and for all nations of the earth as a result—how happy I should be to get the hearing and emotional contact of the great Russian peoples. To whom, now and here, I waft affectionate salutation from these shores, in America's name.

(*Prose Works*, Camden Edition, Putnam, 1902, pp. 259–261.)

The tone of this greeting is characteristically exalted and emotional; it is a development of the greeting in *Salut au Monde*:

'You of the might Slavic tribes and empires! you Russ in Russia!'

But Whitman had spent much time studying the facts about Russia; and his interest in Russia forms, in the words of C. J. Furness, who edited *Walt Whitman's Workshop* (1928, Harvard University Press), 'a fascinating unwritten chapter in the dawning of Whitman's inclusive international consciousness'. It may have been some particular Russian that roused his interest; an old Russian count is mentioned in the record of conversations at the

Gilchrist home (see MS. Notebook of Herbert Gilchrist in a private collection), of whom Whitman said: 'He let me into a good deal about Russians. He was a wild old fellow. He had been a great duellist. Had a scar.' That Whitman really investigated Russian material is proved by his Notes in the MS. Division of the Library of Congress; they include a detailed geographic survey of Russia, statistics and notations about various races there, observations on trade, education and society, and his own ideas on how to improve conditions. For example, this—quoted in the *Workshop:* 'The serfs have been freed, and now trade, intercommunication with the world is all that is needed.' And speaking of church missions, he comments, 'What are all the missions ever built, sent forth, in comparison with the benefits that would ensue to nearly a hundred millions of people by the putting of the great Russian empire in rapport with the rest of the world, through ports, trade, travel, science, literature.'

Virtually no one in this later period echoes Whitman in his friendliness, his stressing of likeness, and his eminently wise insistence on the benefits of intercommunication. Differences continue to be the theme. It depended on what one read—either in American or foreign sources—whether the differences looked attractive or terrifying. Whether these differences actually existed was a question seldom raised. People who did not read Harriet Preston in the *Atlantic*, with her French and her passion for German opera and Russian romance, and her perception of the mystical and exalted piety of the Russian, might soon be harvesting very different ideas about the Russians from a little book in the Twentieth Century Library, a monthly publication of the Humboldt Publishing Co., in New York. The book, entitled *Russian Traits and Terrors—A Faithful Picture of the Russia of Today*, was an 1894 reprint of a publication that appeared in 1891 (Boston, B. R. Tucker). The 'faithful picture' came originally from the *English Fortnightly Review*, and its author was 'E. B. Lanin'—pen-name for E. J. Dillon. To him the Russians were indeed different. Among the titles under which they are discussed are Lying, Fatalism, Sloth, Dishonesty, Sexual Morality, Censure (i.e. Censorship), Russian Prisons, Jews in Russia, etc. The documentation is largely from Russian newspapers, and the general impression is that things could not possibly be worse. There are sweeping generalizations. Here is 'a vast empire peopled by undeveloped types of humanity welting [*sic*] in chaotic ignorance and misery, in various degrees of disintegration from the action of that fearful solvent nameless in the English tongue and which Russians now term Oblomoffism. (From Goncharov's novel *Oblomov*.) This combination of fatalism, will-paralysis, indifference, and grovelling instincts . . .' 'The foreigner who visits Russia ignorant of the language and the people as are most, has little difficulty in gleaning data enough during the first few days of his sojourn to enable him to gauge with tolerable accuracy the abyss that separates Russian notions of morality and decency from those which prevail in the West.' And no doubt, the more ignorant the foreigner, the less difficulty! It is interesting to learn that one 'frequently meets' types like some of the most famous heroines of the greatest writers—Anna Karenina, Irene (Turgenev's *Smoke*), Natasha (Dostoevsky's *Humiliated and Oppressed*), Katerina (Ostrovsky's *Storm*). And they are appreciated, glorified, and imitated in Russia; 'in this country they might be silently pitied and would be inexorably ostracized'. Tolstoy's *Kreutzer Sonata* is an accurate picture, and it would be correct to judge Russian society in the words of Gibbon passing sentence on the Merovingians: 'It would be difficult to find anywhere more vice and less virtue'.

A very different picture of Russia had been published in New York in 1889, translated from the Danish—*Impressions of Russia*, by Georg Brandes. (Published in Copenhagen in 1888.) The translator, Samuel C. Eastman, testifies in his introductory note to 'the great interest taken at the present time in the literature of Russia and in everything which relates to that great country'. Everything that aids in giving a correct impression of its political and social conditions is therefore acceptable. Brandes had gone to St Petersburg in 1887 to lecture in French at the invitation of the Russian Authors Association, and later went to Moscow at the invitation of the curator of the university. He explains in his book just where he went and whom he met, and adds: 'I am not unmindful of how little of what I did see I was able to understand fully, nor of how inconsiderable a portion of a country like Russia and its inhabitants was placed before me. But naturally I believe in my capacity for observation and in the soundness of my judgments.'

We are most concerned here with his interpretations of Russian literature—having sound reasons to respect his judgment as literary critic. But his general account—based on Leroy-Beaulieu's *Empire of the Tsars*, and Elisée Reclus's *Universal Geography*—gives a good background for the literary interpretation. He cannot resist the geographical analogy: apparently because the steppes are monotonously uniform and the great Volga is sluggish, sluggishness and uniformity are Russian characteristics—at least while he is talking about geography. We meet our wolves again, in statistical form: there are 175,000 in European Russia, and they destroy annually 180,000 head of cattle, 560,000 sheep, 100,000 dogs, besides (a minor detail) 150 human beings. Each wolf is estimated to consume annually the value of about 80 roubles.

In a chapter on the ignorance and superstition of the people, he pays tribute to the young men and women who go among the peasants 'with an untiring heroic zeal which is beyond all praise and without parallel in any land'. This active element of the intelligentsia is a 'pure young world', with the 'fiery faith of youth and the passive character of Russian heroism, constant even in torture. The faith in their historic mission and the consciousness of their spiritual power sustain them'. He makes the distinction, so seldom recognized, between the few hundred terrorists and the 'Nihilistic force', which is that of profound scepticism in regard to existing institutions in their present form—the royal prerogative, the church, marriage, property—a scepticism not confined to Russia. He gives a temperate and sensible account of the friendship between men and women, not to be interpreted as free love in the sensual sense, but rather 'a mental and moral attitude that has no connection with frivolity and thoughtlessness'. One seventeen-year-old girl took issue with him when he called Rudin (Turgenev's hero) a typical representative of Russian weakness, reminding him that Russian literature was only an incomplete reflection of the life and character of the Russian people. Brandes still insists that the study of Rudin's inconsistency is so exhaustive that through the weakness of this one character we understand the weakness of Russian character everywhere. But the girl herself he admires as a personality 'impossible to find in a Scandinavian girl of that age—and a will gleams out through the words, flashing like a steel blade, a will which is full of promise'. (Page references—60, 62, 291.)

Brandes examines critically popular ideas about the Russians, such as that they are unoriginal and great borrowers; he notes the beauty of the *troika*, of many handicrafts and decorative arts, and of architecture. He gets rather mixed up with the realistic and the mystical traits of the Russian character, and falls into the pattern of contradictions. 'They are radicals in everything, in faith and in infidelity, in love and hate, in submission and rebellion.' They are the most arbitrary oppressors and the most reckless liberators. Their receptiveness betokens more decided originality in the future. 'The question presses itself upon us whether when we are striving to penetrate the secrets of this land, we are not gazing into the very future of Europe.' (Page 34.)

His account of the literature goes back to the early periods: to Slavic mythology and popular ballads, with many cross references to Scandinavian mythology and ballads. There is much on the Russian language, which, of all living and dead languages, he asserts, is richest in expressions of love—all sorts of love. His references to Russian writers must have been somewhat startling to the American reader; for not only are the now familiar Turgenev, Dostoevsky, Tolstoy, Gogol, Pushkin dealt with, but Lomonosov, Derzhavin, Zhukovsky, Lermontov, Shevtchenko, Chernishevsky, Belinsky, Nadson, Fet, Gleb Uspensky, Goncharov, Griboyedov and Garshin. His tribute to Turgenev, the first Russian author who became cosmopolitan, is that for the cultured readers of Western Europe he peopled the great empire of the East with human beings of the present time. For Dostoevsky, he relies obviously on de Vogüé; Dostoevsky knows 'as no other person knows the irresistible attraction of the gulfs' into which men fling themselves—whether of crime or self-sacrifice. When he explains the discontented youth of Russia, Brandes, having the historical sense, advises us to forget Bazarov, at one time a true conception, and the young people in *Virgin Soil*, who were never a true representation, and also Dostoevsky's *Possessed* —'an ultra-reactionary caricature of a tendency in which he participated in his youth, but to which by the lapse of time he had taken an aversion'. (But that is precisely the novel that the West has continued to look to, for prophetic insight into the Russian Soul.)

The conclusion of this deeply interesting book is a description of Repin's portrait of Tolstoy, guiding the plough. 'What is it that he cultivates? What is it that all these, young and old, the men with good will, prepare and cultivate? Black land, fertile land, new land, grain land . . . the broad unlimited expanse which fills the mind with melancholy and hope . . . the incomprehensible, darkly mysterious, the womb of new realities and new mysticism . . . Russia and the future.' (Pages 352–3.)

iii

Travel, journalism, scholarship, popular education: Edmund Noble, Isabel Hapgood, the Chautauqua Circles

THE GENERAL point of view of Brandes—on the Nihilists and Terrorists, the Russian character and Russian culture—has so much sanity to recommend it that one regrets that it probably influenced fewer people than the sensational *Russian Traits and Terrors*. But another writer, as sane as Brandes, must have reached a much wider public. He was a Scotsman, who received his training in journalism in excellent schools. Edmund Noble (1853–1937) was reporter and editorial writer for the *Liverpool Courier* from 1873 to 1882, correspondent in Russia for the next two years for the *London Daily News*, the *London Daily Globe*, the *Manchester Guardian* and the *Glasgow Herald*. In 1887 he was foreign editorial writer for the *New York Herald*, and on the staff of the *Boston Herald* for forty-six years; a contributor to the *Atlantic Monthly* from 1885, through the '90's; secretary of the Society of American Friends of Russian Freedom from 1892 to 1904; and author, among other books, of two on Russia: *The Russian Revolt*, 1885, and *Russia and the Russians*, 1900.

Many of Noble's articles were in the form of reviews of books on Russia. In an *Atlantic Monthly* review (1894) of the first part of Leroy-Beaulieu's *The Empire of the Tsars and the Russians*, he speaks of the difficulty of understanding even the peoples close to us, and characterizes earlier books on Russia, from Herberstein to Haxthausen, as having descriptive but little critical value; referring to the wild hearsays in the old books and the mad stories in the daily Press about Nihilists, he says: 'Emergence from this habit of treating Russia as a Scythian country rich in Slavonian marvels has naturally been slow, but the process has proved not less certain than that of growing civilization and the progressive unification of the nations'. (I fear that quoting this 'not less certain' passage in 1953 is an invitation to cynicism.)

Or take his review of Stepniak's *Russia Under the Tsars* (*Atlantic*, August, 1885). He praises Stepniak as an unequalled gatherer of information on the domestic struggle in Russia and a collector of anecdotes of Government oppression and the sufferings of conspirators, but as an expositor of 'so-called Nihilism' signally unreliable, because he throws no light on the psychology of 'the strange enthusiasms of Nihilism, its indomitable courage, its power of enlisting the sympathies of women, its nobilities of character, its sublime capacities for self-sacrifice, its saints, its martyrologies, its relics, its perplexing consciousness of a high morality even in the prosecution of tasks obviously unrighteous'.

In his own books, Noble attempts an interpretation that will throw light on this puzzling psychology. The earlier revolt was a gospel of negation that had at first no political character, and that owed much to the influence of Saint-Simon, Proudhon and others. He gives a good account of the Narodnik movement, and distinguishes among the parties, theories and activities of the movements from 1861 to 1878; noting how the Narodniki failed to move the peasants, and how Government reprisals drove people to extremes, he describes the formation in 1879 of the Executive Committee of Terrorists, and the party of the People's Will. After picturing the external features of the dynamic protest against absolutism, he turns to the inner side revealed in personalities like Chernishevsky, whom he visited in his exile at Astrakhan—warning the reader that this interview was held in Astrakhan, not London, and was with an exile with shattered nerves. Selecting four of those who had been involved in the assassination of the Tsar—an aristocrat, a peasant (born a serf), a priest's son, and a student—he sketches their lives, shows how they were united by intense love of country, and were sublimely reckless and willing to die, however misguided their methods.

The Slavic masses look considerably less grey and uniform after Noble has made an historical analysis. He, like Brandes, generalizes freely on the basis of geography, but his geography is much more varied and consequently, so are his Russians. He stresses migratory tendencies and extremes of climate, and in *Atlantic* articles like 'By River and Road in Russia', and 'Island Democracy in the Caspian' (September and December, 1887) he takes his readers to unfamiliar and interesting places, where the customary generalizations do not fit. He spent weeks on some of the islands that were the centre of fishing industries, in the lower Volga and the Caspian Sea. There was a family of entrepreneurs of a singularly enlightened character, the Sapozhnikovs, who had established a sort of primitive democracy on the islands. There were no police or priests or passports or classes; all were well-to-do, all worked. He ends on a note of fear, lest the corrupting influence of civilization reach this spot, with its 'wonderful democracy-compound of Russian, Tatar, and Calmuck'. Noble (like George Borrow) *likes* Russians, and their democratic friendly travelling habits, with the mingling of classes. Commenting on the Russian word *poputchiki* (fellow-travellers), he says, 'that Russian should be the only language in Europe which expresses companionship of travel in a single word, alone suggests this unique thriving of democratic manners in unfavourable soil'. It is sad to reflect that this nice word has become, especially in the West, an insult and an accusation.

Noble has his prejudices; he has little use for the Greek Church —or for Puritanism either, for that matter. He thinks the early Slav system had the freedom of the individual as its foundation, and that the Byzantine Church and the Tartar conquest brought in the principles of autocracy and centralization, and that the 'unification' of Russia was simple usurpation. He makes much of Old Believer revolts as truly popular protest, a hidden rebellion against autocracy, in spite of the ostensible and superficial ritual disputes; 'the motive force of the revolt called dissent was Russian individuality'. (*The Russian Revolt*, page 142.)

One of Noble's *Atlantic* articles (December, 1885) is an admirably descriptive piece on 'Life in St Petersburg', well-balanced between the magnificent and the sordid aspects of the capital. He sees democracy of a sort in the mingling of all kinds of people on the Nevsky (again like Borrow). He describes the vast apartment houses of a thousand rooms, with perhaps two thousand people dwelling in them, and the house-porter in the capacity of police spy over these aggregations of cells. This cloud of police control, he thinks, has moulded literary expression and wrought 'that inimitable language of moods which enabled writers like Pushkin, Gogol, Lermontov and Dostoevsky to play an important part in awakening the national consciousness against the forces of oppression and wrong'. 'A Call on Mother Moscow' (*Atlantic*, August, 1888) is equally interesting and vivid, with all its contrasts to St Petersburg. He refers, in a review of Isabel Hapgood's *Epic Songs of Russia* (*Atlantic*, November, 1886), to the new interest beginning to manifest itself in Russian things; ten years earlier it would have been impossible to issue a volume such as this, so widespread was the incredulity even among educated readers, concerning native Russian literature. 'Nor is it at all doubtful that the thanks for the revived attention to Russia are due much more to the political pamphleteer with his war sensationalism and jingo spirit, than to the Slav scholar and ethnologist, whose aim is the union of races by knowledge, as the purpose of others is the separation of men by prejudice.'

In his earlier book (*Russian Revolt*) he gives support to the already familiar notion of Russian pessimism, as a tendency really universal in Russia: 'Not to be pessimistic in Russia is to be divorced from all contact and sympathy with the national life; to be cut off, either by foreign birth or by some monstrous denial of nature, from the tree of national development. All influences and epochs have contributed to this tendency. A monotonous landscape, the loss of free institutions, Byzantinism, with its cruel law giving and ascetic tyranny, the fiscal burdens of the new State, the antitheses suggested by European culture, the crushing of the individual, the elimination from Russian life of all those healthy activities which engage citizenship in other countries, the harassing restrictions upon thought and movements, the State-created frivolities of society—all these have contributed to the gloom of the mental atmosphere, until today pessimism may be said to be the normal condition of Russian thought.' Yet this Russian sadness is unobtrusive in social spheres; there is surface gaiety, and this lends the charm of versatility to Russian society. This, we must remember, was that famous decade of the '80's—the lull before the storm, the period of depression among the intellectuals, soon to be so wonderfully interpreted by Chekhov. So Noble's emphasis is not misplaced. But when he wrote on 'The Future of Russia' in the *Atlantic* in December, 1900, it is not pessimism that he singles out for comment in a very shrewd forecast: 'The Russians possess a degree of the power of self-adaptation to new conditions not met with, perhaps, in any other country of the world. They have been "changing all that" from the earliest periods of their history'; and he cites the religious revolt of the seventeenth century, the reforms of Peter, the changing of the capital, the abolition of serfdom and so on. And he notes how frequently the term 'new generation' is used—'it being well understood that a single generation usually suffices to give some new and important direction to the intellectual or social tendencies of the people'.

Whatever else it was doing, the literary movement which the *Dial* (August, 1886) termed the Russian invasion of the realm of fiction was helping the French invasion to give the American reader a taste for strong meat, instead of 'the pastry of our home-made fiction' (*Dial*, May, 1886), and make him painfully aware of the limitations of American novelists. He was considered to have a squeamish taste, but this was no longer regarded as wholly admirable, and William Morton Payne criticizes Nathan Haskell Dole's translation of *Anna Karenina* for modifying, in deference to this taste, certain portions where the realism is too intense: 'if we are to have translations of the masterpieces of literature at all, we have a right to demand that they shall be as accurate as scholarship can make them', and 'if Puritan taste cannot take the great writers as they are, so much the worse for that peculiar species of taste. Literary and artistic taste have quite as good claim to be considered'. Scholarship was really beginning to count for something. Isabel Hapgood's translations of Gogol and of the epic songs of Russia (with an introduction by that authority on ballads, Professor Child) led Payne to suggest to Miss Hapgood that she retranslate Turgenev, since with one or two exceptions the existing versions from the French were 'miserably inaccurate'. And this eventually she did.

Isabel Hapgood spent two years in Russia, just at the close of the 1880's, and published many articles in such magazines as the *Nation*, *Century*, *Scribner's*, *Lippincott's*, the *Independent* and the *Atlantic*, many of them later included in her book *Russian Rambles* (1895). In her introduction, she writes not otherwise than one might today: 'In spite of all that has been written about Russia, the common incidents of everyday life are not known, or are known so imperfectly that any statement of them is a travesty. . . . I am told that I must abuse Russia if I wish to be popular in America.' People, she reflects, find it more interesting to hear bad than good things of their neighbours. 'People too frequently go to Russia with the deliberate expectation and intention of seeing queer things. That they do frequently contrive to see queer things, I admit,' and she gives an amusing example of something an American thought he saw: a man going along the streets of St Petersburg, tearing off bits of a live chicken and eating them, feathers and all; what he really saw neither she nor her Russian friends had any notion. 'The general idea of foreign visitors seems to be that they shall find the Russia of the seventeenth century. I am sure that the Russia of Ivan the Terrible's time, a century earlier, would precisely meet their views.' But finding the reality tame, they supply the missing spice. 'A man who would see Russia clearly must strip himself of all preconceived prejudices of religion, race, and language, and study the people from their own point of view. If he goes about repeating Napoleon's famous saying—scratch a Russian and you will find a Tartar—he will simply betray his own ignorance of history and facts.' Knowledge of the language she declares indispensable. 'I have not attempted to analyse the "complicated" national character. Indeed I am not sure that it is complicated. Russians of all classes, from the peasant up, possess a naturally simple, sympathetic disposition and manner, as a rule, tinged with a friendly warmth whose influence is felt as soon as one crosses the frontier. Shall I be believed if I say that I found it in custom-house offices and gendarmes? For the rest, characters vary quite as much as they do elsewhere. It is a question of individuals in character and morals, and it is dangerous to indulge in generalizations. My one generalization is that they are as a nation too long-suffering and lenient in certain directions, that they allow too much personal independence in certain things.'

Dr Babey, in her study of American travellers (previously referred to), considers Miss Hapgood prejudiced in favour of the autocracy—the reason being, perhaps, that she never had any trouble with the police, 'either genuine or manufactured'. She thought that many stories about spies forever in attendance were made up by guides, for the obvious purpose of extorting handsome gratuities for protection, but Miss Hapgood, knowing the language, never employed guides. She made several trips to

Russia, the last in 1916–1917. Dr Babey gives her due credit for her effort to give the American public an idea of the ordinary conditions of Russian life and character, illustrated by anecdotes 'from her vast personal experience'; 'she began her work before anyone else had attempted to render systematically Russian writers into English and so broke the ground for a number of others who later won distinction'.

The titles of some of her *Atlantic Monthly* articles over a period from 1887 to 1893 will give an idea of the range of the experience: 'Count Tolstoy and the Public Censor', 'Count Tolstoy at Home', 'A Journey on the Volga', 'Kazan', 'Harvest Time on the Volga', 'Passports, Police and Post Office', 'Russian Summer Resort—Tsarskoe Selo'. In this last nice gossipy paper, we learn what later travellers have often taken pains to tell us—and the traveller who is writing this book noted the fact in 1946—that the basins had no stoppers; but Miss Hapgood gives the reason—'running water is cleaner to wash in'. What could be more sensible? If there is enough water? Finding the Russian children of all classes behaving well in the parks, she thinks they are born more agreeable than Western children. The account of her summer visit at Tolstoy's estate, Yasnaya Polyana, is detailed and pleasant, and shows rather more sympathy with the Countess than with the Count, whom she sometimes rather shrewdly pushes into a corner in an argument; whereupon he just became silent, and wouldn't be drawn out any farther. She quotes the countess's opinion of her husband's disciples—all 'small, blond, sickly and homely, as like to one another as a pair of old boots'.

Miss Hapgood later played a valuable part in popularizing knowledge of Russian writers through the Chautauqua Circles. The assembly grounds at Lake Chautauqua offered entertainment shading into instruction, with conferences to discuss practically everything, and home reading courses in history, literature, art and science, worked out in some instances on a four-year plan. There was a Chautauqua Press and a monthly magazine, *The Chautauquan*. It is impossible to estimate the number of culture-seeking Americans who must have acquired in the first years of the twentieth century at least a few fairly accurate notions of Russian literature under the guidance of Isabel Hapgood. Her *Survey of Russian Literature with Selections* was published by the Chautauqua Press in 1902; she goes back to earlier periods, relying for the history on Rambaud and on W. R. Morfill's *Story of Russia*; draws upon the work of C. E. Turner and Sir John Bowring, and makes a point of giving 'exclusively' the views of Russian critics upon their own literature, quoting from Belinsky, Dobrolyubov and others, and especially praising Belinsky's brilliant critical articles, which 'educated the minds of that whole generation and prepared men for the social movement of the 'sixties'. And she is abreast of the new literature, with interesting things to say of Gorky, whose *Foma Gordeyev* she translated. At that time he was in what she calls polite banishment in the Crimea, where she hopes the Russian Government will keep him, so that he will develop his immense genius, 'instead of meddling with social and political questions'. Her views of the service rendered to literature by the Russian Government are not as funny as they sound. Others (including Noble, just quoted) have borne testimony to the stimulating effect of censorship, forcing writers into artistic ingenuities of expression, and saving them from the flatness of factual statement, and what Henry James would call *pièces de circonstance*. 'If,' says Miss Hapgood of Gorky, 'he can be kept there or elsewhere out of mischief, the Russian Government will again render the literature of its own country and of the world as great a service as it has already more than once rendered in the past by similar means.' Her chapter on Dostoevsky is notable for the absence of the excited rapture that became so fashionable later. But at this time only four translations are listed, as compared with the now easily accessible Turgenev and Tolstoy. Anyone who faithfully followed the study guide would have known also of Saltykov-Schedrin, Ostrovsky, Leskov, Nekrasov, Uspensky and others.

Along with articles on literature in the magazine, there was from October, 1902, to June, 1903, a *Reading Journey through Russia*, with papers by Hapgood, Noble, and others, that would take one from Kiev to Odessa, from St Petersburg to Vladivostok, to Turkestan, the Crimea, the Caucasus and the land of Tolstoy. These were illustrated and supplied with a glossary of terms, a guide to pronunciation, questions for review and a bibliography. One wonders if the daughters of the ladies who discussed Turgenev on the veranda in the 1880's emulated the culture of their mothers, with more attention to facts now available and less to emotion. More and more knowledge was becoming accessible. In the *Dial* (November 16, 1902) is a notice of the first volume of the important *Anthology of Russian Literature*, edited by Leo Wiener. 'While we can hardly agree with the editor in thinking that Russia is soon destined to take an important place in the American educational curriculum, we are aware that he has done us a valuable service in supplying this generous representation of the literature of his country, for English translations from the Russian have thus far been few in number (except for the novelists) and poor in quality, and the history of Russian literature from the earliest times down to the last century is practically a sealed book to most of our readers. Pushkin we know, and Gogol and their successors.'

The *Chautauquan* has a series of speculations on the theme of Saxon *vs.* Slav running along in the same months with the Reading Journey. The October 1902 article poses a very interesting query: 'The British Empire and the Russian present by all odds the most imposing political spectacles of today, as well as the most stupendous problems for tomorrow. Shall it be the Saxon in the person of the Englishman, or the Slav in the person of the Russian, who shall ultimately civilize and institutionalize the great undeveloped world?' That it might be the Saxon (by courtesy) in the person of the American had scarcely as yet entered the field of speculation.

iv

Condemnation and Prediction: Mark Twain, Henry Adams, T. S. Perry

THE FUTURE of Russia was something to ponder over, and the

growing interest in Russian literature fed these speculations. There was beginning to be a suspicion that this literature had an intimate connection with social and political conditions, and owed some of its significant characteristics to this connection. But until about 1905, American critics of Russian literature continued to direct the attention of their readers chiefly to artistic and moral qualities. The contrast with British criticism—the British being very much aware of the activities of a rival power—will be pointed out later.

Russia, to Americans, was a country where exciting things happened, more and more exciting as the nineteenth century drew to a close and the twentieth dawned. Spectacular events associated ith the imperfectly understood Nihilist movement, and the later vement 'to the people', the assassinations and attempted assas-tions by Terrorist groups, the mass trials (like those of the ayev conspirators in 1871 and that of the 193 in St Petersburg 8), the assassination of Alexander II, the eastward expansion sia, famines and pogroms—all these events strengthened ressions long associated with Russian history: crimes and absolutism and ignorance, contradictions and mysteries. arper (*The Russia I Believe In*) states that about the turn tury, the only book on Russia written by an American cured wide currency was George Kennan's *The Siberian tem*, which gave full details of the worst features of but which also introduced to American readers the Russian liberal and revolutionary thought, whom ad interviewed. But these happenings in Russia did not affect the United States. They were to many an appeal to tarian sympathies, as well as a source of satisfaction, in Americans had so much earlier recognized and dealt with the s of arbitrary power. There was no fear as yet of contagion m revolutionary movements in Russia; this country had had s revolution.

It is true that the difficulties—economic, social, political—attendant on the rapid industrial expansion of the United States were beginning to bring unrest and questioning. But Russia was very far away. Political prisoners—if they were in Siberia—were objects of compassion; kings were anachronisms to enlightened republicans; bombs hurled at Russian despots exploded in quite another world from that of the Haymarket tragedy in Chicago. Perhaps it is not going too far to say that Americans who bothered at all about Russian tyranny and the right to revolution (in Russia) shared the simple view expressed by Mark Twain in his famous piece, *The Tsar's Soliloquy*, published in the *North American Review*, March, 1905. It is an example of the blithe spirit in which Americans were wont to call for the assassination of those they considered despots in other countries. It is a habit we have not lost up to the present day. 'Why does nobody kil Stalin?' inquired *Collier's Magazine* from its cover in June, 195 'The rank and file American', observes Professor T. A. Bailey his study of Russian-American relations, 'while deploring mu has normally looked upon the removal of monarchs, by v means or otherwise, as an incident in progress.'[3]

Mark Twain's piece begins with a quotation from the *Times Correspondence*: 'After the Tsar's morning bath, habit to meditate an hour before dressing himself'. So Ma presents the Tsar, contemplating himself, without his the mirror, and reflecting, in the fashion of Carlyle, t make the man—clothes and titles make the man 140 Russians worship. What a curious and unaccountable the human race is! 'Because in civilized countries it is remove oppressors otherwise than by due process of law that the same rule applies in Russia where there is no s as law except for our Family. . . . We do as we please, done as we please for centuries. Our common trade h crime, our common pastime murder, our common bev blood, the blood of the nation. Upon our heads lie million murders. Yet the pious moralist says it is a crime to assassinate Is the human race a joke? And that is Mark Twain's reflectio though put in the Tsar's mouth.

Had Mark Twain completely forgotten the delightful hours the Innocents had spent at Yalta with an earlier Tsar and his family?

'Among the infinite subjects of my misunderstanding,' wrote Henry Adams to Cecil Spring-Rice, May 31, 1897 (*Letters*, II-128), 'that of everything Russian is conspicuous.' In 1901 Adams paid a visit to Russia, staying three weeks, and perhaps mitigating his misunderstanding somewhat; but his letters written from Russia, interesting as they are, leave that in doubt. Before his visit, he had made many casual references, in letters to his brother Brooks Adams, Henry Cabot Lodge, John Hay and others, to Russia. These are interesting because they come from Henry Adams, and because they illustrate the confusing and confused predictions which one can find scores and scores of less illustrious people venturing to make during the period we have been surveying.

Writing to Henry Cabot Lodge from Sydney, N.S.W., August 4, 1891 (*Letters*, I-511), Adams expresses himself as satisfied that America has no future in the Pacific; 'her best chance is Siberia. Russia will probably go to pieces; she is rotten and decrepit to the core, and must pass through a bankruptcy, political and moral. If it can be delayed another twenty-five years, we could Americanize Siberia, and this is the only possible work that I can still see open on a scale equal to American means'. It was delayed twenty-six years. On June 5, 1895 (*Letters*, II-70), writing to Brooks Adams, apropos his book, *The Law of Civilization and Decay*, he says: 'I fear Russia much! Why can one never penetrate that polar mystery? What chance is there of repeating the diplomacy, the blunders and the disasters of 1813? What chance is there of achieving that success on which Madison had a right to reckon, and which nothing but the unripeness of the age prevented his achieving? Our true point of interest is not India but Russia, yet Russia is impenetrable and *any intelligent man will deal with her better, the less closely he knows her*.' (Italics mine.) In a letter to Worthington Ford, February 2, 1899 (II-213), he speaks of Russia and America as 'the two future centres of power; and of the two, America must get there first. Some day, perhaps a century hence, Russia may swallow even her; but for my lifetime I think I'm safe.' (He died in 1918.) In another mood, April 3, 1900 (to

Charles Milnes Gaskell), he amuses himself with foreign affairs and says Russia is a perpetual joy to him; 'the Russian is an entrancing study'—in the forms of stupidity and brutality that are somewhat different from familiar American, English, French, German varieties. Like Mark Twain, he is finding the human race something of a bad joke.[4]

And then, in the latter part of August and early September, 1901, with Cabot Lodge and some members of the Lodge family, he visited Russia. On the way, in Vienna, he and another member of the party 'plunged' into the Russian language, so they could at least read street signs. His first impressions were that Russia dwarfs Europe, and is like America in that small things do not seem at home in it; but it is at least three generations behind us economically and socially, 'so that nothing much will come of it in my time. I'm satisfied already. *Years of study would not make the thing any clearer. Just looking out of the car window is enough*'. (Italics mine.) August 21—he had been in Russia since the 17th—he writes to Mrs Cameron in the mood of many a tourist to the Louvre or the Uffizi—that's over; done; wipe out Moscow. He had seen the Kremlin which he had been wanting to see since 1858; and it left a queer taste, like caviare and vodka, semi-barbarous, yet *manqué*. The Kremlin is just Byzantium barbarized; the bulbous domes are weak—'the turnip with its root in the air is not so dignified as the turnip with its root in the earth. The architecture is simply ignorance. The builders built in 1600 as they built in 1200 because they knew no more.' Obviously the Kremlin walls and its cathedrals, for the building of which famous Italian architects had been brought to Russia from about 1480 to 1527, did not have the interest for Adams of Mont St Michel and Chartres. Yet he was fascinated by High Mass in the new cathedral; it gave him 'almost a sensation'. Watching the Russians crossing themselves before shrines, he decided they were completely passive. He failed to see a sign of individuality anywhere—'all are run in the same tallow more or less'. But he reflects that in the long run the passive character exhausts the active.

Arriving in St Petersburg on a Friday, he had enough by

Sunday; it was dark, raw and rainy. The fact that his grandfather had been there from 1809 to 1814 gave a family interest to the place; he pities him, then remembers that John Quincy was twenty years younger than he, and 'had been in the U.S. Senate, which ought to have reconciled him to most atmospheres'. Only Catherine's palace at Tsarskoe Selo evoked enthusiasm—its amber room was a joy and Catherine a great woman who knew what was good. Writing to John Hay (August 26) he declares that nature has done nothing for Russia and art almost as little; 'Moscow was amusing for twelve hours. . . . Petersburg is distinctly *vieux jeu*; it reminds me of my grandmother; it says next to nothing of my own world. I am still asking where the deuce Russia is. Thus far I have seen only log cabins in dense forests; or cities without industry separated by 500 miles of barrens. Of Russia I know nothing.'

Knowing, then, nothing about it, he ventures to predict: 'I think that for three generations we can look ahead with very little anxiety to rivalry on the part of Russia. She will need us more than we need her. As yet she has made no progress that I can see towards being economical. She is still metaphysical, religious, military, Byzantine; a sort of Mongol tribe, almost absolutely unable to think in Western lines.' (II-344). To Mrs Cameron, September 1, 1901, he writes: 'The sum of my certainty is that America has a very clear century of start over Russia, and that Western Europe must follow us for a hundred years before Russia can swing her flail over the Atlantic.'

Where indeed was Russia for Henry Adams? Brooks Adams also made a prediction, but publicly, in an *Atlantic Monthly* article (December, 1900) on 'Russia's Interest in China', in which he examines data on Russia's finances. To straighten them out, she must either undergo a social reorganization or else keep on expanding. 'The Russians are Asiatics and therefore less vigorous, energetic and inventive than Western races,' he generalizes, with the familiar Western complacency. 'What a social revolution in Russia would portend transcends human foresight, but probably its effects would be felt throughout the world.' But he adds that the conservative instincts of the race are very strong and likely to prevail till the last extremity. Brooks Adams was troubled by Russia as a problem in the interpretation of world history. In his book, *The Law of Civilization and Decay*, published in 1895, he saw human society oscillating between barbarism and civilization. His ideas had been much discussed in the influential circle around Henry Adams in Washington—a circle that included John Hay, who became Secretary of State in 1898. The importance of this group in shaping official attitudes towards Russia has been pointed out in *American Russian Relations* 1781–1947, by William Appleman Williams (1952). Mr Williams makes clear the dilemma in which Brooks Adams was placed by his own theory: since concentration would soon reach its highest level in the United States, how could the fate of disintegration be avoided? 'More and more he inclined to two conclusions: that the next centralization of world economic power would occur in New York, and that the expansion of the United States into Asia was the only technique by which *The Law* could, in effect, be repealed. The problem then became Russia, since in his view England was already becoming an economic vassal of the United States. But Brooks did not believe that Russia would acquiesce in American control of Asia; so the question became how to defeat that great economic entity and take control of China. Well aware of his brother's new interest, Henry shared Brooks's concern with St Petersburg. "I fear Russia much!" he admitted to Brooks; and then concluded that "you ought to be—like your grandfather—minister to St Petersburg".' (Page 33.)

There were others at this time who advised collaboration with Russia, and the situation must be seen in the light of the long history of American-Russian relations. These, according to Mr Williams, have been determined in large measure by the interplay of three factors: the territorial and economic expansion of both countries; the actual or potential value of each nation to the other in terms of a world balance of power; and—after 1917—the ideological considerations involved in the economic, social and political challenges of the Revolution. From time to time, a mutually acceptable *status quo* has dulled 'the antagonisms engendered by the conflict of two destinies—both expanding and both avowedly manifest'. (Pages 3–4.)

To conclude this survey of American attitudes, fears and generalization, let Thomas Sergeant Perry (whom we have quoted before) have the last shot at prophecy. Perry learned Russian, and possibly he learned something about the Russians, too, from their language. In his *Evolution of the Snob* (1887, page 177), Perry wrote: 'It should be said that if *le monde s'américanise*, as desponding European writers are prone to say, it will alter slowly, for one peculiarly American quality is its intense conservatism; it adheres with, on the whole, wonderful tenacity to what has won the approval of Europe. These questions, it seems, will rather be decided by the Russians, who appear to be destined to take the place long held by the French: that, namely, of becoming the Greeks of modern times—in other words the people who shall carry out their ideas in action, who put their theories into practice. We are least of all a nation that lives on ideas.'

[1] In 1911 Aylmer Maude, in his *Life of Tolstoy*, wrote that nearly half of Tolstoy's works had never yet been put into English 'which at all adequately represents the spirit of the originals'.

[2] Translated by J. L. Edmands, Boston, 1887, under the title *The Russian Novelists*.

[3] T. A. Bailey, *America Faces Russia*, Cornell University Press, 1950, page 120.

[4] In a letter of April 2, 1900, concerning some diplomatic manoeuvres, he writes: 'Of course no one believes a Russian under any circumstances, but I am always interested in speculating why an Oriental tells one lie rather than another.'

CHAPTER VI

ENGLISH ATTITUDES TOWARDS RUSSIAN LITERATURE, AS CONTRASTED WITH AMERICAN, 1880–1905

i

English Interest More Politically Conscious than American

THOSE WHO have made special studies, involving contrasts between English and American criticism of Russian literature in the nineteenth century, are in general agreement that the English was the more political, the American the more aesthetic. Dr Muchnic states that the early interest in England came 'in the wake of closer economic relations and of an enforced political concern'. After glancing at the effects of the Napoleonic, the Crimean and the Russo-Turkish (1877) wars, she concludes: 'It was not until she began to be feared that Russia came to be known'. And Dr Gettmann, noting how the flurry of interest in Turgenev in the Crimean War period died down, remarks: 'Nothing short of a war or a revolution could induce the English to read Russian fiction'. In 1877, the Russian war with Turkey woke the English up again. And from that time on, the Russians were obliging and the English had little opportunity to lapse into indifference. England and Russia were competitors for markets and influence in the Balkans, the Far East and Afghanistan; Russia was expanding to the East in the movement that led to the Russo-Japanese War; and her internal crises became increasingly frequent and lively, from the assassination of Alexander II in 1881 to Bloody Sunday and the abortive revolution of 1905.

Turgenev, who received an honorary degree from Oxford in 1879, had published his *Virgin Soil* two years before; and when in 1878 a young Russian girl shot a prefect of police and a trial of 193 agitators took place in Russia, people turned to Turgenev's book to find answers to the questions raised by these spectacular events. A review of the novel in the *Academy* (September 14, 1878) by Richard Littledale might very well be the review of a political treatise: 'an account from the pen of an exceptionally shrewd and thoughtful writer, of the political condition of Russia, so far as it is affected at present by the secret societies which ramify in every direction and are preparing the way for a series of changes which even the most practised and keen-sighted statesmen cannot forecast'. He indicates the complications that make forecasting difficult in a social system with no organic unity, 'mechanically composed of factors which touch but do not mingle, and the only thing certain is that it cannot last'. He praises Turgenev for giving us in a few graphic touches the men and women 'who are the soul of the secret societies', and for telling us what notions have succeeded in their minds to the doctrines which Herzen preached in his *Kolokol* not so long ago; 'but even he cannot lift the veil by so much as a corner'. The recent war had concentrated attention on the foreign policy of Russia, but her internal condition is of far more moment politically, 'and it is only books like the present that enable outsiders to guess at it with any approach to correctness'. He indulges in the familiar generalization that a true Russian book must have a ring of sadness and failure, but he finds something noble and hopeful in the struggle for freedom and reform, 'however wild and chimerical may be the dreams of those who begin it'.[1]

This is to treat fiction as if it were fact. Turgenev, after all, was a novelist, not an historian, and there is much question whether in his Narodniks he caught the 'soul of the secret societies'. To pay regard to the *race*, *moment* and *milieu*, in interpreting a work of art, is one thing; and nineteenth century American criticism of Turgenev did less than its duty in this respect. But to accept a novel as history is not infrequently an act of wish fulfilment, not of criticism. Such acceptance is illustrated again and again in the story of English and American comment on Russian fiction. It is one source of the bewilderingly contradictory interpretations of the Russian Soul. It helps to explain the passion with which

Western criticism embraced Dostoevsky's *Possessed* as the true Revolutionist's Handbook. It is a habit that persists down to the present moment, as we see for example in the comment on the novel of a Russian exile, *All Hope Abandon*, reviewed in the *Herald-Tribune Books* (October 9, 1949): after noting how the lives of all three main characters in the novel are ruined by the collision of their virtues with a malign system, the review concludes, 'more than a shelf of treatises and travellers' accounts, this simple and terrifying novel will carry the reader into the heart of life in the land where "the revolution in permanence" has become a permanent purge'. The shelf of treatises and travellers' accounts if subjected, of course, to tests of accuracy such as are applied to historical documents, might prove far more reliable, if less picturesque, than a terrifying novel.

As part of the political stimulation of interest in Russian literature, the role of Russian exiles in England must not be overlooked. E. H. Carr, in his *Romantic Exiles: A Nineteenth Century Portrait Gallery* (1933), deals with the group around Alexander Herzen, who resided in London from 1852 to 1865, and published (1857–1862) his famous journal *The Bell* (*Kolokol*), which voiced the aspirations of enlightened liberal Russian opinion. But Herzen struck no roots in England, where he had found, in Professor Carr's words, a haven of refuge, but not the arms of friendship; 'the English had been toleration itself. They were too busy with their own affairs to interest themselves in his'. He did have a brief exchange with Carlyle, as noted in Chapter III. But there was little that was specifically English which he regretted when he left—except (says Professor Carr) Colman's mustard, English pickles and mushroom ketchup. He associated chiefly with the other European refugees who flocked to England after 1848—'the one spot where they could still live and talk and conspire in peace'.

But it was another story with the exiles of the latter part of the century. Prince Peter Kropotkin was influential in the political, philosophical and literary fields. His *Memoirs of a Revolutionist* was published in 1899; his essays on Russian literature, first delivered as lectures in the United States, were persuasive and scholarly interpretations of the Russian writers, seen in close relation with the political and social order. Kropotkin, a philosophical anarchist disposed to believe the best of human nature, expressed the strongest kind of preference for Tolstoy and Turgenev over Dostoevsky, whose visions of the evil in man disturbed his faith. Then there was the exiled Stepniak, who collaborated with Edward Garnett on the introductions to Constance Garnett's translations of Turgenev, and whose books and articles on the Russian peasantry and the revolutionary movement were widely read. Thomas Hardy attended a lecture of his on Tolstoy in 1893. The reviewer of one of Kropotkin's books on Russian and French prisons (*Saturday Review*, May, 1887) remarks glumly: 'The sickening horror of Russian prison life as presented by the Prince fills one with a strong desire to know as little as possible of a country where such things are possible.' But his is a lonely dissenting voice, and on the whole the contribution of the Russian exiles was to spread information about Russia and her special problems, and to deepen sympathy for the liberal and even revolutionary aspirations of the Russian people. After the Bolshevik revolution, still another generation of Russian exiles found hospitality in England, and their experience and points of view directed a strong current of opinion against the new régime. Yet the old sympathy with revolutionary ideas and figures continued, mixed with a vast deal of bewilderment and distress.

Edward Garnett wrote to Galsworthy in May, 1905, when the Russo-Japanese War was not yet over and the revolutionary movement had just been marked by the Bloody Sunday massacre of unarmed petitioners (January, 1905), that Gorky was really selling now; 'it's strange, but people have an idea that Gorky lays bare the depth of Russian depravity, and so the Britishers are buying him'. What a seasoned old critic thought of Gorky at this time can be found in Saintsbury's *Later Nineteenth Century* (1907), where, after some discussion of Turgenev, Dostoevsky and Tolstoy, he remarks: 'The later and actually contemporary Maxim Gorky need only be referred to as an advance in grime.' And he thought Tolstoy and Dostoevsky grimy enough, for he discusses them under the general heading of 'studies of the repulsive', to which they were driven by what he calls some curious over-mastery of impulse. Not, apparently, by any distressing political and social conditions in their country, though he admits, in one of the most engaging understatements one could find, that 'the political state of Russia may not have been and may not be, of the most gracious'.

Gracious or not, we have seen its importance in affecting English reception of Russian literature.

ii

The Work of Charles Turner

ENGLISH CRITICISM, seeking political significance in Russian fiction, was close to what had become, since Belinski, the dominant attitude of Russian critics. This English emphasis derived from the English concern with what was to be hoped and feared from Russia; but perhaps, too, it owed something to an interpreter of Russian literature in the last quarter of the nineteenth century, who was far more informed and competent than any person in the United States during the 1870's and 1880's. This was Charles Turner, already mentioned in Chapter III. Long residence and employment in Russia gave him advantages which observers like Noble and Hapgood lacked. Turner went to Russia in 1859, at the age of twenty-eight, and in 1864 was appointed Lector of the English language at the Imperial University in St Petersburg, holding the office for life—till 1904. Between 1865 and 1897, he produced for his Russian students seven works on English literature. In 1869, in the *British Quarterly Review* (vol. 50), appeared the first long essay on Turgenev, assigned to Turner by the two researchers—Royal Gettman and Carl Lefevre—into the fortunes, respectively, of Turgenev and Gogol in England. In the same periodical in April, 1868, is the first long English essay on Gogol, by Turner. In 1873 Turner's translation of Turgenev's *On the Eve* appeared. In 1877 *Fraser's Magazine* published nine instalments of Turner's *Studies in Russian Literature*, written in St Petersburg, and dealing with twelve Russian authors. Turner came to London in 1881, and lectured at the Royal Institution on the Russian novelists; these articles and lectures formed the basis of his book, *Studies in Russian Literature*, 1882, the first book-length history of Russian literature written in English. In 1883 he lectured at the Royal Institution on Russian life, and in 1888 on Tolstoy, publishing in the same year *Count Tolstoy as Novelist and Thinker*; and six lectures in 1889, at the Taylor Institute in Oxford, were included in the book *The Modern Novelists of Russia* (1890). In 1899 he published both in London and St Petersburg a Birthday Memorial edition of translations from Pushkin. In the light of all this activity, he certainly merits the praise of Carl Lefevre—'a strong cultural link between England and Russia during a tentative and difficult period', 'a true pioneer'.

Turner's aim, stated in the preface to *Modern Novelists of Russia*, was 'to contribute to a better understanding of Russian life, and to promote a friendlier and juster estimate of the character, faith and aspirations of the Russian people'. And, as Lefevre remarks, he was the first English critic to approach Russia and Russian literature with such humility; his criticism stands alone 'not only in volume and historical importance, but also in quality and in its special tendency of reflecting Russian scholarship and criticism'. This last tendency necessarily meant an emphasis on the 'art for life' creed set forth by the most influential school of nineteenth-century Russian criticism. Turner availed himself, as he said in the 1882 book, of the labours of the more eminent Russian critics—Belinsky, Dobrolyubov, Grot, etc. Dr Gettman, the champion of Turgenev against some hostile Russian criticism, thinks Turner uncritical in accepting the view of the Russian critics, but Dr Lefevre makes a convincing documented defence of Turner's scholarship and intellectual integrity. Fiction, as Turner emphasizes, was carefully studied by those interested in political and social conditions, because the censorship operated to keep such matters out of the area of free discussion. This elementary fact was seldom given its due weight in foreign attempts to interpret Russian fiction.

Turner writes factually, simply and with reference to the broad background of Russian life; when, for example, he criticizes Tolstoy's attitude towards women, he supports his case with facts about what Russian women had been accomplishing in medicine and in work among the people. Lefevre, familiar with later excesses of psycho-analytic criticism of Gogol, admires Turner's handling of key material, his stress on the 'human quality of Gogol's unhappiness, not the clinical'; and the 'humane matter-of-factness' of Turner's plain, sensible, well-documented literary biography.

How rarely can the terms *plain*, *sensible*, *well-documented* be applied to the appraisals, generalizations and speculations about the Russians and their culture and literature, which we have been noting through the years!

iii

Edward and Constance Garnett

BOTH THE English Constance Garnett and the American Isabel Hapgood completed translations of Turgenev's novels towards the close of the nineteenth and the beginning of the twentieth centuries. A comparison of the introductions to *Virgin Soil* points up the characteristically different English and American emphasis. Miss Hapgood speaks of Turgenev's discouragement at the reception of the book; his resolution to stop writing; his attitude towards the 'movement to the people', which evoked the 'usual interminable disputes'; his way of sedulously following up all the new phenomena of Russian life; she then comments on the characters, and especially upon the weakness of Nezhdanov, illustrating the recurrent Turgenev theme of the man surrendering himself to the superior woman; and on the divergence of critical opinion on Marianna—either the most brilliant, or the least successful of his portrayals. The reader would get little light on the actual issues at stake in the Russia of Marianna and Nezhdanov.

Edward Garnett, however, in his introduction plunges into the Russian question, building up an interesting article on Anonymous Russia—the term is borrowed from the novel—that is, the Russia of resistance to the autocracy. Marianna is 'the incarnation of that Russian fight for progress, which though half-hidden and obscure to foreigners has thrilled the nerves of Europe. This pure girl, with passionate courageous soul, is in fact the Liberty of Russia. . . . In her figure is personified the flower of the Russian youth, those who cast off from their generation the stigma of inaction, which is the vice of the Russian temperament, as her great writers tell us'. He reminds the English reader of the difficulties under which Turgenev wrote, with 'Silence' standing in official writing above the doors. But 'Anonymous Russia had arisen to mine the doors; the doors must be shattered by secret hands that Europe might for once gaze through'. He then devotes eight pages to explaining that 'going to the people' was the last resort when all other channels of activity were shut; it was the outlet of many liberal ideas; and although there were many cliques in Russia, there were really only two big parties: either you were part of Government Action or you were part of Liberal Ideas, and sooner or later every disciple of liberal ideas was forced into opposition. Among them were not only the writers, the students, the teachers, the Press and the more intelligent of the professional world, but discontented spirits even from the military and the nobility and people with axes to grind. Is Russia to be more Orientalized or more Europeanized?—This is the struggle between a strongly organized bureaucracy armed with the modern weapons of centralized power and the public opinion of a large body of educated subjects with advanced views. Garnett considers the Russian mind very susceptible to European thought, naturally quick and sensitive, moving rapidly to conclusions when once it has started. The Nihilist rising (he uses the word in a very broad sense) is the long-threatened 'revolt of idealism and of the

Russian conscience against Russian cowardice . . . the fermentation of modern ideas in the breast of a society iron-bound by officialism . . . the generous aspiration of the Russian soul against sloth and apathy and greed'.

This introduction was written in 1896. The year before, Garnett had prefaced his wife's translation of Turgenev's *On the Eve* with some very wide-ranging speculations on the Slavs and their future. First he makes the point that this novel, read by the English chiefly for its charmingly drawn picture of a quiet Russian household and its delicate analysis of a young girl's soul, is to the Russians also a 'deep and penetrating diagnosis of the destinies of the Russia of the fifties'. Turgenev is a psychologist not merely of men but of nations. Garnett chooses a minor character, Uvar Ivanovich, as a symbol of the sleepy, slothful Slav of today, yesterday and tomorrow. Asked—'will there ever be men among us?'—Uvar Ivanovich stares enigmatically into the far distance. The Bulgarian hero of the novel, it will be remembered, dies before he can fight on the Balkan battlefields. In telling the story of Elena's love and loss, Turgenev, according to Garnett, has managed 'faintly but unmistakably to make spring and flourish in our minds the ineradicable, though hidden, idea at the back of Slav thought—the unification of the Slav races. How doubly welcome that art should be which can lead us, the foreigners, thus straight to the heart of the national secrets of a great people, secrets which our own critics and diplomatists must necessarily misrepresent. . . . *On the Eve*, of all the novels, contains perhaps the most instructive political lessons England can learn.' He then says Europe and England have always had their watch-dogs on the political premises, ever ready to bay at Slav cupidity, treachery and intrigue, and give noisy tongue whenever the Slav 'stretches out his long arm and opens his drowsy eyes'. They are useful. 'But how rare it is to find a man who can teach us to interpret a nation's aspirations, to gauge its inner force, its aim, its inevitability. Turgenev gives us such clues.' And whatever England's interest may be in relation to Russia's development, 'it is better for us to understand the force of Russian aims, before we measure our strength against it'. Garnett concludes: 'For us, *On the Eve* suggests the existence of a mighty lake, whose waters, dammed back for a while, are rising slowly, but are still some way from the brim. How long will it take to overflow? Nobody knows; but when the long winter of Russia's dark internal policy shall be broken up, will the snows, melting on the mountains, stream south-west, inundating the valley of the Danube? Or, as the national poet, Pushkin, has sung, will there be a pouring of many Slavonian rivulets, towards a common centre, to create an era of peace and development within, whereby Russia may rise free and rejoicing to face her great destinies? Hard and bitter is the shaping of nations. Uvar Ivanovich still fixes his enigmatical stare into the far distance.'

iv

The Academic Note

AS THE fifteen volume edition of Turgenev's novels in the Garnett translations was nearing completion, E. A. B. (Arnold Bennett) wrote an article, 'Ivan Turgenev, An Inquiry', in *The Academy* (November 4, 1899); he considered him appreciated rather by men of letters than by the general reading public, which was not 'gripped' as by Tolstoy and Dostoevsky. But as to Dostoevsky, Garnett said six years or so later in the same periodical (vol. 71, 1906) that the present generation did not know Dostoevsky, and that it was apparently impossible to procure then any of the translations of his works put out by Vizetelly twenty years earlier; so the 'grip' was not very tight as yet. Bennett's emphasis is on Turgenev's artistic qualities; 'when a thing is supreme', he remarks of the story *Byezhin Prairie*, 'there is nothing to be said'. But he finds the moral basis that every work of art must have just about where Garnett, in the passage quoted above, found the political: 'They (the novels) are the muffled but supreme utterance of a nation's secret desire. But what is that to the West? The West cannot feel what Russia feels—cannot even intellectually comprehend the profound surge of emotion which barely agitates the surface of that giant's life'. Garnett was at least making the effort at intellectual comprehension; Bennett was retreating to that fortress of the Slav Soul, which later became so attractive a hide-out for the Western mind. He thought Turgenev a true Slav, marked by 'melancholy, inconclusiveness, and patient inactive faith'—Oriental he was born, and remained. George Moore, by the way, who found Turgenev clear and deep, once played with the idea that he had come from the Crimea and was Greek. So much for the true Slav, the born Oriental.

Among the *Academy* reviews of the '90's a new note begins to be heard; a dry, informed, academic note. Dostoevsky's *Poor Folk*, with an introduction by George Moore, is noticed in vol. 46 (1894), by William Morfill. The translation is well done; he has compared it with the original; George Moore has furnished a preface; 'we will not quarrel with him for what he has written, but a good wine needs no bush'. Exit George Moore! A review of Gogol's *Inspector General*, February 25, 1893, gives the translator credit for a scholarly and spirited version and a useful introduction; then goes back to the 'Home Life in Russia' fraud, 'protested by the late W. R. Ralston'; mentions an earlier translation by Hart Davies; and concludes: 'The English people are gradually "discovering" Russian literature'; three or four years ago, when the translation of *War and Peace* made a sensation, our reviewers spoke of it as a recent work; 'but the present writer remembers first reading it in a Russian country house upwards of twenty-two years past'. And not long ago a reviewer of a Dostoevsky novel recommended that the author improve his style, though Dostoevsky had died years before. 'No one in England read Russian; ergo, there was no Russian literature to read.' After that crack, Morfill relents enough to mention T. Watts, of the British Museum, who wrote the accurate and scholarly lives of Russian authors in Knight's *Encyclopedia*, and W. R. S. Ralston, whose two valuable books ought not to be forgotten.

Professor William Morfill (1834–1909) was the pioneer in Slavonic studies at Oxford, where in 1887 the Lithu-Slavonic languages were admitted into the curriculum. Professor Neville

Forbes (1883–1929) laid the basis of the Oxford School of Russian, which won an equal footing with other Modern Language Schools. These two men were the first to acknowledge the Slav world as a cultural unit, worthy of a scholar's attention, apart even from political and economic considerations. 'Morfill,' said Professor Konovalov in an address at Oxford, November 26, 1946, 'was among the first to recognize that the ideals proclaimed in nineteenth-century Russian literature form an inseparable part of Western humanism.'

Any reader who has followed this rather long story, and who recalls the reflection of Edmund Noble's, quoted in Chapter V, on the aim of the scholar and ethnologist—'the union of races by knowledge, as the purpose of others is the separation of men by prejudice'—cannot but be pleased at the entrance of the professors into the field we have been surveying. Bernard Pares built up a school of Russian studies at Liverpool University, inaugurated in 1907; and in 1915 a School of Slavonic Studies was set up at King's College, London, with which Pares was associated. In *A Wandering Student* (1948) Pares tells how the quarterly, *Russian Review*, was started, publishing articles mostly by Russian scholars or public men, and how Harold Williams in Russia helped to obtain these articles. Co-operation grew between American and British students of Slavic. Professor G. R. Noyes established a centre of Slavonic studies at the University of California; and when in 1943 a volume of Slavic Studies was issued in his honour, with essays contributed by friends, colleagues and former students, an impressive number of American universities, along with the universities of London and Liverpool, were represented through the contributors. The book was published by the Cornell University Press; and this is a good place to recall that Eugene Schuyler, the translator in 1867 of Turgenev's *Fathers and Children*, left to Cornell his collection of Slavic folk-lore, literature and history.

Eugene Schuyler (though not a professor) presents such a pleasant picture of what is desirable in cultural relations between nations that one feels like pausing a moment to contemplate him.

His interest in things Russian proceeded from friendly contact; he learned the language; he selected for translation literature of the first quality; he had the permission of the authors and he made their acquaintance; his interest continued and led to writing of his own, interpreting the other nation; as a diplomatic attaché in Russia, he made friends with all sorts of people, pursued investigations into trade and industry, undertook on his own initiative a dangerous and extensive trip, and published his findings with such honesty and objectivity that they were not questioned; and, as a final gesture, left his collection to a university. If only more diplomats were as versatile—if only more scholars had so wide and beneficent a range! And so, with a caution that all scholars and professors are not without fear and without reproach, we turn back to literature.

V

The English Critical Debate over Realism in the late Nineteenth Century

MATTHEW ARNOLD was quoted some chapters back to the effect that in 1887, the novel of Russia, a 'country new to literature, or at any rate unregarded till lately by the general public of readers', had inherited the vogue lost by the French novel. The general public of readers was probably not too interested in the precise definition of the 'realism' they had been enjoying in French fiction and were now beginning to enjoy in Russian fiction. But the critics and reviewers were, and they filled the pages of the periodicals with nice distinctions.

'We have been in a world,' wrote Arnold in the essay on Tolstoy first published in the *Fortnightly Review*, 1887, 'which misconducts itself nearly as much as the world of a French novel all palpitating with "modernity"'; but in this world of Anna Karenina, we are not made impatient as we should be in a French novel by fine sentiment; we are not asked to believe that Anna is exalted and ennobled by her passion for Vronsky. 'Our Russian novelist deals abundantly with criminal passion and with adultery, but he does not seem to feel himself owing any service to the goddess Lubricity. . . . Much in *Anna Karenina* is painful, much is unpleasant, but nothing is of a nature to trouble the senses, or to please those who wish their senses troubled. This taint is wholly absent.' By comparison, in *Madame Bovary*, the taint is present, though to a much less degree than in more recent French novels, 'which will be in everyone's mind'. This last assumption is rather discreditable to the Victorian reader.

The distinction Arnold draws between French and Russian realism is made again and again by other critics, with varying degrees of felicity or ineptitude. Turgenev, Tolstoy and Dostoevsky shared with Zola and with Ibsen the honour of modifying and broadening the Victorian conception of realism in literature; the critical debates have been thoroughly gone over by special students of the period,[2] and a few quotations will suffice here.

Reviewing *War and Peace* in the 1887 Vizetelly edition, a writer in the *Spectator* (February 5, 1887) declares: 'If one must label Tolstoy, then he is a realist, but not realistic with the repulsive realism of the modern French school, which seems to consist largely in dragging forward and exposing to the light that shameful side of human nature which it should rather be our interest to hide and duty to conceal'. In the *Westminster Review* (September, 1888) Tolstoy is praised for looking straight at the facts of life; his realism, 'unlike that of the declining French school, is not the realism of the gutter. From the gutter, indeed, he does not recoil, but in it he sees the image of the sky.' Captain R. G. Burton, Indian Staff Correspondent, writes an appreciation of Russian fiction that goes back to Pushkin and includes the contemporary Korolenko (*Westminster Review*, December, 1895), excluding Tolstoy's *Kreutzer Sonata*, but finding it generally refreshing to turn from the degenerate modern novel and the inane indelicacies of fashionable fiction and the hysterical emanations of the unhealthy imagination of the New Woman—the Captain is clearly no Ibsenite—to the 'luminous pages of a literature that has in it all the life of true realism'. He considers *War and Peace* the greatest historical novel in any language. Reviewing a French translation of Dostoevsky's *Crime and Punishment*, a writer in the *Spectator* (July, 1886) calls Raskolnikov a 'Hamlet of the madhouse', thinks the novel unlikely to be very popular, being written without much regard to the prejudices of the Philistines, and not suitable for young people. 'We question whether young people would care to read it, but most people would probably be better for reading it, and no one who knows the difference between good and evil would be worse.' Dostoevsky is a realist who calls a spade a spade, but he is not Zolaesque. The hero is an assassin and the heroine a prostitute, but the first repents and the second is one of the noblest characters in fiction.

These quotations illustrate the point made by Clarence Decker that 'the Victorians were less concerned with aesthetic than with moral and religious considerations in their reaction to the realist and naturalist movements of the age'. (*PMLA*, June, 1937.) But George Gissing's understanding of Russian realism was more artistic and more profound. The deep interest he took in Dostoevsky—whose sombreness, according to his biographer Miss Yates (*George Gissing*, 1922), may have helped to deepen Gissing's despondency by the shadow of a shade—finds expression in his study of Charles Dickens (1898). The difference, writes Gissing, between the way Dickens deals with the life of the poor and the way several foreign contemporaries (like him, preoccupied with social questions) deal with it, involves the use of 'that very idle word *realism*'. Dostoevsky's work shows a sombre colouring beside the English novels, sombre, yet not without humour. Gissing seems to be the only English critic before Lytton Strachey to appreciate Dostoevsky's humour. *Crime and Punishment* 'abounds in Dickens-like touches in its lighter passages. Extravagances of character delighted him, and he depicted them with a freer hand than Dickens was permitted or would have cared to use. Suppose the English novelist born in Russia, he might well have been the author of the long scene at the beginning of the book where Sonia's father, the eccentric drunkard, makes himself known to us in his extraordinary monologue. For that matter, with such change of birth and breeding, Dickens might well have written the whole book, which is a story of a strange murder, of detective ingenuity, of a ruined girl who keeps her soul clean, and of a criminal redeemed by love and faith in Christ. . . . Dostoevsky is invariably pure in tone and even decorous from our own peculiar point of view; his superiority as a *realist* to the author of *David Copperfield* consists merely in his frank recognition of facts which Dickens is obliged to ignore or to hint, with sighing timidity.' Gissing admits that Sonia could in fact not have been used by Dickens at all, except in some stagy fashion that would have made glaringly unreal a girl who was exceptional, but not impossible. 'The crucial chapter of the story, the magnificent scene in which Raskolnikov makes confession to Sonia, is beyond Dickens as we know him; it would not have been so but for the defects of education and the social prejudices which forbade his tragic gift to develop. Raskolnikov himself, a typical Russian [*sic*], a man of brains maddened by hunger and the sight of others hungry, is the kind of character Dickens never attempted to portray; his notives, his reasonings, could not be comprehended by an Englishman of the lower middle class. And the murder itself—Bill Sikes, Jonas Chuzzlewit, show but feebly after we have watched that lank student, with the hatchet under his coat, stealing up the stairs; when we have seen him do his deed of blood, and heard the sound of that awful bell tinkling in the still chamber.'

By the beginning of the new century, the debates over realism, French and Russian, were well summed up by A. T. Quiller-Couch (*Pall Mall Magazine*, February, 1901): 'French realism and Russian realism reached us together or almost together and, by the second realism, the first stood condemned. Zola observed no more carefully than Tolstoy; de Maupassant directed his observation no more exquisitely than Turgenev; and beside the two Russians, the two Frenchmen were no less evidently shallow than muddy. To say that Turgenev and Tolstoy saved the novel would be (I believe) false. The novel would have saved itself. . . . But these two men did impressively, and in the sight of Europe, uphold, vindicate and establish the truth that the concern of fiction is with things spiritual, intimate, deep; not with things material, external, shallow; with interpreting the hearts of men, not with counting their buttons; with ideas, not with phenomena; that it uses phenomena, as all arts must use them; but as a means only, to arrive at stability, peace and law—or at least such glimpses as may be got of eternal law.'[3]

Russian fiction did not come to an end in 1901, nor was the precise nature of the realism of the older novelists settled in this debate. It was just the end of a chapter that Quiller-Couch recorded. Gorky, Chekhov, Sholokhov were to pose new problems of definition; and eventually Soviet criticism, with its Socialist realism, was to upset a cart full of strange apples for English critics to sort out. Some of the questions will be considered in later chapters. Here, just to show how alive and how puzzling the meaning of Russian realism continued to be, consider a couple of widely-separated pronouncements.

Nearly two decades after Quiller-Couch, Virginia Woolf, discussing realism, is similarly insistent on not counting the buttons; but it is not the French that she charges with this practice, but those English novelists, Wells, Galsworthy, Bennett, who had become the leading English novelists. They are, she says, materialists, 'concerned not with the spirit, but with the body. . . . They spend immense skill and immense industry making the trivial and the transitory appear the true and the enduring'. (*Modern Fiction*, 1919.) If we want understanding of the soul and the heart, where shall we find anything of comparable profundity with what the Russians give us? In her address in 1924 at Cambridge, on 'Character in Fiction', with its well-known speculations about an imaginary old lady, Mrs Brown, sitting in a corner of a railway carriage, and what different novelists would make of her, she said: 'The English writer would make the old lady into a "character"; he would bring out her oddities and mannerisms; her buttons and wrinkles; her ribbons and warts. . . . The Russian would pierce the flesh; would reveal the soul—the soul alone, wandering out into the Waterloo Road, asking of life some tremendous question which would sound on and on in our ears after the book was finished.'

Skip another twenty years, and a new critical generation is still mulling over Russian realism, still finding something more than buttons, but not quite the same things as its predecessors. 'If,' writes V. S. Pritchett (*New Statesman and Nation*, April 25, 1942), 'we try to define the quality which has given the Russian novel its extraordinary prestige, *realism* is our clinching word. . . . There has always been a subject beyond the immediate subject, which has lifted Russian realism a few inches above the earth. That subject is the fate of Russia itself. In this hour, the novelist seems to say, as I wash my feet, mortgage my estate, or seduce the station master's daughter, the fate of Russia is in the balance. And who says Russia, says humanity.' And in another article (January 17, 1942), he says: 'It was to the great advantage of the Russian novelists that they had to react to the Russian question, a great advantage, too, that the Russian question was to become a universal one—the meaning and necessity of the rise of the masses.'

We recall the words of Henry James: 'Those vaguely-imagined multitudes whom we think of more and more as waiting their turn, in the arena of civilization, in the grey expanses of the North.'

[1] W. R. S. Ralston, who translated some of Turgenev's novels and visited him in 1870 at his Spasskoye estate, wrote an article in *Nineteenth Century*, May 1877, on 'Russian Revolutionary Literature', using *Virgin Soil* to help explain the 1877 trials.

[2] See, for instance, Clarence Decker: 'Victorian Comment on Russian Realism', Publications of the Modern Language Association, June 1937.

[3] This distinction between French and Russian realism, established in the late nineteenth century debates, is echoed from time to time in the following years. Edith Hamilton, as quoted in *Theatre Arts Monthly*, January 1926, expresses it when she says that the greatest realistic fiction was written by French and Russians; but to read one of the great Frenchman's books (referring to Flaubert) is 'to feel mingled despair and loathing for mankind, so base, so trivial and so wretched'; whereas to read a great Russian novel is a very different experience. 'The baseness, the beast in us, the misery of life, are there as plain to see as in the French book, but what we are left with is not despair and not loathing, but a sense of pity and wonder before mankind that can so suffer.'

CHAPTER VII

ON THE EVE—1905–1917

i

IN 1905—and it is less arbitrary to fix this date than it often is in history—the 'vaguely-imagined multitudes' stopped waiting their turn. They stopped being passive, dreamy, vacillating, indolent, submissive, patient, enduring, unenterprising; they disregarded their pre-eminence in the talent of obeying, so much praised by Carlyle. They gave one of the few demonstrations in modern history of a successful general strike; they got themselves a parliament. From the assembling of the First Duma, Russia was no longer truly an absolutism. The Sphinx began to talk—and it was hard to persuade people that everything she said was a riddle, though that effort continues to the present; the polar mystery began to melt; the 'mute veiled Colossus'[1] lifted a corner of the veil; the nightingales, to some listeners at least, began to sing. And the reporters, the travellers, the interpreters, the exiles multiplied.

The troubled events between 1905 and 1917 had more English and American observers in Russia than at any preceding period, and some of them were brilliantly qualified for selecting and recording significant aspects of the scene. Many were moved by a most sincere liking for the country and the people, usually some particular class of the people, peasant, aristocrat, or intellectual; and by the desire to promote in any way possible understanding and friendship. There were more channels of communication open than ever before; more witnesses; swifter and more complete reporting; and more eager interest in wider circles in England and the United States. This interest, thanks to the extensive circulation of some of the greatest Russian fiction, was, in several important ways, quite intelligent. We must assume, from the evidence offered in preceding chapters, that people did read these books, as well as the articles of Schuyler, Noble, Kennan, Hapgood, Ralston, Turner and the rest; and that they did listen to the Chautauqua and the Lowell lectures. Of course, they also read the sensational press. But the manipulation of public opinion for political purposes, benevolent or sinister, was not yet in this period the skilled art it has since become. A certain innocence lingered on. And though the winds of revolutionary doctrine were let loose, Truth, so many people still thought, was in the field, and in the encounter with Falsehood would not be put to the worse. Both cynical disbelief in the possibility of finding out the truth about Russian affairs, and automatic acceptance of sedulously propagated opinion, were rather unusual up to the Revolution.

It is sad to leave innocence behind us in our chronicle, and before we do, let us illustrate it by the famous episode of Gorky's visit to the United States, and by the English enthusiasm over the Russian Soul.

ii

The Innocents at Home

THE SETTLEMENT of the Russo-Japanese War in conferences at Portsmouth, N.H., in 1905, drew the United States into the orbit of European-Asiatic imperialistic struggles in the flattering role of peacemaker. William Dean Howells, who dined with the Russian envoys, was pleased to find that Baron Rosen had read his books and that Count Witte had said at the sight of his name, 'Ah, Mr W. D. Howells! Then I shall see him.' The revolutionary disturbances in Russia found much sympathy in the United States, and even when they were crushed for the time being, there was still so strong a feeling in favour of the revolutionists that the visit of Gorky to raise money for their cause had a good chance of success.

Some of Gorky's work had already appeared in translation and been well received: *Foma Gordeyev*, *Three of Them*, and a collection of stories, including *Orloff*. The tramps he introduced into Russian literature were compared to American tramps, with stress upon likenesses rather than differences. His realism was labelled Russian in the critically accepted sense of the moment—not exaggerating ugliness, but presenting the truth as it is. Biographical information accompanied some of the criticism, although his work was only vaguely related to his environment, and his career was explained by 'restlessness of soul and a longing for the unfettered life of the fields'. The critic James Huneker[2] saw a little farther into Gorky's realism when he described him as a naturalist to whom Zola might have gone to school to learn the alphabet of his art. Huneker had seen Gorky's *Nachtasyl* (*Lower Depths*) performed in Berlin and Vienna: 'an almost indescribable *mélange*—for it is not a play—of men and women whose very lives smell to heaven'; but with all his hatred of life, pity oozes from his pages, and 'compared with the drama of lubricity manufactured in Paris and annually exported to America, this little study of a group of outcast men and women is a powerful moral lesson'. This was doing rather well for a writer whom Huneker calls a 'lycanthrope'. The Russian wolf again?

Abraham Cahan wrote a sometimes confused but interesting article in the *Bookman* ('The Mantle of Tolstoy', 1902), including Gorky in a survey of old and new Russian writers, and describing his message as a persistent panegyric of strength, of master spirits, not victims; his 'Napoleons of the Gutter', Cahan thought, would not meet with lasting favour among a people always complaining, sighing and wailing. He generalizes in the familiar way about the all-forgiving pity of the 'typical' Russian, and considers the Russian tendency to be lenient towards crime one of the keynotes to the psychology of 'this curious people in whom the world is so keenly interested these days, but whom it seems at a loss to make out'. Having decided that Turgenev's *Rudin* is a distinctly Russian novel, Mr Cahan has no choice but to label Gorky's very different stories 'decidedly un-Russian, all his atmosphere and the vividness of his characters notwithstanding'. And they are not likely to have enduring fame, or to please the Russians. For the 'average Russian' has been 'correctly' described by foreign observers as one 'in whom the simple sincerity of the child is combined with the intuitive wisdom of the prophet. Born to be sad, mere cleverness for its own sake would be lost upon him, and a work of art, which is straining for effect, be it ever so lofty or subtle, is sure to weary him.' So Gorky, 'although a child of the very heart of his people', is the least Russian of all the writers of note in the modern novel. Quite an achievement, when one is a child of the very heart of one's people! Mr Cahan comes down to earth at the end and gives a very good picture of certain conditions in Russia in 1902, referring to the completion of the trans-Siberian railway, the development of Russian industries, the political demonstrations that united in protest wage-workers and university students. All these events might have made him reflect that 'Russian' would have to take on some new meanings.

Gorky, then, was known as a writer. We have already quoted Isabel Hapgood's friendly account of him and his work. And ever since that famous Sunday in January, 1905, his name had figured 'prominently and sympathetically' in Press dispatches. The late Alexander Kaun in his book *Maxim Gorky and His Russia* (1931) gives a full account of the whole fantastic episode of Gorky's visit to the United States and of the reasons for the failure of his mission. There was excellent advance publicity and, as Kaun says, 'Gorky's sojourn in this country promised to be a series of banquets and public meetings, with the participation of many literary and political notables. An invitation to the White House from President Roosevelt was rumoured to be pending.' He arrived on April 10, 1906. A few days covered his rise and fall. He was the victim partly of the advice of American friends, who had him sign a telegram of sympathy for the Idaho miners under criminal indictment; partly of rivalries between New York newspapers; partly of the effective under-cover activity of the Russian Embassy; and partly of the moral hysteria of the American public, aroused by the headlines that Gorky was travelling with a lady to whom he was not legally married. That, under Russian law concerning divorce, he could not be, was not explained.

Gorky was bewildered, but scarcely more so than two of the most distinguished of the older writers who had planned to welcome him at a great dinner—Mark Twain and William Dean Howells. Mark Twain had written a letter to be read at a public meeting of three thousand persons, declaring his sympathy with the Russian revolution, his hope that it would succeed, and his very low opinion of the Russian Government; 'some of us, even the white-headed, may live to see the blessed day when Tsars and grand dukes will be as scarce there as I trust they are in heaven'. When the scandal broke, Mark Twain, as his biographer Albert Bigelow Paine tells the story,[3] paced up and down in his study among drifting wreaths of cigar smoke, very unhappy and completely uninterested in a cartoon picturing him as upsetting the Tsar's throne. An army of reporters pursued both Clemens and Howells, and the Russian Revolution was entirely forgotten 'in this more lively, more intimate domestic interest'. Mark Twain said about the affair—'Custom is custom. It is built of brass, boiler iron, granite.' A visiting stranger has to find out a country's customs; to Dan Beard he said: 'Gorky made an awful mistake, Dan. He might as well have come over here in his shirt-tail.' Howells, in a letter to his brother, April 16, 1906, writes: 'We were going to give him a great literary dinner, but he has been put out of three hotels with the lady who was not his wife, and M. T. has been swamped in reporters wanting to know "how about it" . . . It seems to have blown over, together with the revolutionist committee which Gorky has hopelessly damaged. He is wrong, but I feel sorry for him; he has suffered enough in his own country, except for the false relations which cannot be tolerated here. He is a simple soul and a great writer, but he cannot do impossible things.'[4]

Exiles had been generously received before. Longfellow, one remembers, entertained Bakunin. Stepniak, a decade or so before the Gorky episode, had lectured in Boston on Siberian prisons and had dined at Howells's home. On their way there, Howells and his guest had passed a fire-house and Stepniak had insisted on sliding down the brass pole as the firemen did. 'A big man in a black ulster, he looked like a bear on a pole.'[5] But Gorky had chosen the wrong kind of participation in American life: he should have climbed poles, not sent telegrams to miners. He did after all, however, find staunch friends in the United States, and he spent six months in the Adirondacks, where he wrote *Mother*. But one cannot expect after this to find much disinterested criticism of Gorky as an artist. The *Bookman*, commenting in June, 1906, on 'the eclipse of Gorky', is not content with deploring Gorky's tactlessness in violating the social and political prejudices of a country not his own. He must be wiped out as an artist: 'Gorky himself is no one in particular—a product of the slums, for years a tramp, he has written some books which have a certain morbid interest because of their brutality'; like the books of so many Russians, they are permeated by a hopeless cynicism, which has at least the power of making the reader feel unhappy and depressed. But one has a little sympathy with the *Bookman's* disgust with what it calls the really unsavoury spectacle of amateur Anarchists and pink tea Nihilists of American extraction who greeted Gorky with maudlin enthusiasm and looked with pleasure on a revolution far enough away not to hurt them; yet became offended by his social mistakes and sympathy with miners. 'Their myopic minds cannot realize the appalling horrors which would attend the general uprising of a population that is almost brutish in its incapacity for self-rule.' So the Russian people and other Russian writers all go down with Gorky.

iii

The Russian Soul

TWO FOREIGN critics, one French and one Russian, both profoundly impressed by Dostoevsky's genius, made the English aware of the Russian Soul. Melchior de Vogüé was first in the field. Edmund Gosse, writing from the standpoint of 1908, remembered *Le Roman Russe* (1886) as a revelation of the 'most blazing order'. Up to then little was known or conjectured in Western Europe about 'the mysterious soul of Russia'. Conjecture was further stimulated by the publication in 1902 of a partial translation of Dmitri Merezhkovsky's study of Tolstoy and Dostoevsky; and from then on, references are frequent to the man-God, God-man, the Christ-anti-Christ, antitheses that Merezhkovsky stressed in his interpretation of Dostoevsky, and worked into the stylized pattern of his own novels. Enthusiasm for Dostoevsky and the Russian Soul kindled slowly, but finally blazed up with the publication of the Garnett translation of *The Brothers Karamazov* in 1912. The enthusiasm continued at fever heat for some years. This Dostoevsky cult, which was a large part of the cult of the Russian Soul, was, writes Dr Muchnic in her study of Dostoevsky's reputation, 'a complex intellectual phenomenon—composed partly of war-time sympathies, partly of mysticism, partly of a new interest in abnormal psychology and in the revelations of psycho-analysis, partly of an absorbed concern with artistic experimentation. Dostoevsky represented an ally, a mystic, a psychologist of the unconscious, a designer of a new fictional form'. The Russian Revolution even for a time increased his prestige as a prophet (in *The Possessed*). The Russian Soul, on the other hand, declined in value, having developed the bewildering traits of a split personality. But by degrees new critical material on Dostoevsky began to temper uncritical enthusiasm. The biography of Dostoevsky by Professor E. H. Carr (1931) makes use of such material, and swings away completely from the Russian Soul. Rozanov, the husband of Dostoevsky's ex-mistress, Pauline Suslova, is credited by Carr with being 'the real founder of the school of criticism which discovered in the great novelist's life and work a profound mystical significance and elevated Dostoevsky into a great religious teacher—the school which found its most brilliant representative in Merezhkovsky and the last but not least of its disciples in Mr Middleton Murry'. (*Fortnightly Review*, October 1, 1929.) These dry scholars take the bloom off innocence.

While the fever lasted, Mr Murry ran perhaps the highest temperature, although Dr Gettman picks John Cowper Powys for the distinction. 'I know,' writes Mr Powys in his *Autobiography*, 'that in certain subterranean motions of my spirit, I am much more like the

Idiot of Dostoevsky than I am like Cagliostro. I daresay I have a touch of Ivan Karamazov in me, too'. Mr Murry's very feverish state in 1916, when he published his book on Dostoevsky, provoked some coldly sensible remarks from D. H. Lawrence, about people who dig their heads in the sand like the disgusting ostrich and see a revelation there.

It must not be forgotten that, in the gradual development of rhapsodic attitudes towards the Russian Soul, went much that was based on sound observation of Russian realities. Between the Russo-Japanese War and World War I, English travellers of experience, students of the people and of the language, like Maurice Baring and Stephen Graham, published popular books on Russian life and literature. Baring covered the Russo-Japanese War as correspondent for the *Morning Post*, and found time to read *The Idiot* and *The Brothers Karamazov*: 'these two books were a revelation'. He remained for a time in Russia after the war, and in the years up to 1914, made several other long stays. Three of his books—*Landmarks in Russian Literature* (1910), *The Russian People* (1911), and *The Mainsprings of Russia* (1914)—made a deep impression; Arnold Bennett reviewed the first with enthusiasm, and it helped to stimulate the growing interest in Dostoevsky. To the understanding of the Russian character, Baring made the doubtful contribution of a division of all Russians into two types—Lucifer and Ivan the Fool, the latter being the hero of Dostoevsky's novels and the aim and ideal of Tolstoy's teaching. But he deserves the praise given him by Carl Lefevre: 'Before Baring, only Turner in England had made such prodigious efforts, including mastery of the Russian language, to effect a cultural liaison between England and Russia'.

Stephen Graham specialized in pilgrimages and peasants and wrote a series of books just before and during the World War—*Undiscovered Russia*, *Changing Russia*, *The Way of Martha and the Way of Mary*, *With the Russian Pilgrims to Jerusalem*, etc. He must accept some responsibility for creating that impression of the Russian amusingly described by Hugh Walpole—'a blessed sort of Idiot unable to read or write, but vitally conscious of God'—

and of Russia herself as 'a land of snow, ikons, mushrooms and pilgrims'. A review of *Changing Russia* in the *New Statesman*, October, 1913, gently rebukes Graham for being so sad at the inevitable processes of change; he knows the people as few do, he is right to love the adorable unlettered peasant, but if Russia is to hold its own with the West, this peasant has got to be spoiled and it is no use to implore the Tsar and his advisers to 'keep the peasant living simply and sweetly on the land'. The enthusiasms of Baring and Graham helped prepare the ground for the English propagandists who had to justify the alliance of democratic England with autocratic Russia in World War I. They did it on a religious basis and clothed the old imperialistic designs upon Constantinople in a mystical garment: the 'second greatest day in the history of humanity' would be that wonderful day when Russia entered the holy city of Constantine, 'for there will begin the reign of peace—peace on earth, good-will among men'. Russia was the nation to whom Christ had committed His secret.

Graham, who was in Russia after the war began, found Maxim Gorky busy writing articles of which several attacked Dostoevsky on the ground that he was bad for Russia, because his outlook was concentrated on suffering and death, and Russia must cease to be mystical, suffering, melancholy, and become instead clear-minded and mistress of her soul. Graham, with disarming candour, comments: 'The Russia which Gorky attacks is just that which is spiritually interesting to us in England—the mystical and impractical Russia, Russia on pilgrimage, artistic Russia; and that which he wants Russia to be is just what would have least spiritual interest for us—Russia optimistic, cocksure, business-like, well dressed, smart and Western.' Gorky had referred to Graham's *The Way of Martha and the Way of Mary* as meeting with English approval, because 'in picturing us as holy lazy-bones and impractical persons, it allowed the English capitalist to rub his hands with glee, seeing in Russia a future British colony such as Africa and India'. Graham sees the point, but refuses to back down from his position that England does receive spiritual aid from Russia to help redeem her from commercialism and materialism, and so—for the sake of England—he clings to his Holy Russia.

Some years before (1902), Gorky's novel *Foma Gordeyev* had been characterized by Arthur Symons (*Saturday Review*, vol. 93, article 'The Russian Soul') as a strange, chaotic, attractive book, 'which we may read either for its story or because we want to find out something more about the mysterious Russian Soul'. From about 1910, when Pavlova appeared in London, the Russian Soul was enlivened by the Russian ballet. Frank Swinnerton, recalling in *The Georgian Scene* the early years of George V's reign, describes how the Ballet Russe 'infected letters': Diaghilev and Nijinsky created a new state of mind. 'Its rich décor, so bold and at times so bizarre, the triumphs of its strangeness and its beauty, the unfamiliar rhythms of its musical contributions'—all had the glory of a new world. And there was the opera, too, never before performed in London, writes Sir Osbert Sitwell (*Great Morning*, 1947), until these years, which 'relieved one suddenly from the Viking world of bearded warriors drinking blood out of skulls, that had been for so long imposed by Germany. They pleased the eye at last, as well as the ear.' Chaliapin, 'in the towering and magnificent frame that housed his voice . . . seemed to embody the immense spaces of his native country'. The word genius had to be used almost with monotony in speaking of Stravinsky, Nijinsky, Diaghilev, Karsavina, Fokine. The music of 'Petrouchka'—'traditional yet original, full of fire and genius, complication and essential simplicity, held up a mirror in which man could see, not only himself, but the angel and ape equally prisoned within his skin'. (Pages 263 ff.)

The opera rescued social intercourse from disaster in the days just before the assassination of the Archduke, as a review in the *Spectator* (June 27, 1914) of Rosa Newmarch's *The Russian Opera* informs us: 'Russian opera is perhaps the only topic of the hour on which educated people can meet on a common ground of admiration. Ulster, the suffrage, Lloyd-Georgian finance, Mr Winston Churchill, are all dangerous subjects which divide house against house and estrange lifelong friends. Even golf has begun to develop fissiparous tendencies.'

Those who some years later recall the period write a little in the spirit of the morning after, but through the half-mocking tone, the extent of the infection is apparent. Somerset Maugham, sent to Russia in 1917, to prevent (as he says in a preface) the Bolshevik Revolution, despatches the hero of his 1928 novel, *Ashenden, or The British Agent*, to St Petersburg on the eve of the fall of the Kerensky Government, where he meets an old love of his, and remembers the time in London 'when Europe discovered Russia . . . and Russian art seized upon Europe with the virulence of an epidemic of influenza'. 'Everyone was reading the Russian novelists, the Russian dancers captivated the civilized world, and the Russian composers set shivering the sensibility of persons who were beginning to want a change from Wagner. . . . New phrases became the fashion, new colours, new emotions, and the highbrows described themselves . . . as members of the intelligentsia.' Ashenden, like the rest, had hung an ikon on the wall, read Chekhov, and gone to the ballet. His Russian love Anastasia then lived in London with her husband, and literary folk came and gazed with humble reverence at 'pale-faced bearded giants who leaned against the wall like caryatids taking a day off; they were revolutionaries to a man and it was a miracle that they were not in the mines of Siberia. . . . Now and again like a peach blossom wafted by the breeze, Pavlova herself hovered in and out.' They talked of Alyosha and Natasha and Anna Karenina. Anastasia tells Ashenden that her husband will kill himself, should she divorce him to marry Ashenden, who is startled but thrilled: 'It was really very much like a Russian novel and he saw the moving and terrible pages, pages and pages, in which Dostoevsky would have described the situation. He knew the lacerations his characters would have suffered, the broken bottles of champagne, the visits to the gipsies, the vodka, the swoonings, the catalepsy, and the long, long speeches everyone would have made.' (Page 276.) When Ashenden looked into Anastasia's dark melancholy eyes, a little protruding like a Pekinese's, he saw 'the boundless steppes of Russia, and the Kremlin with its pealing bells, and the solemn ceremonies of Easter at St Isaac's, and the forests of silver beeches and the Nevsky Prospekt. It was astonishing how much he saw in her eyes'.

It was just as astonishing how much the English saw in the Russian Soul just then. Before Middleton Murry had got around to presenting the Karamazov brothers as epochs in human consciousness, a writer in *The Fortnightly Review* just before the outbreak of the war (J. A. T. Lloyd, reprinted in *Living Age*, May 2, 1914) had done rather well with the brothers as symbolic of Russia: 'Russia inarticulate, dreaming her great Byzantine dreams, half choked, half strangled by barbarism, and yet retaining always a vision that sweeps upward into vistas beyond the morass of her passions'.

Havelock Ellis, who greeted 'with religious joy' the coming of the Russian ballet,[6] admitted in May, 1915 (*New Statesman*) that Russia was still a little barbarous—implying no depreciation. But then she was so vast, and the psychological implications of vastness are gentleness. 'We are told of that very typical Russian, Turgenev, that he was a man of enormous build and extremely gentle manner, almost feminine in his impressionability and delicacy. That is the typical combination presented by Russia herself; like the elephant, enormous and delicate.' Having achieved this striking transformation of Bear into Elephant, Ellis discourses on the Russian genius: it flows out and lacks clear outline, like its landscape; it is attracted to the mystically vague; it has difficulty in concentrating its will power; it is indifferent to conventional moral rules; it has its *nitchevo*, or 'it doesn't matter' moods; but its most profound trait is humanity. 'All modern literature from the days of Gogol bears the seal of this mingled temper, variously proportioned, but always this seal of ruggedness which finds its issue in an infinite sweetness, a revelation of human tenderness never before seen in the world.' The Russian character is marked by 'the strength that brings forth sweetness'. Certainly at this point, Samson's lion broke into the Havelock Ellis zoo.

About the same time, Rebecca West published some reflections

—'The Barbarians'—in the *New Republic*, January 9, 1915, reflections inspired by reading here and there in *The Brothers Karamazov*, while browsing in a bookshop in a 'delicate spirited suburb' of London. That England, with her habit of judging other nations by their political institutions, should be an ally of Russia could be explained only by the fact that 'wherever people who write and think gather together, Russian literature is loved and praised'. Russia was to the young intellectual of today what Italy had been to the Victorians; as they, their imaginations stimulated by Turner and the Brownings, had dreamed of the 'crumbling richnesses' of Rome and Venice, so 'we today think of that plain of brown earth, patterned with delicate spring grass and steel-grey patches of half-melted snow and cupped in a round unbroken skyline, which is Russia'. (At last the snows are melting.) 'We are deeply and affectionately familiar with Russian life,' and after a number of little pictures of that life, suggesting Chekhov and Turgenev and the rest, Miss West concludes: 'We have arrived at intimacy with a people extraordinarily like the English, in their untidiness and their inflexible conviction that there are other things in the world besides efficiency, but sweeter in their hearts, beautifully devoid of the sense of property, and beautifully troubled by consciences that are sharp-edged like a child's. And from this literary friendship there has sprung the immensely important comradeship of the nations which today keeps civilization together.' Miss West in thus explaining the Anglo-Russian alliance was relying pretty heavily on the political innocence of her American readers. She is somewhat troubled by the thought that perhaps Tolstoy and Turgenev, being aristocrats, had not given us the soul of Russia, the accomplishment of that task being left to the starvelling Dostoevsky, the shopman's son, Chekhov, and the hawker Gorky. 'In Russia all men kiss one another on Easter Day, because Christ has risen, and this religious sense of brotherhood lingers throughout the year.' As she turns the pages of her Dostoevsky, she is reminded that there was sometimes cruelty in Russia and political servitude and lack of education; barbarism—but not the barbarism of the Germans. She reflects how many of the great writers of both countries had been afflicted with ill-health; 'but in the one nation suffering has turned to sweetness, to a rapturous embrace of life, to a determination to clean the world before death comes. In the other it leads to a snarling at the mildness of health, to a sick aggressiveness, a mad desire to spoil the world.'

One does not like to think of the distress of Havelock Ellis and Miss West when, very soon, Russian strength brought forth Bolshevism, and the sweet-hearted Russians, so like the English, became beautifully aware of property and began taking it over. On the very eve of this change, a fine performance of *Boris Godunov* led W. J. Turner in the *New Statesman* (January 16, 1917) to say: 'This opera once again makes us feel how much more we English have in common with the Russian people than with any other nation in Europe.'

Occasionally in these early war years, the voice of common sense strikes a little coldly on the ear. Bernard Shaw saw nothing mystical about the Russian alliance. In a famous pamphlet, 'Common Sense about the War', published as a supplement to the *New Statesman* (November 14, 1914) he expressed the deep uneasiness over this alliance felt by 'all disinterested and thoughtful supporters of the war'. Up to 1906 it was generally recognized that the Tsarist Government was the enemy of every liberty England boasted of, but newspapers have ceased to report examples of Russia's disregard of the political principles England stands for. Why? The answer is simple. It was in 1906 that we began to lend Russia money and Russia began to advertise in *The Times*. 'Since then she has been welcome to flog and hang her H. G. Wells's and Lloyd-Georges by the dozen without a word of remonstrance from our plutocratic Press, provided the interest is paid punctually. Russia has been embraced in the large charity of cosmopolitan capital, the only charity that does not begin at home.' But Shaw had, as he put it, to save his face with his personal friends, who were either Russians, 'or discoverers of the soul of the Russian people'. So he declares to Sasha Kropotkin and Cunninghame Graham: 'my heart is with their Russia, the Russia of Tolstoy and

Turgenev and Dostoevsky, of Gorky and Chekhov, of the Moscow Art Theatre and the Drury Lane Ballet, of Peter Kropotkin and all the great humanitarians, great artists and charming people, whom their very North German Tsars exile and imprison and flog'.

E. M. Forster was not in sympathy with turning to Russian literature to find out what 'animates our great Ally'. Reviewing (*New Statesman*, July 24, 1915) some translations of stories by Chekhov and Sologub, he remarks, 'Russian literature will scarcely come to its own until we cease to seek in it for the Russian spirit. We still read it for information, just as we used to read French literature for information about that other local product, *la femme*.' No use turning to literature for what it seldom provides — a generalization. Comparing the art of Sologub and Chekhov, he notes how to Sologub's ingenious mind, nothing means much unless it means something else, mostly psychic; it is a relief to turn to Chekhov, to his character Savka who is Savka, and to Savka's supper, which is supper.

But supper was not supper in those days. If not a feast of reason, it was certainly a flow of soul. In 1916 Macmillan published a very handsome book, illustrated with colour plates, to aid the fund for Russian refugees. The title was *The Soul of Russia*, the editor Winifred Stephens, and the contributors, both British and Russian, form an impressive list. The Soul is presented in many aspects; excellent articles give information about Russian drama, folk-lore, folk-song, music, painting, poetry, language, peasant industries; there are poems by Balmont and Bryusov, stories by Kuprin and Sologub. It is propaganda in the interests of humanitarianism, but it illustrates the great variety of interest in things Russian on the eve of the Revolution. The editor in her introduction refers to Russia's 'noble, but sometimes unfathomable soul', and also to 'our great and unfortunate ignorance of the Russian language'. G. K. Chesterton manages to attack the English Party System in connection with the Russian Soul; but admires 'the long heroism of that outpost of Christendom against Asiatic anarchy', and hopes that 'in the better days after the War, we shall approach the great Russian people with an open mind, if necessary as an entirely new people discovered on the other side of the moon'. Harold Begbie, 'After-Dinner Memories', recalls wonderful late parties in the salons of Petrograd, among the most charming people in the world—these Russians, who are nearer to the English than any other nation, and singularly modest, earnest and intelligent.

Contributions by Russians help us to understand how the English, relying upon them, could go off the deep end. Olga Metchnikoff, widow of Elie Metchnikoff and a lady of letters, writes how 'in the first months of the War, the Government made itself one with the people . . . all divisions of class, party and nationality disappeared. The whole country had but one thought, one desire, one object. Morals were reformed, alcoholism vanished. . . . To the mystic soul of the people it seemed that in war-time, as before the Holy Communion, one ought to be in a state of grace. And in those days we realized of what infinite goodness and moral force the Russian people are capable.' Shakespeare's influence on the soul of Russia is described by Nestor Kotlyarevsky; until recently Russian life was a stranger to passion; Russians 'hardly knew the meaning of passion in the inward world of ideas'; Russian life was characterized by tranquillity, passivity; but all that was changed when Shakespeare's plays became familiar on the stage; he showed that man is the sport of his passions—by the free action of his own heart and mind. Colonel Peretts, a Russian staff officer, does his bit: in Russian military science, which originates in the defensive, is expressed the soul of the Russian people, 'ever deeply convinced that God is not with the aggressors'. But 'in the defence of God's anointed, for the sake of his Tsar, the head of all the Russian army, the Russian soldier, himself a member of Christ's army, will boldly march into the greatest danger'. The officer, the colonel tells us, sees to it that the soldiers are well fed, that they are clean and barbered, that they are warmly clothed, and he himself inspects their linen. One turns away with reluctance from this idyllic picture of Russian military life, to the moving plea of Rimsky-Korsakoff: 'Has not the time come for the spiritual union of Britain with the folk-art of Russia, which reveals the breadth and depth of the people's soul? Is not a friendly and careful study of the creative work of the folk the truest way in which to arrive at that reciprocal penetration which should inspire all the external forms of union between great nations?'

The Russian Verb might seem a little apart from the Russian Soul, but Jane Ellen Harrison, author of *Russia and The Russian Verb*, a book published in 1915, established the relationship. The reviewer in the *New Statesman* (December 11, 1915) is somewhat sceptical about the spiritual significance of imperfective aspects. 'The Russian verb is poor in tenses, but rich in aspects. It is constructed in fact for the benefit of people who want to know *how* a thing is done, rather than the time *when*. . . . Because action is habitually spoken of as incomplete, it is regarded as incomplete, and so Russians (and particularly their novelists) refuse to pronounce moral judgments or to add up results. Some call this reluctance mere moral slackness; others, including Miss Harrison, call it literary objectivity.' The *quality* of the action is of the greater importance to the Russsian; but the reviewer does not share the enthusiasm which drives Miss Harrison to declare, 'I want to use these aspects; I long to be able to, I need them, they feed me spiritually.' He congratulates her on the good time she is going to have 'when she arrives at the stage of attempting the translation of a really skilled artificer in imperfective aspects, such as Chekhov'.

A reviewer ('A Study in the Untranslatable', *New Statesman*, August 26, 1916) of Mme Jarintsov's *The Russians and Their Language* notes the publication of *The Slav Soul*, *The Soul of Russia*, *The Russian Soul*, and is amused: 'Ever since Miss Jane Harrison caused a boom in the imperfective aspect of the Russian verb by declaring that in it lay the clue to the soul of the Russian people, there has been much amateur psychical research into the manners and customs of the latter'. Mme Jarintsov, however, laughs at the soul traders, and gossips delightfully about her language.

iv

Translations: Evidence of Increased Interest

AFTER SWIMMING about in this sea of soul-rhapsody, let us climb out upon dry land for a brief rest and find out what new light was being shed on Russian literature during these war years by new translations.

The most important happening in this field was of course Constance Garnett's translations of Dostoevsky's major works, beginning with *The Brothers Karamazov*, 1912, followed by *The Idiot*, *The House of the Dead*, *The Insulted and Injured*, *The Raw Youth*, *The Gambler*, *The Possessed*, *Crime and Punishment*—in all, twelve volumes by 1920. And the second most important was Mrs Garnett's *Tales of Tchehov*, in thirteen volumes, 1916–1922. (In 1921, Arnold Bennett notes in his *Journal* that he was buying another set of Chekhov for his town flat, so that he would not be without his Chekhov either in town or country.) Separate stories of Chekhov's by various translators had been appearing since 1891; and a good critical evaluation by R. E. C. Long, in the July 1902 *Fortnightly Review*, is considered by Vivienne Koch[7] the best up to 1911. But the cumulative effect of volume after volume, in a reliable translation, was marked both in England and the United States.

Other translators were busy, and the book reviews talk with an informed air of Andreyev, Gorky, Garshin, Artzibashev, Sologub, Kuprin, Korolenko. It was called a 'catch-as-catch-can' era by Julius West in the *New Statesman*, August 14, 1915, partly to be explained by the fact that international copyright agreements did not apply to Russia—no permissions needed, no royalties paid. Fiction held the first place, especially short stories, which were preferred by publishers because the chance against two translators making the same selection was a safeguard against wholesale duplication.

Of the other Russian writers, Aksakov was translated, the first two volumes of his autobiographical work appearing in 1916 and

1917, in a good rendering by J. D. Duff. But Goncharov's *Oblomov* (1915) was labelled 'an impertinent substitution' by the reviewer, who considered that 60,000 words instead of the original 160,000 represented 'wreckage', and that it was scandalous to publish a travesty when it was of such great importance that the English should understand the Russian mind. (*New Statesman*, October 2, 1915.) Vladimir Solovyoff's *Three Conversations on War, Progress and the End of History*, issued from the University of London Press, appeared in 1915. The early diaries of Tolstoy, letters of Dostoevsky, the autobiographical volumes of Gorky (*My Childhood*, *In the World*), a Russian Anthology, compiled by C. E. Bechhofer, with twenty-five no longer living Russian writers represented by extracts, a volume of *Russian Poets and Poems*, including Pushkin, Lermontov, Tyutchev—these publications, all during the years 1914–1917, suggest a public interest, which was also being stimulated by reprints of such older interpretations of Russian literature as those of Edward Garnett and Kropotkin and by new books by Baring and Serge Persky (*Contemporary Russian Novelists*).

Of the three great Russians, Turgenev, the first to have had his novels offered in a complete translation, was temporarily much less interesting to English readers than Dostoevsky. As for Tolstoy, it was not until 1928, when the Centenary Edition of his works began to appear (under the editorship of his biographer Aylmer Maude), that his stature as man and artist could really be measured. Yet Havelock Ellis, reviewing in 1917 (*New Statesman*, September 22) the diary—*Youth* 1847–1852—entitles his article 'The Supreme Russian'. Tolstoy is a profound seer, a supreme artist, a dominating and representative personality, but not a great thinker; Ellis emphasizes his childlikeness, quotes Merezhkovsky—that Tolstoy is a Titan, but also a fledgeling fallen from the nest and wailing in the high grass, 'like you and me and all the rest of us'—and concludes: 'The image of Tolstoy as the *colossal and eternal child, the symbol of Russia herself*, may well be the final image he leaves on our mind'. (Italics mine.)

Certainly in this period, the English had a wide choice of interpreters of Russian literature and a quite considerable body of translations, good and bad. How many people—leaving out of the picture the no doubt huge army of the indifferent—believed in the Russian Soul, who can say? Many, reading the stories of Artzibashev, Andreyev, Sologub, Kuprin, Gorky, were possibly troubled, like Gerald Gould who reviewed many of them, by a discrepancy between Russian fiction and what little they knew of Russian fact; 'my Russian friends', he wrote (*New Statesman*, April 8, 1916), 'are without exception perfectly sane; yet almost all the Russians I read about in books are as mad as hatters'. Perhaps, he reflected, only the madder books get translated.

[1] The expression is George Moore's from 'Two Russian Realists', *London Quarterly Review*, April, 1888.

[2] *Iconoclasts: A Book of Dramatists*, by James Huneker, 1905.

[3] *Mark Twain: A Biography*, by Albert Bigelow Paine. Vol. 3, pp. 1282-5.

[4] *Life in Letters of William Dean Howells*. Ed. Mildred Howells, 1928. Vol. 2, pp. 219-220.

[5] *Ibid*, Vol. 2, p. 13, letter of January 1891.

[6] *Havelock Ellis, Philosopher of Love*, by Houston Peterson, 1928, p. 327.

[7] *Chekhov's English Reputation*, Columbia University Master's thesis, by Vivienne Koch, 1933.

CHAPTER VIII

THE PARTIAL ECLIPSE OF THE RUSSIAN SOUL

i

The Secret City

ADMIRERS OF the Russian Soul were bewildered by the events of the revolutionary year 1917. The novelist Hugh Walpole had worked with the Red Cross in Russia and had been in St Petersburg during the days of the February Revolution. In 1916 he had published *The Dark Forest*, staging a drama of rivalry in love in the 'dark forest' at the Russian front. One of the rivals is the sinister Semyonov, a Dostoevsky stereotype, sensualist-idealist, sadist-masochist, who reappears in the sequel, *The Secret City* (1919). The woman he loved had been killed and he seeks to burst the barriers of the flesh and be united with her spirit; but unwilling to adopt the simple method of suicide, which Russian fiction had made almost pleasantly familiar, he works out an intricate plot in order to get himself shot by a man he tortures. The 'secret city' is the St Petersburg of Dostoevsky, with a red sun, evil and secret and cunning, or a creeping smoky dusk, monstrous buildings towering overhead and figures slipping in and out of doorways like furtive shadows. But it is also the secret heart of man, and more especially the Russian Soul, that Walpole is engaged in exploring. The narrator—an invalid Englishman also carried over from the earlier novel—makes a very sensible opening observation: 'This business of seeing Russian psychology through English eyes has no excuse except that it is English. . . . Of Russia and the Russians I know nothing, but of the effect upon myself and my ideas of life that Russia and the Russians have had during these last three years I know something'. Walpole plays off one young Englishman, who has read Dostoevsky and thinks he knows all, against another, resident for many years in Russia, who just says 'rot' when the first talks of the mysticism of the Russian peasant as destined to save the world; 'he had formed, from the reading of the books of Mr Stephen Graham and others, delightful pictures of the warmest hearts in the world holding out the warmest hands before the warmest samovars'. The narrator preserves a certain amount of critical detachment for a while, as he puzzles over the Russian character. The Russian, he believes, 'lives in a world of loneliness peopled only by ideas. His impulses towards self-confession, towards brotherhood, towards vice, towards cynicism, towards his belief in God and his scorn of Him, come out of this world; and beyond it he sees his fellow-men as trees walking, and the Mountain of God as a distant peak, placed there only to emphasize his irony.'

But when the Utopian glow of the first hours of the Revolution begins to fade, and the spectre that haunts Europe—Communism—raises its head, the real gulf between Russia and the Western world becomes visible: 'For more than three years we had been pretending that a week's sentiment and a hurriedly proclaimed idealism could bridge a separation which centuries of magic and blood and bones had gone to build. For three years we tricked ourselves (I am not sure that the Russians were ever really deceived) . . . but we liked the ballet, we liked Tolstoy and Dostoevsky (we translated their inborn mysticism into the weakest kind of sentimentalism), we liked the theory of inexhaustible numbers, we liked the picture of their pounding, steam-roller like, to Berlin . . . we tricked ourselves and in the space of a night our trick was exposed.' At a great mass meeting, he looks at the faces—'wave on wave of faces, or rather the same face, repeated again and again and again, the face of a baby, of a child, of a credulous cynical dreamer, a face the kindest, the naïvest, the cruellest, the most friendly, the most human, the most savage, the most Eastern, the most Western, in the world'.

Russia had slipped back behind her veil of mist and shadow; 'we may trade with her, plunge into her politics, steal from her

Art, emphasize her religion—she remains alone, apart, mysterious'.

ii

The Morning After

THERE WAS still that Russian literature. Two articles in *The Contemporary Review* (April and June, 1918) seek to account for the disconcerting events in Russia by re-examining her literature. They typify the sharp divergence of opinion about the Revolution that appeared at once and has continued through the succeeding years. The Reverend G. W. Thorn (June number), 'Sidelights on the Psychology of the Russian Revolution', seems to know something about Russian literature, but prefers to linger in what Merezhkovsky called Dostoevsky's laboratory. After quoting some of the most hair-raising passages from *The Possessed*, he concludes that Dostoevsky had foreseen what such tendencies would lead to when allied to revolutionary doctrine, and that though his prophecies had seemed a gross caricature at the time, recent events had fully justified them. He still thinks the Russian Soul has a mission; it is hard to say what he thinks it is, since excess of impulse and sympathy with crime (prominent marks he believes of the Russian character) augur ill for a spiritual mission.

Hagbert Wright, 'The Rebirth of Russia' (April), bases his generalization upon a broad survey of most of the important writers from Pushkin on, many of them still no more than names —if that—to the English. 'They must be read as an indictment of a State system, and no more terrible indictment of the kind has ever been penned.' Contrasting the great literature of England, nurtured in health, with the modern literature of Russia, he calls the latter 'the cry of a soul sick unto death'. That the revolution has disappointed us in one way or another is no excuse for misrepresentation, misunderstanding and aloofness. The Bolsheviks, everywhere condemned, have constructive purposes—a commonwealth based on the common right. Most people are abusing

Russia and think they are witnessing the downfall of a people, but that people is being reborn. 'The Russian Revolution is the culmination of a secular effort which engages the very soul of a people, which reaches down to the very depths of life and to the sources of hope. We shall do Russia radical injustice unless we remember that.' We should remember that to the English, bent on winning the war, the revolution is an episode in the war; to the Russians, the war is an episode in the revolution. In a later article (*Quarterly Review*, 1921), Wright, commenting on some seven books, in French, Russian and English, on Russian literature, goes much more deeply into the history of that literature, as far back as the epic songs of the eighth and ninth centuries. Gogol, Turgenev, and Tolstoy are the three pillars of the temple of Russian literature; they prepared the way for a social revolution. 'The Russian writer's idealism shows itself in a continual search for inner truth and for the highest pinnacle of justice.' In Dotoevsky, too, this search is everywhere evident; but great as he is, 'he is a psychopathologist of universally acknowledged genius who devotes himself to the abnormal. . . . His people are Russians, but Russians seen in a mirror which gives to those it reflects an appearance of malformation'. It is in other writers that he finds the national types that are at once critical and just.

Edmund Gosse, who in 1887 had spoken in a letter of *Crime and Punishment* as a 'masterpiece of psychological study', the subject 'distressing enough but most thrilling and entrancing in its carrying out', was pleading in 1926 to André Gide to release himself from his bondage to the Russians and particularly to Dostoevsky. 'We have all in turn been subjected to the magic of this epileptic monster. But his genius has only led us astray, and I should say to any young writer of merit who appealed to me, "Read what you like, only don't waste your time reading Dostoevsky. He is the cocaine and morphia of modern literature".'[1] Gosse was finding Chekhov delightful in 1921—some of his letters had just been published—but looked back with some distrust upon the infatuation, about 1910, 'with what we supposed to be the genius of Russia'. He approves of Chekhov's respect for science, and lack of prophetic ardour, but cannot resist applying even to him phrases about the inscrutable Russian mind and the languorous Russian temperament, admitting, however, that there is much to be done before we can pretend to understand the mind of Russia. Among the books Gosse discusses in these essays, *Books on the Table*, is Gorky's *Reminiscences of Tolstoy*—considered by later criticism one of Gorky's most brilliant achievements, but found by Gosse to be without discretion; an instance of Bolshevist literature destroying the tomb of its prophet. Gosse's own opinion is as disconcerting as he found Gorky's portrait: 'Intellectually, spiritually, during the close of his life, Tolstoy was a hippopotamus rolling about in a clouded pool.' (This hippopotamus should be joined by that other one, picking up a pea, in H. G. Wells's famous characterization of Henry James.)

'Clouded pool' is not a bad term for things Russian at this period. English writers looked into it, and were not at all clear about what they saw. The soul, yes. 'If we want understanding of the soul and heart', wrote Virginia Woolf, 'where shall we find it of comparable profundity'—outside of Russian fiction? 'It is the soul that is the chief character in Russian fiction. Delicate and subtle in Chekhov, subject to an infinite number of humours and distempers, it is of greater depth and volume in Dostoevsky, liable to violent diseases and raging fevers.' And, in Dostoevsky, this soul is alien to an English reader, having no sense of humour, no form; we go down into Stavrogin, Mishkin, and other Dostoevskian characters, 'as we descend into some enormous cavern; lights swing about; we hear the boom of the sea; it is dark, terrible, uncharted'. His novels are 'seething whirlpools, gyrating sandstorms, waterspouts which hiss and boil and suck us in'. In every great Russian writer Mrs Woolf discerns the features of a saint; they see farther, without our 'gross impediments of vision'. But can the English, for all their enthusiasm, understand Russian literature? There is the language barrier, and the blind dependence upon translators: 'of all those who feasted upon Tolstoy, Dostoevsky and Chekhov during the past twenty years, not more than one or two perhaps have been able to read them in Russian'; and so we have judged a whole literature, stripped of its style. What remains—'as the English have proved by the fanaticism of their admiration'—is something very powerful and impressive; but 'how far can we trust ourselves not to impute, to distort, to read into them, an emphasis that is false?'[2]

D. H. Lawrence was one of those who did not trust themselves very far. When he read *The Brothers Karamazov* in 1913, he was 'fascinated but unconvinced'. In 1915 he wrote (to Lady Ottiline Morrell) that he had been reading *The Idiot* and did not like Dostoevsky, who was like a rat, 'slithering along in hate, in the shadows and, in order to belong to the light, professing love, all love; but his nose is sharp with hate, his running is shadowy and rat-like, he is a will fixed and gripped like a trap. He is not nice.' He read *The Possessed* in 1916 and decided he had 'gone off' Dostoevsky; nobody in the novel was 'possessed' enough to interest him. 'They are great parables, the novels,' he wrote to Middleton Murry, 'but false art. . . . All the people are fallen angels, even the dirtiest scrubs. This I cannot stomach. People are not fallen angels, they are merely people.' Among the posthumous papers of Lawrence, collected in *Phoenix*, are two prefaces: one prepared, but never published, for the English translation of a novel by Giovanni Verga and the other written for a special edition of 'The Grand Inquisitor', from *The Brothers Karamazov*. The first raises the question of why the Russians are so popular, and finds the answer in the Russian fashion of making every man his own hero: 'The merest scrub of a pickpocket is so phenomenally aware of his own soul that we are made to bow before the imaginary coruscations that go on inside him. That is almost the whole of Russian literature: the phenomenal coruscations of the souls of quite commonplace people. Of course your soul will coruscate, if you think it does. . . . No matter how much of a shabby animal you may be, you can learn from Dostoevsky how to have the most tender, unique, coruscating soul on earth.' Though he could not stomach Dostoevsky, he could not stop thinking about him; the reflections on 'The Grand Inquisitor' are often penetrating; Dostoevsky is 'always perverse, always impure, always an evil thinker—and a marvellous seer'; his 'amazing perspicacity is mixed with ugly perversity'.

William Gerhardi had never had the Russian Soul fever, although in his novels, *Futility* (1922) and *The Polyglots* (1925), and in his study of Chekhov (1923), he had displayed more expert knowledge than most of the soul-worshippers possessed, of certain aspects of the Russian temperament. He was not therefore suffering any morning-after revulsion in 1926, when he exclaimed: 'Oh, the great Russian soul! Oh, the colossal Russian mind! It is overwhelming. It is like some gigantic machine of marvellous design and construction—with a hitch that prevents it from working; like a born orator, with an impediment in his speech. Russia will not change. There will arise some new Peter the Great, who will conceive a new plan, let us say, for electrifying the whole of Russia, with a stroke of the pen. On the margin of the ministerial report he will write the words: "Electrify Russia at once". And the contractors will duly bribe the authorities and supply rotten material, get rich, and the scheme will be crippled at birth. In this lies the humour and genius of the race. It needed a Chekhov to see it, a Chekhov who seemed a little weary of people knocking at the window of his bedroom at about half-past two in the morning, anxious for a "soul-to-soul" talk'.[3]

Perhaps Russia would never change. Opinions will continue to differ as to Mr Gerhardi's place among the prophets. But for the moment, in the middle of the 'twenties, the new day looked very bleak to some of the intellectuals. The apparent changes were repellent to 'Crites', reviewing in the *Criterion* (October, 1924) L. Trotsky's *Problems of Life*. The *Criterion* usually held itself above the political battle: 'To the point of view of a periodical like *The Criterion*, much of what has been said and written in impeachment and in defence of Soviet Russia is of minor interest. Not that it is possible, or even right, for any individual to regard such matters from the point of view of pure intelligence alone; but it is well that we should all regard them from that point of view now and then'. 'Crites', like anyone aware of culture at all, knows that there are and have been different cultures; and while we may not like the notion of cannibalism or head-hunting, we do know that they formed part of a tenable culture in Melanesia. So 'Crites' was prepared to find in Mr Trotsky's book 'an exposition of a culture repellent to my own disposition; but I hoped that it would be distinct and interesting. A revolution staged on such a vast scale, amongst a *picturesque*, *violent and romantic people* (italics mine), involving such disorder, rapine, assassination, starvation and plague, should have something to show for the expense: a new culture horrible at the worst, but in any event fascinating. Such a cataclysm is justified if it produces something really new:

Un oasis d'horreur dans un désert d'ennui.

It is not justified by the dreary picture of Montessori schools, playing fields, plasticene, club-houses, communal kitchens crèches, abstinence from swearing and alcohol, a populatioı warmly clad (or soon to be warmly clad), and with its mind filled (or in process of being filled) with nineteenth-century superstitions about nature and her forces. Yet such phenomena as these are what Mr Trotsky proudly presents as the outcome of his revolution; these form his "culture". Here is the Eastern prophet of the new age speaking in the smuggest tones of a New Bourgeoisie: "The cinema amuses, educates, strikes the imagination by images, and liberates you from the need of crossing the church door". It remains only to observe that there is no mention in Mr Trotsky's Encheiridion of Culture of such an institution as the ballet, and that his portrait shows a slight resemblance to the face of Mr Sidney Webb.' A ballet on the edge of a volcano in eruption is evidently the image of the new Russia that would assuage the thirst of 'Crites' in the waste-land.

The *Criterion* in the next few years, very much to its credit, did not cross Russian culture off its books. It published translations, especially of letters and anything relating to Dostoevsky, and full notes on the contents of Russian literary periodicals, published by the exiles in Paris, Brussels, and Prague. (*Versti*, *Volya Rossii*, *Contemporary Annals*.) One of the *émigré* editors and critics was D. S. Mirsky, who soon came to England, and whose articles began to appear in the *Criterion*, where his *Russian Literature to 1881* was very favourably reviewed (January, 1928). Sir Oliver Elton, in his Taylorian Lecture at Oxford, 1929, calls Mirsky 'our best guide'.[4] By 1928, the *Criterion* is reviewing Soviet periodicals with what seems to be a high degree of objectivity, and continues to do so in the years following—including *Novy Mir*, *October*, *Zvezda*, *Krasnaya Nov*. The controversies that preceded the dissolution of the Association of Revolutionary Writers (RAPP) in 1932 are reported, with many quotations; the work being done by Soviet poets, novelists, and playwrights—Mayakovsky, Ivanov, Leonov, Kataev, Alexei Tolstoy, Fadeev, Pasternak, Gladkov, Lidin, Prishvin—is described and briefly criticized. Soviet writers show, on the whole, more vigour than their *émigré* contemporaries; 'literary Russia is the devil's own seething kettle of energy'.[5] (January, 1928). In May, 1927, T. S. Eliot became the editor of what was now, after one or two variations in name, the *Monthly Criterion*. In 1929 T. S. Eliot and A. L. Rowse were exchanging views on Marxism and Communism, rather as if what was said about Soviet Russia were of major interest. The discussion is on a high level of good manners, very instructive and important in the matter of the development of Mr Eliot's political ideas. It is referred to here because Mr Rowse makes a statement that the writer of this study believes to be true, but very much neglected by all those who have found it convenient through the centuries to talk of Russia as an enigma, a mystery and so forth. Mr Rowse (April, 1929), discussing the Literature of Communism, remarks: 'The pretence that it is impossible to get reliable information is itself a propaganda move against Communism'. And in this period, we see that it was possible to get reliable information in what at first glance might have seemed a rather unlikely spot—T. S. Eliot's *Monthly Criterion*.

iii

The Soul becomes, more modestly, the soul

'THE ONCE notorious Russian Soul,' V. S. Pritchett called it in 1942. Although all these simplifications must be qualified, there is a good deal of evidence to support the statement that as the Dostoevsky cult waned, the Chekhov cult grew among the English. The great importance of Chekhov's literary influence is a subject for a later chapter. Here one may guess at the effect Chekhov's popularity had in replacing the capital *S* in soul with a small *s*. Chekhov's soul was a modest one; it was also—or was so considered at this time—a non-political and a non-prophetic soul. D. S. Mirsky (*Criterion*, October, 1927) explores the reasons for Chekhov's appeal to the English intellectuals: their mood is out of tune with heroic values; and Chekhov's attitude to civilization—at least as expressed in his letters—is one of negative values; and his style is free from everything sharp and glaring, bathed in a perfect and uniform haze, with a narrative method allowing nothing to happen, but only 'smoothly and imperceptibly to become'. His despair is compared to that evoked by E. M. Forster in *Passage to India*, in Mrs Moore's experience in the cave—ultimate and absolute, but mean and devoid of vastness and tragic grandeur—'the undying worm itself'. Chekhov lulls and soothes with an art nearer to that of the hypnotist than to that which begets human values. 'To the stripped and cast-out mankind of today Chekhov is the arch-seducer. To succumb to him is as sweet as it is for the worn-out wayfarer struggling with the blizzard to go to sleep in the snow—it is the sweetest of spiritual deaths.' Sir Oliver Elton, in the lecture already referred to, brings out the subtleties of Chekhov's art in felicitous phrases—'the luminous grey texture, full of sparkles when it is held in the right light'—and also, significantly, finds the problems of the Russians not so alien to those of the English. There are many stories of Chekhov in which the theme is some kind of a fatal error or impasse or spiritual deadlock; a conception made familiar by his plays, where there is only the wish to escape, the ineffectual vision of some window or outlet which is too high to reach. The healthy Briton is impatient; 'he fingers his moral muscles, and he says, "Why don't they *do* something? How Russian!"' But look around, and you will see that an impasse in life is not a specifically Russian thing; look at Hardy, at Gissing, at George Eliot, whose Dr Lydgate in *Middlemarch* is a thoroughly Chekhovian figure. What *is* Russian is the artistic method and its power of suggestion.

When in 1930 (June 5) the London *Times Literary Supplement* published an article on 'Dostevsky and the Novel' that is a very important summing-up of the Russian influence on European, not merely English, fiction, it did not neglect the soul. 'The agitation of mind and spirit which the Russian novel expressed seemed suddenly to communicate itself to novelists in other countries; the infection spread until, in one or other of its various forms, the problem of representing the soul, reality, the intangible world—one name serves as well or ill as another—became an obsession with the European novelist.' Some of the conclusions of this article will be taken up later. But note here the phrases—the 'naked soul', 'the metaphysical sensation of existence'—'thrillers where the soul is substituted for the dead body'. Dostoevsky did not bring the soul into fiction—'he merely sought to exclude everything else from it'. Some English novelists (Virginia Woolf, David Garnett), who most readily assimilated the Dostoevsky tradition, have discovered that 'as material for literature, the soul is formless, it lacks variety, it has no sense of humour'.

Enough has been set down, I think, to convince anyone that the Russian Soul has been more rather than less at the mercy of the political climate. Even V. S. Pritchett, that very sensitive critic of Russian literature, who joked about the Russian Soul in 1942—clearly perceiving the nonsense that has been uttered about it—could actually say in 1948, comparing, unfavourably, Koestler's *Darkness at Noon* with Dostoevsky's *Possessed*: 'It is evident from our post-war contacts with them that the Russians are as Dostoevsky drew them: a people living by wont in a natural atmosphere of suspicion and mistrust and consumed by fantasies.'

(*Harper's Magazine*, January, 1948.) Perhaps all who were not consumed by fantasies were killed defending Stalingrad.

The climate in the fall of 1945 was more favourable to the soul, and it figures in many of the answers by British writers, in a London Brains Trust broadcast, to a question about the influence of Russian literature, old and new, on British literature. Ten other Brains Trust programmes were being held at the same time, in Birmingham, Leeds, Newcastle, Cardiff, Bristol, etc. The participants make an impressive list, and some of the opinions will be quoted later on in the discussion of Russian influence. But at the moment it is the soul we want. Marjorie Bowen said Russian literature 'caused our writers to get down to what happened to men's souls'. Phyllis Bentley found the general contribution of Russian literature in the past to be the stress on immaterial values; whatever happens, it is always why it happens and the effect on the soul of the person that is presented as important, rather than the material results—an extraordinarily important contribution, especially to our somewhat material British civilization. Lovat Dickson, publisher and editor, said, 'We owe Russia thanks for the fact that since the great Russian novels thrilled us at the end of the nineteenth century, we have been able in our own novels to talk about the soul without blushing. None of Dickens's or Thackeray's characters ever talked about the soul. The soul became interesting when it was found that it was possible to talk about it decently.'

A recent novel by Christopher Sykes, *Answer to Question 33* (1948), records the puzzled wonder of the hero over the magic that for some people, including Englishmen, lies in Russia's very name: 'It is undeniable that in Russian gatherings there occurs a certain glow of soul, a thing very easy to parody, and best suited, one might say, to an adolescent taste, yet whose force is not easily resisted even by the sceptical. Perhaps this explains a very curious phenomenon: that English people of the most conventional kind, young middle-class spinsters, for example, who in the old days went out to Russia to become governesses to great families, engineers with the shape and outlook of John Bull, or British consular representatives, sometimes enter that land and never return English again.' He has known cases where they forgot their own language and even grew to look like their Russian neighbours. Ordinary Western people like himself come nearest to understanding this enchantment in 'passages of Russian music and literature, in the haunting magic that sometimes seems to flash and play round the gentle Turgenev, or in those disturbing digressive episodes in Moussorgsky's opera of Boris Godunov, or in some scenes of Chekhov's plays in which that great writer appears to be describing something which is familiar to you, though it is a thing you have never seen or experienced'. He describes the last scene in *The Three Sisters*; 'the impression the scene makes on you is not an ordinary sentimental one; you feel, at the end of the comedy, the immensity of human fate, *the enigmatic character of Russia, its vast expanse, and its soul*'. (Italics mine.) A late bulletin on souls appears in a review entitled 'The Art of Turgenev' in the London *Times Literary Supplement* for July 7, 1950: 'All who love Russia, not only in her past, but in her difficult present, recognize her most characteristic mood as self-absorbed and sombre—a wrestle of souls, some obscure travail taking place in a darkened corner'. The darkened corner on this subject, it may seem to some of us, is the Western mind.

iv

American Postscript

THERE WAS no such excitement among intellectuals in the United States over the Russian Soul, as among the English. That at least is the impression derived from a rather cursory reading of periodicals, roughly corresponding in the United States to those in England that yield such a rich harvest of enthusiasm. Americans had no need of the Russians to teach them how to talk of the soul without blushing; they had had Emerson; even the Russians had not had the Over-Soul. The *New Republic* published articles by Rebecca West, H. N. Brailsford, Hugh Walpole and other English writers, but some of them were criticized rather severely. Professor Samuel Harper of Chicago University, for example, found Brailsford's interpretations of Panslavism and Slavophilism confused, and added that Brailsford represented an important group of English Radicals whose views and statements with regard to Russian politics 'coincide most strangely with the views and statements of the Russian reactionary'. (March 13, 1915.) And Jacob Zeitlin, in an article, 'Dostoevsky the Reactionary' (March 20, 1915), marshalled a number of facts about Dostoevsky's prejudices which Rebecca West ignored, and found something 'amusingly fatuous in the indiscriminate admiration which the English have developed for things Slavic simultaneously with the growth of the German terror'. Somewhat later Louis Friedland in *The Dial* (September 27, 1917), in the course of a review of Graham's *Russia in* 1916 and Arthur Ruhl's *White Nights*, calls upon Heaven to protect a people from those 'who love them for being rather interesting. It is so difficult to be heroic, odd, mediaeval and bizarre in this workaday world. And all to please the fancy of a few alien pilgrims who seek the balm of Gilead in a crass and material age.'

The American intellectuals were not immune to the Dostoevsky fever, however, during these years when, as Randolph Bourne put it, a new Dostoevsky came along every few months so that he seemed a living author. When his *Letters to his Family and Friends* was reviewed in the *New Republic* (December 5, 1914), he was called 'as disturbing to the spirit as any Hebrew prophet or early Christian saint' and yet his novels in the Garnett translations had been received 'most graciously'. 'One can but wonder at the general amiability when the first result of reading him would seem to be a dazed surprise that ordinary life should be so comfortable and unquestioned an affair for so many ordinary and cheerful people. . . . The effect of Dostoevsky is like that of a dangerous and delirious fever; the convalescent does not easily feel readjusted to the general life.' Philip Littell took the opportunity afforded by the appearance of a new edition of Baring's *Outline of Russian Literature* to reminisce very pleasantly about the accidental sort of way in which Russia had taken shape in his mind, from his childhood when Russian leather was to other leathers as Guava to common jellies, through the usual notions about wolves, snow and steppes, to the Turgenev sportsman listening to the peasant boys around the fire; then came the great novelist—Tolstoy—who made all other novelists, even the other Russians, seem 'arranged'. And now there was 'the master of hallucination in comparison with whose intensity your own life seems unrealized and unlived'. (*New Republic*, March 6, 1915.)

Randolph Bourne, quite surprisingly, finds that Dostoevsky's 'superb modern healthiness' is becoming more apparent. The older classic fiction kept the dividing line clear between queer and normal, sane and insane, virtuous and villainous, but now we are trying to close up that dualism. Dostoevsky knows no dividing line, and that gives a very salutary jolt to the American imagination. True, *The Idiot*, read once, remains a stream of fairly incomprehensible people and unintelligible emotional changes, but Bourne is sure he would understand it, if he read it again. Dostoevsky's stories have the *tempo* of the inner life which we know, 'with its ceaseless boring into the anxious future and its trails of the unresolved past'. They leave an after impression of rich kindness, born of suffering and imperfection, and of man 'as a being with his feet in the mud and his gaze turned towards the stars'—(an echo of the old gutter image)—'yet always indissolubly one in feet and eyes and heart and brain. If we are strong enough to hear him, this is the decisive force we need on our American creative outlook'.[6]

Van Wyck Brooks discovers in the hero of Waldo Frank's *The Unwelcome Man* an American Oblomov, describes Goncharov's hero as 'one of those archetypal characters that add so to the weight of Russian literature', and then strikes out a bold generalization: 'America is simply Russia turned inside out. Russia is the richest of nations in spiritual energy, we are the poorest; Russia is the poorest of nations in social machinery, we are the richest'. (*Dial*, March, 1917.)

Our social machinery came into action very effectively after the

October Revolution and the withdrawal of Russia from the war. The *Dial* noted in June, 1918, that 'Russia-baiting' had become the favourite sport of polite newspapers and polite society, and had extended to include Russian literature. In that connection, a few sentences from Professor Paul Shorey's address before the American Medico-Psychological Association are quoted: 'Tolstoy, if not insane, has been a prolific source of insanity in others,' and the study of Russian literature is impairing the sanity of American literary criticism and the sobriety of American opinion. By November 30, the *Dial* notes how the sales of Russian literature had fallen off, Dostoevsky suffering, presumably, for the sins of Trotsky; and is worried lest the publication of the volumes of Gorky's autobiography should be discouraged. Chekhov, fortunately, 'not tainted anywhere with politics or views', continues to appear.

The *Dial* editors kept its columns open to correction of various lies and distortions, and published favourable reviews of the books of Edward A. Ross, Charles Edward Russell, Albert Williams, and others, reporting on events in Russia. In December, 1918, they issued a plea to withdraw from Russia; among the editors at this time were Harold Stearns, Thorstein Veblen, John Dewey. They spoke of the 'poisonous atmosphere of lies and slander and intrigue and double-dealing'. 'When a really first-rate analysis of what the Soviet Government is doing is published, like *The Soviets at Work*, by Lenin—we are informed by Postmaster-General Burleson that it is unmailable.'

But to follow the political history of the period is outside the purposes of this study. Flagging interest in Russian literature was of course part of the picture, but that interest was far from expiring, and Chekhov actually benefited from the reputation he had acquired of leaving to others the solution of the riddles of the universe—and society. The volumes of the Garnett translation continued to appear, and the American short story began to lose some of its familiar characteristics and turn Russian. And after the 'Chekhov story' came the 'Chekhov play', and other Russian plays. Enthusiasm for the Moscow Art Theatre had begun before the Russian Revolution and was at its height when the company paid its 1923–1924 visits to the United States. No Postmaster-General declared it contraband. In those days artists still had certain privileges.

We now turn to the complicated question of literary influences.

[1] *The Life and Letters of Sir Edmund Gosse*, London, 1931, p. 493.

[2] *The Common Reader*, by Virginia Woolf, 1925, essays 'Modern Fiction' and 'The Russian Point of View'.

[3] Preface by William Gerhardi to the English translation of P. Krasnoff's *From Double Eagle to Red Flag*, 1926.

[4] Later scholars agree in the favourable estimate. Professor E. J. Simmons says of Mirsky (*New Republic*, Nov. 28, 1949) that there has never been 'a more eloquent and perceptive interpreter' of Russian literature, 'though there have been more scholarly ones'; Mirsky is a critic with a sense of values enriched by a wide culture; with some annoying crotchets, but with an original and sensitive mind.

[5] 'J. C.' (John Cournos?) in the *Criterion*, Sept. 1928, writes that there are many voices in the Soviet Union and many quarrels and conflicts; 'in short men are not machines'.

[6] Randolph Bourne, 'The Immanence of Dostoevsky', *Dial*, June 28, 1917.

PART TWO

CHAPTER IX

THE RUSSIAN INFLUENCE: SUBJECT-MATTER, THEMES AND VARIATIONS

i

Russia as Subject-matter

THIS STUDY has so far followed, in the main, a chronological plan. Knowledge of Russian literature has been shown as part of a complex pattern of increasing interest in Russian culture, from Elizabethan times to the second decade of the twentieth century. The travellers and reporters have had their place with the translators and the literary critics, and the Russian influence on English literature has been implied or indicated rather than analysed. In the following chapters some analysis will be attempted, and the treatment will be topical rather than chronological, with the aim of suggesting the fields where research is badly needed. Travellers' tales have continued to be in the twentieth century almost as fascinating as those of the Elizabethans, but we shall have to mention them here only to dismiss them. All of us have had, in recent troubled decades, our favourite reporters and observers: churchmen or scientists, theatre experts or educators, politicians or generals, roving correspondents or secret agents, poets or factory workers, labour leaders or ambassadors or the wives of ambassadors. Instead of the single spy of the past—in no derogatory sense—we have had battalions. All of these later observers, like their predecessors, have been subject in varying degrees to those private and collective errors described by Bacon as the idols of the tribe, the den, the market-place and the theatre. And particularly the 'theatre': the theories and philosophies, political, social, and religious, which direct our attention to everything that supports our view of the world and blinds us to the facts that do not. In what they report they often reveal more of themselves and their own country than of Russians and Russia. When they change their views, as they have so often done, we are led to a reflection nicely phrased in a review in the London *Times Literary Supplement* of a reprint of a book by Louis Fischer (August 31, 1951): 'When the enthusiast burns what he once adored and worships what he formerly scorned, it is always a moot point how far the change is in the idol and how far in the worshipper himself.'

The truth to be found in all this material is in that dismembered state Milton once described—her lovely form hewed into a thousand pieces and scattered to the four winds; so that the 'sad friends of Truth, such as durst appear', go up and down, 'gathering up limb by limb, still as they could find them'. Addressing ourselves to governments at large, as Milton did to the Lords and Commons of England, we may echo his appeal: 'Suffer not these licensing prohibitions to stand at every place of opportunity forbidding and disturbing them that continue seeking, that continue to do our obsequies to the torn body of our martyred saint.'

The future historian of our times—that impartial judge we like to conjure up, partly to relieve ourselves of our present responsibility—will have to sift out from all this evidence what he needs to prove that the world as he finds it could not have taken any other shape. He will have at hand the anthologies, probably to be compiled by literary historians, of the most brilliant narratives of events, the most eloquent denunciations, the most moving personal histories, the most heart-rending disenchantments, the most acute political prophecies, the most sinister plottings and the most imaginative fantasies. Scholars will provide comprehensive classified bibliographies, with annotations free of political bias. Meanwhile, the reader of today must choose his interpreters according to his literary tastes and his convictions. A light shadow may fall upon his certainties, if he has permitted himself to know something of the earlier patterns of prejudice and prophecy in the story we have been tracing, of how we come to know our neighbours.

The introduction into English fiction and drama of Russian characters and a Russian setting, whether authentic or synthetic, can be counted as a Russian 'influence'. Without Russia, they would not be there. At present writing (1952) the villain of the 'thriller' or the suspense drama or counter-spy feature on the radio or the screen in the United States turns out to be a disguised Russian 'Red', where a decade ago he was a disguised German Nazi or a Japanese. Much popular fiction presents the current Russian stereotypes on the same level of credibility. The sociologist who studies the comic books and the pulp magazines and the radio and television programmes as material for the understanding of popular culture deals with material of great importance, which the literary study cannot concern itself with. On a literary level, the listing of examples of Russian subject-matter in English and American literature has long ceased to be the simple matter it was when one discovered a character named 'Burris' (Boris) in a Fletcher play (*The Loyal Subject*), with 'Mosco' as a setting, or when the mother who threw her child to the wolves turned up in a poem, or when Catherine the Great took a new lover or murdered an old husband, and was admired or damned by a Byron or a Landor. The Romanoffs, singly or collectively, became subjects for biographies, more or less fictionized, by more or less scrupulous historians and novelists—Eugene Schuyler, Stephen Graham, William Gerhardi, Katharine Anthony, Edgar Saltus and others. Many of the able journalists and observers, besides reporting on the spot and reminiscing in later years, made capital of their experiences in a novel or a few short stories; among them Walter Duranty, Maurice Baring, Edmund Noble, Maurice Hindus, Ralph Fox, Anna Louise Strong.

George Gissing did not visit Russia, but he wove reminiscences of his Russian reading into his novel, *The Crown of Life* (1899). He sends his hero, Otway, to Russia, full of the desire to create better understanding between that land and his own, and Otway found that the more he knew of the country, the more it interested him. 'That huge empire was a mere blank to be filled up by the imaginings of prejudice and hostility. Was it not a task worth setting before oneself, worth pursuing for a lifetime, that of trying to make known to English folk their bugbear of the East?' These and other reflections are introduced into conversations over cigars —about trade and competing markets in China. Otway is particularly interested in the sect of the Doukhobors and the abolition of capital punishment in Russia; he thought that to abolish capital punishment for ordinary crimes was a great advance. He goes to Odessa and studies Russian; the girl he loves has the bright idea of learning it, too, (in secret); and finding an article in a Russian review signed with his name, she appeals to him to be her teacher and read a passage from Tolstoy aloud to her—for the accent. All this furnished Gissing with a very obvious excuse to talk about what interested him. The deeper Russian influence upon him is shown in other ways in his book on Dickens, from which we have quoted, and in the novel *Isabel Clarendon*, 'the undiluted pessimism' of which (according to Morley Roberts, in his introduction to *Thyrza*) 'shows so plainly its Russian affinities and his own temperament'.

Somerset Maugham, as we have seen, made use of his first-hand Russian experiences in *British Agent*. In *Christmas Holiday*, a later novel (1939), a young Englishman meets in a Paris brothel a Russian girl named Lydia, but known as the princess Olga, who tells her story. She is the daughter of a Russian professor who had fled from the Bolsheviks, but later made his peace, went back to Russia, and was murdered by the Cheka—for no particular reason, just as a matter of Cheka routine. Lydia and her mother lived half-starved and roofless in Paris; she married a Frenchman, who turns out to be one of those Gidean eccentrics who commit unmotivated murders. Lydia, like Dostoevsky's Sonya, resorts to prostitution for the purest of motives—to make the money necessary to get Robert out of prison. And she thirsts to atone by her own suffering for the crime of Robert, who can only suffer physically. The narrator has a friend, Simon, who is built up into a *Possessed* stereotype: a tortured fanatic, who tries by rigid asceticism, by freezing every shoot of affection, to prepare himself for the role of first assistant to a dictator in a revolution. Much is said of Derzhinsky, an actual person, who was chief of the Cheka in the early days of the Russian Revolution; he is presented in a most bloodcurdling version. Lydia says of Simon that, if he were a Russian, he would either become a dangerous agitator or commit suicide, but since he is English, it is equally in the cards that he will end up as an editor of *The Times*.

Freer, less imitative handling of Russian subject-matter has given us far more interesting literature.

ii

Fantasias in the Russian manner on English Themes and in the English manner on Russian Themes

SUCH A title as *Reginald in Russia*, when the author is 'Saki'—Hector Munro—promises entertaining variations on the Russian theme. Munro spent a 'delightful two years', 1904–1906, in St Petersburg, as foreign correspondent for the London *Morning Post*; he watched the events of that famous Sunday in January 1905 from various good vantage points; his sister, who also saw some of them, said it was more exciting than any play. Among his articles are amiable speculations on Russian characteristics, such as the all-prevailing inertia of Russians of all classes, for which he thought the long Russian winter could be held partly responsible; they do exert themselves when they have to, but quickly relapse into an atmosphere of congenial torpidity.

The title sketch in the *Reginald* volume (1910) is a dialogue in a St Petersburg salon between young Reginald and a Russian princess on the theme of English and Russian politics. Nothing that you hear about us in England is true, says the Princess; and later, 'Here it is dreadful—everyone goes to such extremes.' 'We go to Albert Hall,' counters Reginald. An invitation from the Princess to stay with her in the country does not tempt Reginald, for 'her particular part of the country was a few hundred versts the other side of Tamboff, with some fifteen miles of agrarian disturbance between her and the nearest neighbour'.

'The Bag' is the only other sketch with a Russian flavour. Vladimir, a youthful Russian guest at an English country-house of the Horseback Hall kind, cannot ride but he can shoot, although he is abysmally ignorant of the rules about birds and beasts and what is game and what is not. He includes woodpeckers among the birds, and finally bags a small furry animal. His bag (with the animal), temporarily tossed up out of the way on a shelf over the tea-table, becomes more interesting than the tea-cake to the fox terrier, who sniffs and sniffs, until the major exclaims—'There's a pretty warm scent!' During the commotion that follows, Vladimir's mind strays back to the youth in an old Russian folk-tale, who 'shot an enchanted bird with dramatic results'. It is suspected that Vladimir has shot a fox—a frightful breach of etiquette at this season. The turmoil finally subsides, and Vladimir asks his young hostess what he is to do with *that*. She says to bury it. And so 'it came to pass that in the dusk of a November evening the Russian boy, murmuring a few of the prayers of his Church for luck, gave hasty but decent burial to a large polecat under the lilac trees'.

Maurice Baring's novel *Tinker's Leave* (1927) is described in the preface as a record of impressions received in Russia and Manchuria in wartime (1905), transposed into a fantasy. It is interesting to compare with the novel his *Puppet Show of Memory* (1922), where in one chapter he tries to analyse the fascination of Russia and the character of the Russians. He saw some of the best and worst of their traits; those he liked seemed the most precious. In 1904 he saw Chekhov's plays acted; he calls *The Cherry Orchard* the most symbolic play ever written, summing up the whole of pre-revolutionary Russia—dancing on the top of a volcano heaving and rumbling with the faint noise of the coming convulsion. It was pleasant there on the volcano, and he had a delightful time 'living the peculiar comfortless comfort of Russian life among the intelligentsia'; everybody seemed to take everybody else and everything for granted; time had no meaning; one long conversation followed another, into which different people drifted. *Tinker's Leave* is a long conversation. The hero, an English wine merchant, falls in with some friendly Russians in Paris and is persuaded to take a long holiday in Russia; these strange people 'seemed to say such unreasonable things so reasonably and to make them sound so plausibly'. Miles's first evening in St Petersburg turns into quite a night, with gipsies and vodka and caviare, wanderings around the city, and a fight with the police. His Russian friend Alyosha Kouragine arranges all sorts of things for him, inventing stories to get him taken on as a photographer for an American publishing firm, to go into Manchuria. As they travel together across Siberia, they discuss different national customs and freedoms; Alyosha pours out the story of his misfortunes, which include killing someone and being imprisoned; they talk of art and literature and the differences between Dostoevsky and Chekhov. Both give us the adventures of the Russian soul, but Dostoevsky's patterns are fantastic and colourful, Chekhov's drab. Chekhov is the first playwright to have made plays out of moods. The talkers improvise amusing versions of *Hamlet*, according to Ibsen and then according to Chekhov.

Somewhat similar in its conception of the Russians, but more effective artistically, is William Gerhardi's novel *Futility* (1922). Gerhardi, who spent his childhood in St Petersburg (his father was a British businessman with interests there), was later attached to the British Embassy at Petrograd and observed the Revolution in most of its early phases, later seeing service with the British Military Mission in Siberia. These and other experiences, later distilled in fiction, are recorded in *Memoirs of a Polyglot*, an autobiography published in 1931. A long introduction to the Collected Edition of his works (1947) contains reflections on art and life, including comments on Chekhov, which suggest what he may have sought to accomplish in his own fiction. Chekhov, he says, penetrates to a level 'immeasurably deeper than the superficial differences of men and race to a bedrock of common humanity where all human beings, as human beings, are frail, irresponsible, weak. Against this their success or failure is shown to be irrelevant.'

Futility is described (in the Collected Edition) as a novel on

Russian themes, 'depicting a father gathering dependants as his hopes rise and his fortunes sink through four succeeding stages of the Russian social scene; the narrator, an Englishman of Russian upbringing, revealing, against this humorously and geographically changing but tragically unchanging background, the pathos of his growing love for the second of three bewitching daughters'. The critic Gerald Gould (*The English Novel of Today*) says of the characters of the novel that they 'dance endlessly, they drink wine and tea endlessly, endlessly they talk'. It is 'a nightmare of mines which cannot pay, doctors who cannot practise, lovers who cannot marry, writers who have never been known to write a line, families which can neither separate nor stop quarrelling while together'.

Futility, Russian—the words belong together. Gerhardi's Russians are those we have come to think of as Cherry Orchard people. After the Revolution, Russian writers give us glimpses of them: Bulgakov, for instance, in his play *Days of the Turbins*, shows them in the confusion of civil war and foreign intervention. But gradually they vanish from play and novel—whether lost or transformed; for Soviet literature, futility is not a Russian theme. For Bernard Shaw it became an English theme, in *Heartbreak House*, to be played with in the Russian manner.

The difference in temperament and in dramatic technique between Shaw and Chekhov produced plays so different that without Shaw's preface to *Heartbreak House*, the 'Russian manner' of the fantasia might have remained unidentified. Behind the mood of Chekhov's plays, Shaw sought the ideas. Behind the obvious differences between Chekhov's Russia before the Revolution and his own England at the time of the First World War, Shaw sought the historical parallels. Implicit in the characters, moods and symbols of Chekhov's plays, Shaw found this idea: that in the evolution of societies, a once strong and able ruling class, which has allowed the power to slip from its hands, is destined to be supplanted by emerging classes and groups capable of governing. Heartbreak House is 'cultured, leisured Europe before the War'. Much earlier than Chekhov, Tolstoy, in his play, *The Fruits of Enlightenment*, had shown us around Heartbreak House in his 'ferociously contemptuous manner', wasting no sympathy upon it; for to him it was the house in which Europe was stifling its soul, and he was not disposed to leave the house standing, if he could bring it down about the ears of its amiable voluptuaries. 'He treated the case of the inmates as one of opium poisoning, to be dealt with by seizing the patients roughly and exercising them violently. . . . Chekhov, more of a fatalist, had no faith in these charming people extricating themselves. They would, he thought, be sold up and set adrift by the bailiffs; therefore he had no scruple in exploiting and even flattering their charm.'

The English, continues Shaw, saw a few performances of Chekhov's plays, stared, and said, 'How Russian!' But as Ibsen's plays fitted every middle and professional class suburb in Europe so Chekhov's intensely Russians plays fitted all the country houses in Europe, in which 'the pleasures of music, art, literature and the theatre have supplanted hunting, shooting, fishing, flirting, eating and drinking. The same nice people, the same utter futility.' These nice people hated politics, though they were precisely the people with the opportunity to share and influence the activities of politicians, newspaper owners and administrators. But 'they did not wish to realize Utopia for the common people; they wished to realize their favourite fictions and poems in their own lives; and when they could, they lived without scruple on incomes which they did nothing to earn'. After an entertaining and devastating description of the alternative to Heartbreak House—Horseback Hall, and a thrust at the way Heartbreak House played with revolutionary ideas (including Shaw's) over the weekend, Shaw sums up: Power and culture were in separate compartments. He pays a tribute to the bravery as well as the charm of this class: though it did not know how to live, it knew how to die—'a melancholy accomplishment which the outbreak of war presently gave it practically unlimited opportunities of displaying'.

Chekhov's dramatic method has been called the orchestration

of moods; Shaw's the orchestration of ideas. In *The Cherry Orchard*, the faint distant twang of a snapping wire and the sound of the first blows of the axe in the orchard deepen the mood of things ending, the threat of destruction; but there is no call to action, no formulation of alternatives. Shaw's Captain Shotover, however, seeing the danger threatening 'this ship of ours, this England', replies to Hector's question, 'what am I to do?' with the vigorous imperative: 'Learn your business as an Englishman—navigation. Learn it and live, or leave it and be damned.'

The two Heartbreak Houses, English and Russian, have likenesses beyond that of being overshadowed by the same doom. Their inmates could have visited back and forth very congenially. Captain Shotover's country place welcomed people as casually as Madam Ranevskaya's. Old Firs in *The Cherry Orchard* and the old nurse in *Uncle Vanya* have their counterpart in the housekeeper at Shotover, interfering with everybody and mothering them, more bustling and aggressive than the Russians, but just as ubiquitous. The Russian guests would have taken part with enthusiasm in the charades at Shotover, and the English guests gathered mushrooms and picnicked in the Russian woods. No Russian would have been at all surprised at the eccentric entrances and exits of the old captain, nor at the way people talked to themselves rather than to each other. Shaw's fantasia *is* in the 'Russian manner', in spite of Shaw himself as the captain popping in and out, as Chekhov never did. The Russian influence did its part in shaping one of Shaw's best plays.

We need not pause over Shaw's *Great Catherine* (1913) and his *Annajanska, The Bolshevik Empress* (1918), both farcical interludes, written especially for certain actresses. He calls them variety turns, bravura pieces, 'of the stage, stagy'. Their purpose is that announced by Annajanska, when she is asked, 'Are you a Bolshevist?' She replies, 'I am anything that will make the world less like a prison and more like a circus.'

In that delightful island of Nepenthe, where the oddest things happened when the south wind blew, Norman Douglas assembled some Russians among all the other eccentrics, each, as the good

Bishop found, so perfect in his or her kind. He plays variations in the English manner on a Russian theme. The Russian Messiah, Bazhakuloff, as Douglas says in the preface to the 1924 edition of *South Wind*, 'obviously derived from Rasputin and another holy Russian impostor whose name I cannot recall'. The Master and his followers, who have named themselves the Little White Cows, to mark their innocence of worldly affairs, have found refuge on Nepenthe after being expelled from Russia. With their scarlet blouses, their fair hair and wondering blue eyes, and the patriarchal simplicity of their manners, they have attracted the friendly interest of Madame Steynlin, who lets them bathe off her promontory and picnic in her grounds, and who falls in love with a strapping young disciple, and asks him to teach her Russian. He comes to her villa at meal-times and stays on for hours, 'while they wrestled with the complexities of Russian genders'. In converse with this child of Nature, she began to understand 'the inward sense of that brotherly love, that apostolic spirit, which binds together every class of the immense Empire; to revere their simplicity of soul and calm god-like faith'.

The Master, his face a mask of placid imbecility, often sits motionless, sometimes making peevish sounds, as if desirous of formulating some truth too deep for human utterance, something that the Epicurean philospher Mr Keith is sure will be about the Man-God. A mock-serious chapter is devoted to the five periods in the life of this ex-monk: the probationary, the dialectical, the political, the illumined and the expiatory. At the end of the second period he had uttered his first revelation: the Man-God is the Man-God, and not the God-Man. The Procurator of the Holy Synod, thinking he might use this inspired monk, then took him on; his connection with the Court developed and, like Rasputin, he became the power behind the throne. An undisclosed scandal brought about his fall and banishment to a remote monastery. He was regarded as a martyr and his followers multiplied. In this illumined period, he had a second revelation: the flesh and blood of warm-blooded beasts is Abomination to Little White Cows. Many of his disciples in the army then refused to eat meat, which was bad business for the Grand Dukes with lucrative army contracts; thus the new heresy endangered the foundations of the Empire. Bazhakuloff, refusing to withdraw his revelation, was given the choice of assassination or expulsion, and chose with his followers to go into exile. But even on Nepenthe there are splinter movements among the faithful, and involvements in other intrigues, and the Master finds himself in jail. This is the expiatory period.

In his prison the poor old Master has dim memories of the old days; of the lusty country folk, the songs and dances at hay-making, the fragrance of the land, the sluggish rivers rolling their brown mud about the plains, the mild long-drawn evenings. 'He felt again that all-pervading charm of sadness, of tender yearning that hangs in the pale Russian sky and penetrates to the very soul of the endless country.' Even the south wind, apparently, cannot blow away the old familiar generalizations about Russian sadness; even Norman Douglas cannot resist them. The Master remembers the monasteries, pilgrims, chants, litanies, sombre ikons with staring eyes; and the smells of cabbage soup, unwashed bodies, incense, and boot-leather—Holy Russia, in short, and 'it all moved before his eyes in a kind of melodious twilight'.

Mr Keith, speculating with his friend the Count on religion, finds in the Russian Orthodox Church a 'repository of apocalyptic nonsense such as no sane man can take seriously, nonsense of the right kind, the uncompromising kind. . . . The paralysing, sterilizing cult of these people offers a far better springboard into the clean element of thought than our English Church, whose *demi-vierge* concessions to common sense afford seductive resting-places to the intellectually weak-kneed.' The Count agrees that the Russians have a better springboard than the English, but the queer thing is that they won't jump, whereas the Englishman often does.

Of all the fantasias on Russian themes, the most delectable is the episode of Orlando's love affair with the Russian princess at the time of the Great Frost in the reign of James I of England. It is a part of Virginia Woolf's *Orlando: A Biography* (1928). Her hero-heroine, whose life spans the centuries from Queen Elizabeth to Thursday, October 11, 1928—at that moment aged thirty-six and a lady—met the princess when she came to the English court in the train of the Muscovite Ambassador. Orlando called her Sasha for short, and 'because it was the name of a white Russian fox he had had as a boy—a creature soft as snow, but with teeth of steel, which bit him so savagely that his father had it killed'. Orlando had heard—perhaps from Master George Turberville or some other Elizabethan traveller?—strange tales of Russia, about women wearing beards and men covered with fur from the waist down and everyone smeared with tallow to keep the cold out. But Sasha has no beard; she speaks French and skates divinely; and when they have grown hot with skating over the frozen Thames, they would sit wrapped in their sables and she would tell him of the snows of Russia and the wolves howling across the steppes—'and thrice, to show him, she barked like a wolf'. To the scandal of the Court—for Orlando is engaged to an English lady—they not only dance at balls, but mingle with the London crowds at carnivals and theatres—where they see a performance in which a black man smothers a white lady—and Orlando is consumed with a jealousy for which he has excellent reason. Sasha had almost cajoled him out of his belief that he had seen her in the arms of a handsome Russian sailor on the Ambassador's ship; 'had not the candle guttered, had not the shadows moved'? But in all she said, 'however open she seemed and voluptuous, there was something hidden; in all she did, however daring, there was something concealed. So the green flame seems hidden in the emerald, or the sun prisoned in a hill. The clearness was only outward; within was a wandering flame. It came, it went; she never shone with the steady beam of an Englishwoman.' When agonies of doubt would seize him, he would blaze out in wrath; perhaps his rages pleased her and she provoked them purposely; 'such is the curious obliquity of the Muscovitish temperament'.

Sasha agreed to fly with him on the first dark night, and together they would take ship to Russia—'there the sunsets are longer and the dawns less sudden and the sentences often left unfinished from doubt as to how best to end them'. But on the agreed night, the great thaw comes, the ice breaks up in the river, and the dazed Orlando watches the appalling race of waters carrying past him on the ice-floes the most fantastic human wreckage. When he looks for the Russian ship, long frozen in the ice, it is gone, and Sasha, he knows, with it. Far off he sees it standing out to sea, the black eagles at the masthead. The soft white fox with the teeth of steel, Sasha is a symbol of Russian ambiguities. But though Orlando hurls insults after her, 'the swirling waters took his words, and tossed at his feet a broken pot and a little straw'.

Among fantasies on Russian themes should be included George Orwell's much admired *Animal Farm* (1945), a brilliant political satire, directed, it seems to be agreed, against Stalin and his commissars. It is an animal fairy-tale, described by an English critic, Tom Hopkinson, in a number of *World Review* (June, 1905) devoted to Orwell, as a 'work of genius in the lofty tradition of English humorous writing'. The trouble with fairy stories, as with symbols, is that the interpretations are not fixed and permanent. Some years before Orwell's satire, Aldous Huxley published *Brave New World*, with its witty forecast of a society of mechanized men. Our critics took it to be directed against the tendencies of Communism. Mentioning this interpretation to a well-read young woman in the Soviet Union, in 1935, I was not too surprised by the good-natured retort, 'We consider it a satire on the tendencies of a decadent capitalism.' We interpret satires and symbols according to the idols of our tribe.

Futility, charm, imbecility, ambiguity, impracticality: it is an odd list of Russian themes that have proved attractive to English writers. They belong to the old Russia, the Russia with a Soul. Nostalgia for that Russia is the mood of a 1946 poem by William Carlos Williams, entitled *Russia*.[1] It opens with an image—'the Williams Avenue Zionist Church (coloured)', 'the cross at the top slapped together (in this lumber shortage) of sticks from an old barrel top, I think'; and then invokes 'Russia, idiot of the world, blind idiot, do you understand me?' He places his dream in her hands:

I am
at home in my dream, Russia; and only there,
before the obliterating blow,
that shall flatten everything
and its crazy masonry,
am I at home.
Inspired by my dream I do not call upon
a party to save me, nor a government
of whatever sort.
Rather I descend into
my dream as into a quiet lake
and there, already there, I find
my kinships, thence I rise by my own
propulsions into a world beyond the moon.
O Russia, Russia! must we begin to call
you the idiot of the world? when
you were a dream the world lived in, you
inviolate—
O Russia! Russians! come with me into
my dream and let us be lovers. . . .

The Walt Whitman note is developed into an invitation to loaf a moment at the edge of destruction. Then the poet remembers Mayakovsky. Does Russia remember him? A good guy—'and killed himself, I suppose, not to embarrass you'. Let Mayakovsky be his sponsor. He recalls a night in a 14th Street New York café, when Mayakovsky read to them—'and it sounded like the outpourings of the Odyssey'. The final image of the poem is a print in a poor kitchen of Leonardo's Last Supper, against a severe and simple background:

It's that background
from which my dreams have sprung. These
I dedicate now to you, now when I am
about to die. I hold back nothing, I lay
my spirit at your feet and say to you—
Here I am, a dreamer, I do not
resist you. Among many others, undistinguished,

of no moment. I am the background
upon which you will build your empire.

When *was* Russia 'a dream the world lived in'? And just how ambiguous can the word 'idiot' be?

There is nothing ambiguous about E. E. Cummings's attitude towards the new Russia. *Eimi* (1933) is a variation on the theme of Cummings, inspired by thirty-seven miserable days in the Soviet Union, a 'non-country' of 'non-men'. In a later chapter we shall take up literary expressions of other attitudes.

iii

Definitions and Distinctions

THE QUEST for sources and influences has a fascination for the literary historian and critic. Russian literature, as possibly affecting the work of English and American writers, came so late into the field that there has been very little sifting of the evidence, except in the relatively few special studies of individual authors. There has not yet been time for the delicate distinctions, refined through the years, that one finds in a good discussion, say, of the influence of Rousseau upon English writers in the eighteenth century, or of the debt to each other of Goethe and Scott. Give the scholar adventurers time, and we may eventually have rectifications of the records, verification or rejection of the guesses, disclosures of the forgeries and follies, recovery of lost papers—all as fascinating as anything yielded up in the pursuit of Byron or Boswell or Sir Thomas Malory. The field of research is wide open, or will be, if the politicians ever cease from troubling.

How is an influence proved? Take for example the supposed Russian influence on Sherwood Anderson. Virginia Woolf apparently started the idea, or gave it currency by her authority, when in 1925, in her essay on 'American Fiction', she said of Anderson's stories: 'The feeling recalls that with which we read Chekhov for the first time'. For 'we' substitute 'Mrs Woolf', and the statement has a certain precision. But what was her feeling when she first read Chekhov? We have a clue in what she says elsewhere about Chekhov; we have already quoted her; something about the soul. Did the feeling come back when she read Anderson, because he too was somehow concerned with the soul? Or because, at the moment of reading Anderson, some 'mark on the wall' started a train of associations in which Chekhov was involved? In any case, that a sensitive critic like Mrs Woolf was reminded of Chekhov when she read Anderson may suggest a possible connection between them. Had Anderson read Chekhov before writing his own stories? Irving Howe, in his biography of Anderson, quotes him as saying that he had not read the Russians until after he had published *Winesburg, Ohio*; but notes that this statement is controverted by two passages in Anderson's letters, a remark in his *Memoirs*, and a recollection in an autobiographical fragment. Anderson's other recent biographer, Mr Schevill, quotes from an unpublished letter written by Anderson to Roger Sergel about 1925: 'I was perhaps thirty-five years old when I first found the Russian prose writers'. This would be about 1911. 'One day I picked up Turgenev's *Annals of the* [*sic*] *Sportsman.* I remember how my hands trembled as I read the book. I raced through the pages like a drunken man. Afterward in Tolstoy, Dostoevsky, I found the same thing. . . . I found in them the love of human life, tenderness, a lack of the eternal preaching and smart aleckness so characteristic of much western writing—nearly all of it in fact.' He noted in his *Memoirs*, about 1932, 'reading for perhaps the twentieth time Turgenev's *Annals of a Sportsman*'. Since likenesses in important respects between the art of Turgenev and that of Chekhov have often been pointed out in Russian criticism, Chekhov may have come to Anderson through Turgenev.

How did the influence reveal itself in Anderson's work? Mr Howe compares his story, 'Death in the Woods', with the stories of Turgenev and Chekhov, in its reliance on effects of mood and devices of pacing; and in the sense it conveys of 'the ultimate unity of Nature . . . an harmonic oneness of all its parts and creatures bunched in the hands of death'. Anderson and the Russian writers look at life in the same way, and have a common faith in 'man's essential decency despite his inevitable tragic fate'. Mr Schevill finds striking differences of style, manner and national background, but feels that, despite the tenuousness of the evidence, 'even in the portrayal of character' Anderson was more closely related to Turgenev and Chekhov and the Englishman, George Borrow, than to D. H. Lawrence—whose influence on Anderson is another story.

A very slight hint by the author puts the critic on the scent. Ernest Hemingway, while on a hunting trip, read Tolstoy's Sebastopol sketches and his *Cossacks*: 'I was thinking how real that Russia of the time of our Civil War was, as real as any other place, as Michigan or the prairie north of the town and the woods around Evans's game farm, of how through Turgenev I knew I had lived there'. (*Green Hills of Africa*, page 108.) Edmund Wilson draws critical conclusions: 'The pages which Hemingway was later to write about American woods and waters are equivalents to the transcriptions by Turgenev—*The Sportsman's Notebook* is much admired by Hemingway—of Russian forests and fields. Each has brought to an immense wild country the freshness of a new speech and a sensibility not yet conventionalized by literary associations.'

Another example, from our older literature. Sarah Orne Jewett found the terms in which Turgenev was spoken of in Stepniak's introduction to the translation of *Rudin* applicable to herself; he loved light and poetry, and was the poet of the gentler side of human nature; yet she says that she did not know 'much' of Turgenev in her earlier years. (1904.) Much earlier, in 1888, she was, according to Vernon Parrington, 'oddly enough persuaded' that she had long been trying to do what Tolstoy was doing. A certain story of his startled her because she had been dimly feeling the same kind of motive in writing *The Gray Man*, and she tells her correspondent that she could name half a dozen stories where she had tried to say it; now she knows what he means 'and I know that I can dare to keep at the work I sometimes have despaired about'. To Parrington, the tie with Tolstoy seems the thinnest of gossamers; her own realism is as dainty and refined as her manners—'bleached out to a fine maidenly purity'; but perhaps the Tolstoy connection lay in her ascribing the gentleness of her Maine fisherfolk to a primitive environment supplemented by an encompassing religion. One can at least say that she drew some kind of sustenance from Tolstoy.

If all critics were as sceptical of influences as Parrington, we should miss some of the thrills of discovery. In Chapter XI of her novel *Night and Day*, Virginia Woolf quotes a reflection upon life, and later in the paragraph says that her heroine had twisted the words of Dostoevsky to suit her mood. An alert critic traced the quotation to *The Idiot*, and stated that *Night and Day* was inspired by *The Idiot*.[2] The passage certainly proves that Mrs Woolf had been reading *The Idiot*, and from other places in her writing we know what the experience of reading Dostoevsky was like to her. As unlike as possible, by the way, to our experience in reading *Night and Day*. The quotation is to the effect that it is life that matters, the process of discovering, not the discovery itself. Virginia Woolf was always seeking to catch the slippery silver fish, life, 'the spirit we live by', in her net. A myriad influences and inspirations working upon her temperament must have confirmed her in this pursuit. *Night and Day* was her last serious attempt to write the novel of social manners, as brought to perfection by Jane Austen and Trollope. Reading *The Idiot* may have helped to convince her that she was on the wrong track; that—as she put it in one of her essays—English fiction had to escape from the perfection represented by *Pride and Prejudice* and *The Small House at Allington*. The Russian influence was working upon her, as upon other European novelists, in the direction of breaking up the old moulds. Her next novel was *Jacob's Room*, in which she did break them.

When authors are asked, often for publicity purposes, who or what influenced them, they are likely to be self-conscious and unreliable, for reasons that will occur to anyone. It is the unpremeditated note in diary or letter that is revealing. Arnold Bennett notes in his journal (November, 1903) that he wished in his *Old Wives' Tale* to catch the 'tone' of Tolstoy's *Death of Ivan Ilyich*;

and whether he succeeded or not, we know what he intended. In February, 1909, being 'more and more struck by Chekhov', he thought of writing 'a lot of very short stories in the same technique'. In April, 1913, reading *War and Peace*, he was enthusiastic over 'the superbly rendered domesticity', and the final thrills inspired him with 'a good basic scheme for *These Twain*'. The result fell far short of the model, but there is no question that Bennett was cultivating the Russian influence.

Conrad talked much about his sources and all that he said has been studied and checked by his biographers and critics. He set out in *Under Western Eyes* to 'capture the soul of things Russian',[3] and admittedly achieved a sinister conspiratorial atmosphere; an atmosphere which, as his friend Edward Garnett pointed out, was coloured by his Polish heritage, by all that he and his family had known and suffered at Russian hands, all that he had read and brooded over. The Russian novelist whom Conrad admired was Turgenev, whose characters were not 'strange beasts in a menagerie or damned souls knocking themselves about in the stuffy darkness of mystical contradictions', like those of Dostoevsky, whom he did not admire. Yet the atmosphere both of *Under Western Eyes* and *The Secret Agent* suggests Dostoevsky rather than Turgenev. In *Joseph Conrad, a Reassessment* (1952), Douglas Hewitt discriminates helpfully among influences, affinities and resemblances in comparing the fiction of Conrad and Dostoevsky. Conrad's praise of Turgenev and Tolstoy was tied up with his rejection of the qualities he himself shared with Dostoevsky; his repudiation of anything in his own work which savoured of the morbid made him hate any other writers who appeared to have this taint. Yet there are striking resemblances between Conrad and Dostoevsky, and the greatest, according to Mr Hewitt, lies at the heart of the best work of them both: 'the recurrent situation of the obviously "good" man who is confronted by a "double" whom he cannot repudiate and who makes him aware of evil or equivocal qualities in himself which he would rather not see'. In Dostoevsky among the paired characters are Raskolnikov and Svidrigailov, Ivan Karamazov and Smerdyakov, Stavrogin and

Verhovensky; and in Conrad, Lord Jim and Gentleman Brown, Lord Jim and Marlow, Marlow and Kurtz, the narrator of *The Secret Sharer* and the fugitive he shelters. Mr Hewitt finds the relationship with Dostoevsky a close one—and 'most significant where there is least a question of "influence"'. Pursuing the comparison throws light on both Conrad's limitations and his achievements. In Conrad's pessimism and his scepticism, Mr Hewitt sees a similarity with the side of Dostoevsky revealed in the questioning and the doubts of Ivan Karamazov and Raskolnikov and Kirillov; but he finds Conrad lacking in the positive elements of Dostoevsky's thought.

Any study involving influences tends to underscore the contribution of the author under consideration: a thesis on Turgenev marshals all the evidence for his influence on George Gissing, and one on Dostoevsky finds that Gissing was most indebted to Dostoevsky. Professor Tindall in his *Forces in Modern British Literature* mentions the probable French influence on Gissing, but says nothing of the Russian. One can only conclude that Gissing was variously influenced. It is easy to commit the reductive fallacy of assigning to one cause a phenomenon only to be explained by the interaction of many. Resemblances may arise as the effect of similar causes, and not from imitation. What looks like an influence may be a parallel or a coincidence. Once an influence has affected one writer, it may affect others through him. The literary family tree branches out. It has been thoroughly demonstrated that Turgenev helped to form the novel of Henry James; but then consider what Henry James has done to later novelists who may never have read a line of Turgenev. No novel dealing with crime and its motives and consequences could be written after *Crime and Punishment* became widely known, which would not seem to be indebted to Dostoevsky. Theodore Dreiser and Richard Wright both read Dostoevsky, and the usual adjective applied to *An American Tragedy* and *Native Son* is 'Dostoevskian'. Yet both novels grew out of profound experience of American life in the depths where social pressures breed crime; they are of our native soil. It would be difficult, however, to convince anyone that they would have been written in just the way they were, had not Dostoevsky pioneered along that path.

Thomas Wolfe, we know, read Dostoevsky. He also read Proust, Joyce and Tolstoy. How disengage the specific Dostoevsky influence? His conception of his own family, fictionized as the Gants, with the taint in their blood, their extravagant appetites, the mother's avarice, is remarkably like Dostoevsky's conception of the Karamazovs, who may well have been present in Wolfe's mind, tempting him to symbolize and romanticize his own tribe. The critic Maxwell Geismar discovers the Russian soul in Wolfe's works:

> 'There was a cultural strain in the hill people—with their involved family histories and their meticulous back-country etiquette, their abundant hospitality and their endless talking, their mountain laughter and their clinging legends of sin and bloodshed—that probably comes closest, among all our rich cultural strains, to what we have labelled the "Russian" soul: I mean, of course, merely the human soul, though at once more deeply enslaved and freer—a soul, as it were, in fetters and in ecstasy.'[4]

When our literature displays souls of this sort, or abnormalities and obsessions, or odd varieties of decadence, we may prefer to regard them as foreign importations. We feel at once more cosmopolitan and more comfortable.

'Modern Southern writing seems . . . most indebted to Russian literature, to be the progeny of the Russian realists,' wrote the Southern novelist, Carson McCullers, some years ago. (*Decision*, 1941.) She goes on to show that the circumstances under which modern Southern literature (with emphasis on Faulkner and Caldwell) has been produced are strikingly like those under which the nineteenth century Russian writers functioned. The South has much in common, sociologically, with old Russia: in both life is held very cheap; in both there is a class structure; in both, great poverty, which sets an exaggerated value on small material things—a mule, a bale of cotton, a samovar. In brief, Russian realism of the past and Southern realism of the present display some interesting characteristics, some close resemblances in method and mood, that are perhaps the literary expression of a certain kind of social order or stage in social development. The resemblances at a certain level are striking. But Mrs McCullers notes that Russian realism rises from this level to the height of the great philosophical fiction of Tolstoy and Dostoevsky, to the posing of basic questions and the exploration of problems, which inform their realism with passion and significance. On the lower level she has stressed the cruelty of both realisms. 'The cruelty of which the Southerners have been accused is at bottom only a sort of naïveté, an acceptance of spiritual inconsistencies, without asking the reason why, without attempting to impose an answer. Undeniably there is an infantile quality about this clarity of vision and rejection of responsibility.'

This last phrase—*rejection of responsibility*—is completely inapplicable to Russian realism, past or present. Just what Russian writers have understood by acceptance of responsibility will be discussed later. If there is this difference between Russian and Southern realism, it is perhaps more important than all the resemblances. In any case, though Mrs McCullers makes some very acute comparisons, she scarcely convinces us that modern Southern writing is 'the progeny of the Russian realists'.

Parenthood is notoriously difficult to prove sometimes. It is safer for the critic to be content with 'inspiration' or with that expression in dedications to wives and professors: without their help, this would never have been written. Or let the parenthood be that of events: *The Iron Heel*, writes Joan London of Jack London's novel, would never have been written, but for the 1905 Russian revolution.[5] The English critic Gerald Gould groups several women novelists, first appearing about 1910, as 'Neo-Russians'; he does not know, he admits, which had studied what Russians, or if everyone *had* studied them, but 'that there was an influence, an emanation, an inspiration, I think certain'.[6] It is perhaps in a recklessly happy mood after completing some very good bit of critical analysis that a critic throws off a generalization, which he never expects to have to support with evidence. Laurie

Magnus (*English Literature in its Foreign Relations* 1300–1800, 1927), having discussed the place of Shakespeare in French criticism, makes an excursion out of bounds into the nineteenth century and into Russia: 'Nor, passing other countries by, can we omit to record in this context, how, in the nineteenth century, Shakespeare's spirit was transfused into Russian literature and the mind of Russia, where the note of philosophical fatalism, which recurs in Russian novel after novel, was derived, finally, from *Hamlet*'. This derivation would simplify the whole question of Russian fiction—if only everybody agreed about the interpretation of *Hamlet*. Perhaps Hamlet was a Russian. 'Hamlet,' wrote William Morris in March, 1888, after reading *War and Peace*, 'should have been a Russian, not a Dane.'[7]

[1] *New Republic*, April 29, 1946.
[2] W. Y. Tindall, *Forces in Modern British Literature*, p. 304, n.
[3] *Letters from Joseph Conrad*, 1895-1924. Introduction and Notes by Edward Garnett. 1928. Letter of Jan. 6, 1908.
[4] *Yale Review*, Summer 1946, 'The Hillman and the Furies', by Maxwell Geismar.
[5] Joan London, *Jack London and His Times*, 1939.
[6] Gerald Gould, *The English Novel of Today*, 1924.
[7] *The Letters of William Morris to His Family and Friends*, ed. Philip Henderson, Longmans, Green & Co. 1950, page 280. Morris is referring to 'the curious undecided turn of the intellectual persons' in Russia.

CHAPTER X

THE RUSSIAN INFLUENCE: NOVEL, SHORT STORY, AND PLAY

i

Turgenev

THAT RUSSIAN realism, variously defined through the years, has been an influence upon Western fiction, is an accepted critical commonplace. Studies of individual writers have explored its precise effect upon their development, and broad surveys of trends in modern fiction have indicated its extent. Critics have disagreed from the first and still disagree over many of the questions at issue; they have stopped arguing about others. Turgenev, for instance, has long occupied a secure position. He has been generally regarded as the most Westernized of the Russians; his work, therefore, most accessible to Western minds, and all the more influential because of his long residence abroad and his personal friendships with Flaubert, Henry James, Zola, George Moore and others.

George Moore, who met him in Paris and discussed Zola and naturalism, remembered how he had condemned as vicious that method which always records what a person felt rather than what he thought. What difference does it make to me, said Turgenev, whether a woman sweats in the middle of the back or under the arms? Moore admired the skill of Turgenev in the fusion of physical details with mental impressions. He preferred the short pieces to the novels, and in his own *Untilled Field* (1903), concerned with the scenery, the people and the problems of Ireland, he is deeply indebted to the *Sportsman's Sketches*.[1] Here is an interesting example of a migratory influence: Maria Edgeworth's stories of Ireland had made Turgenev wish to write in that manner about Russia, and he did; and then his stories about Russia made Moore wish to write in that way about Ireland; and so we come back to Erin. Moore's novel, *The Lake* (1905), with its lyrical descriptions, its brooding over Irish life and tradition, and its thwarted love, recalls *A House of Gentlefolk* and *On the Eve*. Moore's opinions about the Russian novelists are to be found in *Avowals* (1919) and in Volume ii of *A Story-teller's Holiday* (1908). His dislike of Tolstoy is expressed with all the perversity that betrays complete lack of sympathy. Dostoevsky he includes among the men of genius who have written novels, but adds that 'vapour and tumult do not make tales'. He is lyrical over Turgenev whom he links with Corot. Their art revealed to him all he needed to know; they were 'holy places' where 'I rested and rest'. Turgenev proved to Moore's satisfaction that the right creed is Art for Art; that morality is a myth and an academic discussion; and that the artist can only teach 'by giving the world images of beauty'.

William Dean Howells did not derive from Turgenev any notion that morality is a myth, but his own decisive rejection of the creed of Art for Art came only after he had read Tolstoy. His admiration of the artistry of Turgenev was unqualified, but as for any influence upon his work, Mr Van Wyck Brooks is probably right in his cautious statement: 'Howells had developed his own realistic method, and Turgenev rather confirmed than determined this method: he confirmed it with his plotless novels and his groupings of three or four persons whose interwoven fates alone concerned him'.[2] Turgenev's reticence was part of his charm for Howells, 'but Howells's own personality ordained his method'.

So no doubt did that of Henry James, but in the process of developing his method, the influence of Turgenev was both early and strong. James, the critic, analysing and admiring Turgenev's art, guides us in our search for the Russian influence on James, the novelist. Carefully detailed comparisons have been made in the special studies of James's work. Cornelia P. Kelley, in *The Early Development of Henry James* (1930), has traced his interest in Turgenev's technique from 1874 on, and has pointed out many of the parallels in method, attitude, subject matter and even scene, between *Rudin* and *A House of Gentlefolk*, and James's *Roderick Hudson* and *The American*. James perceived that what made a subject morally interesting to Turgenev was adversity, failure: both the failure that comes from within, springing from a flaw in character, and that which comes from without and may ennoble the nature suffering it. Turgenev's Rudin is an instance of the first kind of failure—strong in impulse but weak in will and action; and Rudin was in James's mind when he created his Roderick Hudson, who like Rudin was a moral failure. The lovers in *A House of Gentlefolk* suffer the second kind of failure and accept adversity—'more eloquent', thought James, 'than a pair of lovers grasping at happiness'. *The American* owes much to this novel (as well as to George Sand, Miss Kelley is careful to point out), and there is a striking parallel in the final convent scenes in both novels.

A more recent study, by Daniel Lerner, pursues the comparisons much farther than Miss Kelley, including many short stories.[3] He brings together Turgenev's *Three Meetings* and James's *Four Meetings*: in both, young girls in trouble are observed by detached and helpless onlookers; Turgenev's *A Correspondence* and James's *A Bundle of Letters* and *The Point of View*. (Turgenev gets along with two correspondents, James uses six.) Turgenev's *Dream* and James's *Master Eustace* both have heroes with neat Œdipus complexes. 'Turgenev's other study of adolescence, *First Love*, probably served,' in Mr Lerner's opinion, 'as a partial source of James's *What Maisie Knew*, both in plot and technique'. Turgenev's *The Dog*, a study in auto-suggestion, has likenesses to *The Turn of the Screw*. Then there is Turgenev's way of introducing as a foil—and rival—to the pure young girl, an experienced and not too pure woman, as in *Smoke*, *Spring Torrents*, *Fathers and Sons*. This also James does, in *Roderick Hudson*, *The Portrait of a Lady*, *The Wings of the Dove*, *The Golden Bowl* and so on. But it is well to remember that glamorous sirens have robbed young girls of their lovers from time immemorial, as James might have noticed without Turgenev's help.

Or—still exploring with Mr Lerner—compare *On the Eve* with *Portrait of a Lady*: each with two rejected lovers standing by and watching the rival third carry off the lady to her ultimate destiny, not of happiness but of renunciation and dedication. Isabel Archer and Elena are as different as Albany and Moscow, except in their integrity and their clarity about what they sought in life. And then there are the two 'fatally aesthetic' (James's phrase) young men—Nezhdanov in *Virgin Soil* and Hyacinth in *The Princess Casamassima*, with their revolutionary involvements and their suicidal solutions.

Mr Lerner, making a point of similarity of temperament, considers both novelists characterized by 'cosmopolitan-humanist aestheticism', with the difference that Turgenev had a kind of social conscience that James lacked. But here Mr Lerner is walking on eggs. A discovery insisted upon by some of the later critics of James is that he *had* a social conscience.[4] And a trend in some recent criticism of Turgenev, both English and American, is toward denying that Turgenev had one and asserting that he cared only for art and frustrated love.[5] What *is* a social conscience? A question for further examination in its relation to the artist.

Broadly speaking, the influence of Turgenev's art upon James, as later upon Galsworthy and other masters of the well-made novel, was in economy and objectivity, with the emphasis upon character. But Turgenev had, as James noted, a passion for shifting his point of view, and this must have come to seem to the James of the later novels, with the action centred in one consciousness, a thoroughly illicit passion.

John Galsworthy was reading Turgenev in the Constance Garnett translation when he first met Edward Garnett in 1900. With Turgenev's method in mind, he was writing *The Villa Rubein*. Resemblances between the two novelists have been rather casually noted from time to time. Frank Swinnerton (*The Georgian Scene*) says that Galsworthy 'shared with his master' a sense of beauty and irony, and a feeling for tragic young love. William C. Frierson (*The English Novel in Transition*) sees

Turgenev's influence in Galsworthy's juxtaposition of youth against age, class against class, social philosophy against social philosophy, in *Jocelyn*, *The Country House*, *The Dark Flower* and *Fraternity*; while Dr Gettman questions whether the Russian example influenced Galsworthy in a positive way or merely confirmed his own temperament and gifts.

Virginia Woolf's case is less debatable. Her essay on the novels of Turgenev (*Yale Review*, Autumn, 1933)[6] proves, if any proof is needed, that she was more at home sitting up with Turgenev's lovers and intellectuals, arguing about the future of Russia 'till the dawn rises over the eternal samovar', than descending into some enormous cavern with Dostoevsky's God-men or men-Gods. Her analysis of his art reads in important respects like an analysis of her own. She did not consider that he had a supreme gift for storytelling. Neither did he: 'I lack architecture', he told Henry James, 'but I would rather have too little architecture than too much, when there's danger of its interfering with my measure of the truth.'[7] Turgenev did not see his books, Mrs Woolf goes on, as a succession of events; 'he saw them as a succession of emotions radiating from some character at the centre. . . . The connection is not of events, but of emotions, and if at the end of the book we feel a sense of completeness, it must be that in spite of his defects as a story-teller, Turgenev's ear for emotion was so fine that even if he uses an abrupt contrast, or passes away from his people to a description of the sky or of the forest, all is held together by the truth of his insight. He never distracts us with the real incongruity—the introduction of an emotion that is false, or a transition that is arbitrary.' After observing that his heroes and heroines are among the few fictitious characters of whose love we are convinced, she adds: 'Yet, strangely enough, the individual never dominates; many other things seem to be going on at the same time. We hear the hum of life in the fields; a horse champs his bit; a butterfly circles and settles. And as we notice, without seeming to notice, life going on, we feel more intensely for the men and women themselves because they are not the whole of life, but only part of the whole.' As we read this passage we see, instead of the circling butterfly, an aeroplane writing its message in the London sky over Mrs Dalloway.

The lack of architecture in Turgenev and some of the other Russian novelists is called by V. S. Pritchett 'freedom from our kind of didacticism and our plots'. (*New Statesman and Nation*, January 17, 1942.) 'The characters of our novels from Fielding to Forster get up in the morning, wash, dress, and are then drilled in their roles. They have got to prove some practical point in morality or psychology before the book is done.' Perhaps there was more room to breathe in that simpler Russian feudal society, for in all those Russian novels 'we seem to hear a voice saying: "The meaning of life? One day that will be revealed to us—probably on a Thursday." And the day, not the insistence of the plot or purpose, is the melodic bar. We see life again, as indeed we know it, as something written in days; its dramas not directed by the superior foreknowledge of the writer, but seeming to ebb and flow among the climaxes, the anti-climaxes, the yawnings of the hours.' But this eventless day is haunted; there lies on these persons 'the shadow of a fate more richly definitive than the fate of any individual human being. Their feet stand in time and in history. Their fate is corporate, the fate of Russia itself, a fate so often adjured with eloquence and nostalgia, oftener still with that really mediaeval humility which has been unknown to us since the Renaissance, and which the Russians will equate mystically with the fate of humanity itself.'

But *was* Turgenev concerned with the fate of Russia? Was he really 'Russian' at all? We continue to like him, and in the mid-twentieth century he is being reprinted, retranslated, reintroduced by voices of authority. We want to keep him, but we don't want to keep things Russian. A review in the New York *Times* (March 12, 1950), of an 800-page anthology of his writings, was entitled, 'The Un-Russian Russian'. The reviewer, Mr Alfred Kazin, a well-known American critic, considered that Turgenev, unlike Tolstoy, Dostoevsky and Chekhov, was able 'to dispense with Russia, to convert it into a "background" to his tales of personal frustration, something the other great Russian writers never did'.

His work breathes 'tepid resignation', lyric sadness, disenchantment, disillusionment with men, affairs, Russia itself. Chekhov's characters are frustrated 'by the world they live in, Turgenev's by themselves'. Russia is the background to their quiet ordeal of frustrated love; 'it is not, to their conscious mind, of the ordeal itself'. This collection omits *A House of Gentlefolk* and *Virgin Soil*, as well as *A Sportsman's Sketches*, his most robust work, in Mr Kazin's words, and he admits that the impression of resignation may be deepened by the omission.

That Turgenev was among other things the poet of the doomed love-affair has not been news for a long time; the connection with his own doomed love affair was established a quarter of a century ago. We in the West have come to love frustration as a theme in fiction, as the Russians loved it in the later nineteenth century. And this is fortunate for the continued popularity of Turgenev and Chekhov. That to us, now, Bazarov's story emerges as simply 'an elegy on all human frustration' is perhaps true; but to say that Turgenev saw all the political meanings which he put into his book as just a background to personal frustration may well be to read into the past the desires and emotions of the present. Turgenev, says Mr Kazin, cannot take Bazarov's or any ideas seriously. Isn't it we who cannot? Turgenev did take them seriously; why else did he integrate them with his characters so that we cannot separate them? Hopes and fears for his native land (in James's phrase) were not mere emotions unrelated to ideas. The opposing views of Slavophiles and Westernizers in *A House of Gentlefolk* are more than background. Turgenev makes the Slavophile the sympathetic character, and satirizes the Westernizer—though he himself was a Westernizer—not because he did not take their ideas seriously, but because he was an artist who saw these people as human beings, not as ideas walking.

Turgenev will have to be accepted, not merely as an influence, but as a *Russian* influence. Dr Gettman's conclusion about this influence rests securely on the evidence and makes a modest plea: 'A novelist who contributed to Howells's influence, who played a large part in the development of Henry James, who supplied George Moore with an ideal, and who won admiration or imitation from Arnold Bennett, Frank Swinnerton, Ford Madox Ford and Virginia Woolf—such a novelist deserves some measure of gratitude from lovers of English fiction'.

ii

Tolstoy, Dostoevsky and the 'formless' novel

IT IS easy to make slap-dash pronouncements about Dostoevsky's influence. It is to be suspected wherever in a novel we find 'doubles' and abnormal characters; a thick and murky atmosphere; a prostitute who is somehow pure in spirit; a sordid murder from lofty motives; political conspiracy; confessions that only a Slav Soul would think of pouring out; phoney metaphysics; 'darkness at noon'. A thorough study should be done of the preoccupation of Western critics with their favourite Dostoevsky novel, *The Possessed*, and the connection with political events.

R. L. Stevenson was deeply impressed by *Crime and Punishment* at the time he wrote his well-known short story, *Markheim* (1886). But in spite of the parallels with Dostoevsky, Dr Muchnic thinks that *Markheim* produces 'fear of the naïve ghost story or fairy-tale variety', and does not give the feeling of 'intensity of maddened thought'. *Dr Jekyll and Mr Hyde*, with its theme of dual personality and the conflict of good and evil impulses, suggests Dostoevsky and his 'doubles'. But the peculiar mark of Dostoevsky's psychology—opposite emotions simultaneously manifesting themselves—is absent, and we have two characters, each taking his turn on the stage.

A sound case can be made out for the influence of Dostoevsky's psychology on a fine and somewhat neglected novel: *Maurice Guest*, by Henry Handel Richardson (1908). This novel, one of the few that have music as the main theme, is described by the author's husband, Professor J. G. Robertson, as a book of 'literary provenance'.[8] It gathers up into itself 'the threads of the realistic movement of the previous generation' and is a last link in the chain beginning with *Madame Bovary*. The indebtedness is not only to French, but also to Scandinavian and Russian fiction. 'Readers familiar with the work of the Russians felt a strong kinship here from the beginning; some of its earliest critics saw in it indeed a dubiously Russian novel. And indeed from that first scene before the Leipzig concert hall, which recalls the opening of Turgenev's *Smoke* before the Kurhaus in Baden-Baden, to the ironic anti-climax with which *Maurice Guest* closes, a Russian influence is never far absent. . . . The master that stands behind the most impressive pages of her work is unquestionably Dostoevsky. . . . And it is just this Dostoevsky element which gives *Maurice Guest* its particular niche in literature; it assimilates and reproduces in an English form all which Russia meant for the European novel in the foregoing generation. And as the story merges into tragedy, the Dostoevsky influence grows in intensity. No previous English writer had dared to unveil the holy of holies of the spiritual life, the agonizing self-analysis and despair of a tragic distraught nature with such frankness as here; and none, it is safe to say, could ever have done it without the figure of that "outsider of life", Raskolnikov, before his eyes.' Another likeness, which might be pointed out, is that Maurice, the would-be composer, like Raskolnikov, the would-be Napoleon, suffers his acutest anguish in the realization that he is after all a mediocrity.

In contrast to Turgenev's shapely novels, those of both Dostoevsky and Tolstoy were for a long time considered 'formless'. Matthew Arnold could not take *Anna Karenina* as a work of art. It was a piece of life; Tolstoy did not invent and combine it, he saw it all happening so, he related it, and what his novel lost in art, it gained in reality. Saintsbury, writing twenty years later, agreed in calling Tolstoy's novels pieces of life, but he did not like them: they were in an unlicked, unfinished condition: 'the great war scenes of *War and Peace*, the sketches of society and the autobiographical study of Levin in *Anna Karenina*, the crimes and punishments of *Resurrection*, leave us—all of them, if not all of us—with a sense of the half-digested, the crude'.[9]

'Novels they are *not*,' wrote the American critic Joseph Kirkland in *The Dial* (August, 1886), referring especially to *Childhood*, *Boyhood* and *Youth*, but also commenting on parts of *War and Peace*, then in the course of translation. 'They lack a love-story or other plot, and a heroine; and they are without even a hero, unless we accept a thoughtless child, a bad boy and an absurdly egotistical youth as the hero. Pictures of Russian real life they are—perfect pictures. The only open question is, are the subjects worth the canvas?' Photographic accuracy, phonographic literalness, telegraphic realism in narration—evidently Kirkland was obsessed by new inventions—are his key critical words. He admired photographic accuracy when it was applied to a 'worthy' subject like the battle of Borodino. Howells was not misled by analogies with phonographs and cameras. After a fine tribute to Turgenev's art (in *My Literary Passions*), he nevertheless realized, re-reading *Smoke*, that he now had less than his first satisfaction in its art; this art that for years he had considered had gone as far as art could go; that had made him impatient with the 'deliberate and impertinent moralizing of Thackeray, the clumsy exegesis of George Eliot, the knowing nods and winks of Charles Reade, the stage-carpentering and lime-lighting of Dickens, even the fine and important analysis of Hawthorne'. Tolstoy had made him aware of a finer and truer method than even that of Turgenev, master of the artifice that kept out of sight. After Tolstoy, he was impatient even of the artifice that hid itself; he could not find any artifice, any manner in Tolstoy.

Henry James was distressed to discover, about 1914, that the work of many of the younger English novelists seemed to derive from Tolstoy, 'from whose all but equal companion Turgenev we recognize no derivatives at all'.[10] What does it all mean, he asks about *Sinister Street*, *Sons and Lovers* and *Round the Corner*? The authors of these novels are just squeezing out large round oranges to the last drop, just for the pleasure of squeezing them, without selection or intention. James was left with no discernible values, with just the sense of something going on and on. Tolstoy, he admits, is a great painter of the social picture; but 'from no other great projector of the human image and the human idea is so much truth to be extracted under an equal leakage of value'. In all the length and breadth of *War and Peace*, he could not find the centre of interest or the sense of the whole. Writing to Hugh Walpole, one of the young men who, he thought, were being disastrously influenced, he refers to Tolstoy and Dostoevsky as 'fluid puddings, because the amount of their own minds and souls in solution in the broth gives it savour and flavour, thanks to the strong rank quality of their genius and their experience'. (That experience might have been a sore point with James, who, it seems agreed by his critics, rather held back from experience that could be called strong and rank.) In another letter he speaks of re-reading the 'interminable' *War and Peace*, protesting as much as admiring: 'he doesn't *do* to read over and that exactly is the answer to those who idiotically proclaim the impunity of such formless shape, such flopping looseness, and such a denial of composition, selection and style. He has a mighty fund of life, but the waste, and the ugliness and vice of waste, the vice of a not finer *doing* are sickening.' As a contrast to the formless novels he disapproves of, he praised the selection and method of Conrad's *Chance*, where Conrad displays himself as a 'votary of the way of doing a thing that shall make it undergo the most doing'.

The 'orange-squeezers' had intentions other than the mere pleasure of squeezing. Compton Mackenzie (*Literature in My Time*) writes that the influence of Dostoevsky on him and his contemporaries was profound, and 'to the critic who pointed out that there was no evidence of such influence in our published work, I would reply that the evidence will be found in an anxiety to tell the truth'. Equally vague, and yet significant, is William Gerhardi's statement in his book on Chekhov that modern literature has the great Russian novelists to thank because 'today it is more difficult to pretend, more difficult to keep up an attitude of insincerity in literature, to affect a thing, even if your affectation be sincerity, a professed dislike of affectation'. But how prove that such an influence has been at work?

It took some time before the 'formless slice of life' verdict was thrown out of court, and the selection and intention that controlled the development of Tolstoy's novels, the dramatic dynamism that shaped the novels of Dostoevsky, came to be appreciated. Percy Lubbock, in his *Craft of Fiction* (1922), does his stubborn best to prove Tolstoy wasteful of his subject in *War and Peace*, and to make us see the well-shaped novel Tolstoy might have written, had he known and taken to heart the lessons to be learned from Henry James. But Mr Lubbock defeats his own end by such an admission as this: 'Meanwhile the story has rambled and wandered uncontrolled—or *controlled only by Tolstoy's perfect consistency in the treatment of his characters*'. (Italics mine.) It would be hard to think of a more exacting control. 'He could work with such lordly neglect of his subject', concludes Lubbock, 'and yet he could produce such a book—it is surely as much as to say that Tolstoy's is the supreme genius among novelists'. Robert Herrick, reviewing this book of Lubbock's (*Yale Review*, October, 1922), thinks that Mr Lubbock confuses technique with creation, and himself attempts to define the form of *War and Peace*—'the one great realized epic of humanity under the strange delirium of war and war's chaos'. Referring to 'those mountainous masses of impression and generalization that form the matrix of the book, and from which the creator's intention emerges as the carven figure emerges from the raw marble in the hands of a Rodin', Herrick concludes: 'It is just that craggy background of theory and history and brooding generalization, with which the critic finds so much fault, that gives *War and Peace* its isolated grandeur as a picture of life never to be paralleled by our deft and knowing workers in the craft'.

The vogue of *War and Peace* in the wartime England of the early 1940's produced some more discussion of form. 'It creates an epoch,' writes the *New Statesman and Nation* critic, G. W. Stonier (January 10, 1942), 'and it does this by combining, as does no other book, two realities: the reality of fiction and the reality of history. That the two do *not* mix easily . . . can be seen from the absence of similar works in literature with which to compare Tolstoy's.' One might 'slice life' for an eternity without achieving success of this sort.

But how does an influence from such a novelist reveal itself? It is easier to discover Dostoevskian 'doubles' or to identify Stalin on the animal farm than to trace to Tolstoy an English novelist's 'anxiety to tell the truth'. Dr J. Allan Smith, in his special study of Tolstoy's fiction in England and America, comes to the rather general conclusion that his influence on the novel is to be found in greater seriousness of subject matter, in a realism tempered by a moral interpretation of life, in social criticism, in penetrating psychological analysis, in 'solidarity of specification' in incidents and characters, and in long novels, with submergence of plot and emphasis on the individual scene or incident.

When enthusiasm for Dostoevsky and for the Russian Soul was beginning to cool a little, the London *Times Literary Supplement* (June 5, 1930), in the valuable article already referred to on 'Dostoevsky and the Novel', cast up the critical accounts. His influence on English fiction—'the most insular in the world'—is harder to trace than on the European novel. What is the change from Fielding, Austen, Henry James? The novel is looser, less constricted, more confidential, more like life as we know it. *Crime and Punishment* helped to dissolve the distinction between types, being itself a romantic novel, a realistic, a psychological and a novel of adventure, all in one. What came to seem important was 'the reality, the inward truthfulness and comprehensiveness of the vision'. Dostoevsky discovered 'no new ultimate values; he only affirmed the existence of the ultimate'. It was his technical method as a novelist, 'not the sort of spiritual reality he postulated, which gave the novel new boundaries and a new vitality. He has bequeathed to later novelists the ambition to discover a less questionable reality in the region of experience he so ingeniously explored.' The clearest evidence of the effect he has had, the article concludes, is in 'the looseness and formlessness of the contemporary novel'. But writers in England are trying to restore the balance, and 'it is in the growing emphasis on artistic form that we can detect the failure of his type of symbolism'.

But has it failed? Dostoevsky's technical devices, as Mr Gilbert Phelps points out in a recent article, 'The Teapot and the

Samovar', the rapid shifts of focus, the giddy grouping and re-grouping of the characters, the sudden rises in temperature—have all left their mark in the work of Graham Greene and to a less degree in that of Nigel Balchin, Alex Comfort, and F. L. Green. But Graham Greene has been profoundly influenced not only by the shape, method and atmosphere of novels such as *Crime and Punishment* and *The Possessed*, 'but also by their moral ferment, and above all by the diabolical darkness that surrounds so many of the characters, so that the rare moments of grace and pity break through with almost unbearable brilliance and poignancy'.[11]

iii

The Short Story

FORMLESSNESS WAS also the criticism levelled at first against the Russian short story, which in the end established itself as a new form, with the help of such discerning analysis as that of Mirsky, Gerhardi and others. Katherine Mansfield's work was the main channel through which the Chekhov influence flowed around 1920. She wrote in the Chekhov manner. Though more restricted in her experience and her outlook, she saw many things as Chekhov did. Her deep temperamental sympathy with him is often expressed in her letters, which are full of references to him, especially her letters to Koteliansky, who was doing a great deal of translation from the Russian. Her stories, acclaimed by critics in England and the United States, raised a standard of revolt against the Poe–O. Henry–Maupassant type of short fiction.

In England Chekhov was fairly well known, through scattered volumes of translations, before fresh impetus was given to admiration of his work by the complete Garnett translation. English writers, critics and translators were at that time at work upon Chekhov and in communication with one another: Virginia Woolf and her group, Katherine Mansfield and Middleton Murry, the Garnetts, Koteliansky, Gerhardi—the list is long and distinguished. Stuart Sherman, writing in 1924, declares that the

Russian short story was 'obviously imported from England' into the United States, and that the English had done a good job in presenting Chekhov as a fine conscientious artist, 'whose realism is far more subtle, suggestive and truly profound than that of more flamboyant novelists who have invaded us since the Japanese War; Andreyev and Gorky, for example'.

It was a strong American literary citadel into which Chekhov penetrated with his English reinforcements. For various reasons —among them opportunities for publication in the popular annuals, gift books, women's magazines such as *Godey's Lady's Book*, beginning as early as 1830—the short story had been widely cultivated in the United States, from the days of Irving and Hawthorne, through Poe and Bret Harte, to Hamlin Garland and the school of New England local colourists; and in the early twentieth century the fresh talents of Jack London and O. Henry met the competition of Kipling from England. In the course of time, crystallization into a formula was encouraged by the enormous market of the popular magazines. The formula become lodged in college courses and text-books and was diagrammed. Any short piece of fiction that did not fit into the definition might be interesting reading, but was not a short story. Characteristic of much later criticism is an early verdict on Gorky's stories in *The Dial* (1902): 'Most of these pieces in fact are not stories at all, but realistic sketches of life, portrayals of mood, and psychological revelations'. When finally the 'Chekhov story' became accepted, it gave profound satisfaction to the many readers who were beginning to feel that the formula story had distorted psychology to fit a pattern and had falsified living experience. The little magazines that sprang up helped to satisfy the new taste in fiction. After about 1920, any short piece of fiction, without a beginning or an ending in the Maupassant–O. Henry sense, and without the allurements of suspense and climax, was called in the United States Russian or Chekhovian.

Virginia Woolf and Somerset Maugham, in their different ways, have drawn fine distinctions between Russian and other short story forms. 'The great French masters, Mérimée and Maupassant', wrote Mrs Woolf, 'made their stories as self-sufficient and compact as possible. There is never a thread left hanging; indeed so contracted are they, that when the last sentence of the last page flares up, as it so often does, we see by its light the whole circumference and significance of the story revealed. The Chekhov method is of course the very opposite of this. Everything is cloudy and vague, loosely trailing rather than tightly furled. The stories move slowly out of sight like clouds in the summer air, leaving a wake of meaning in our minds, which gradually fades away.'

Maugham's comment is in his introduction to an anthology of short stories which he edited in 1939.[12] He considered that the immense prestige of the Russian writers in general and of Chekhov in particular had to a large extent 'transformed the composition and the appreciation of short stories'. Critical readers were indifferent to the technically well-made story, and the writers who continued to produce it, 'for the delectation of the great mass of the public', were little regarded. In Maugham's opinion, Chekhov's characters are not sharply individualized; 'his people are shadowy; but because they have not the clean-cut outline of a silhouette, because they are like vapours that rise towards evening from the surface of a lake and lose themselves in the enveloping dusk, though lacking the fine distinction of personality, they have a common humanity. I despair of making myself clear when I say that they strike me less as persons than as human beings. Each one is as it were a part of everyone else and the hurt that one does to another is bearable because in a way it is a hurt that he does to himself. And because they are shadowy they remain secret. We understand them as little as we understand ourselves. And so Chekhov gets the effect which is perhaps the most impressive that the writer of fiction can achieve: he fills you with an overpowering sense of the mystery of life.' This power gives point to stories that otherwise seem pointless, and when his stories come off, they give a feeling of reality which Maupassant's even at their best hardly do, 'for the pattern he has forced upon them prevents your complete surrender; somewhere in your subconscious the recollection lingers that what you are reading is after all only a fiction'.

Maugham is somewhat inclined to take the mysterious and melancholy view of Chekhov. Are his own stories in any way Chekhovian? If they are, he has given us the clue to analysis. Other critics have made more technical points; showing, for example, how Chekhov's art seizes upon significant moments of experience, moments often quite different from those we usually think of as significant. A. E. Coppard says that Chekhov presents his people 'at just the significant moment of their lives when they do for a brief space become universally interesting'. And in his own stories Coppard often does just that. Chekhov has the gift of using imagery to convey the meaning of these moments, integrating subject and object in a kind of mystical synthesis. D. S. Mirsky has plotted the curve of his stories and revealed his skill in marking that precise point—clearly perceptible only after the curve is completed—when the life-line changes its direction. To imitate the Chekhov story, with all these critical aids, has seemed easy to less gifted writers, and has been a great temptation. Only they do not know the significant from the trivial, and the line has not curved around to its new goal, but just wandered on.

Chekhov's mastery of atmosphere has tempted critical seekers after 'influences' to discover a Chekhov inspiration in some story where a certain atmosphere is achieved, a certain mood evoked through imagery, or a certain sense adumbrated of our common and mysterious human destiny. A master's thesis, for instance, brought together as identical in situation and setting Chekhov's 'Lady with the Toy Dog' and Joyce's 'The Dead'. *Identical* would have to be understood in a very Pickwickian sense indeed if this comparison were to be sustained. But both stories have a similar atmosphere; both convey lonely moods of lovers apart in feeling when they should be in communion; both use imagery—the sound of the surf in one, the sound of the falling snow in the other—which suggests the eternal sleep awaiting all of us, the descent of their last end upon the living and the dead. Influence? One suspects the likeness to be 'purely coincidental'—similar responses of sensitive artists to life.

iv

The Chekhov Play

AFTER THE acceptance of the Chekhov story came that of the Chekhov play, received at first with bewilderment but recognized in time as a play depending for its effect upon mood and atmosphere, and dramatizing futility. The Chekhov play is a literary influence, and only a part of the far wider influence of the Russian *theatre*, on acting, direction, staging and organization. These other aspects will be taken up in the next chapter.

Since the critical attempts to define a new form probably lead people to look for certain things, and some of the people are writers who thus become aware of new possibilities for their art, we shall begin with the struggle in the West to understand the Chekhov play. Maurice Baring is one of the earliest reporters, and he has already been quoted on the symbolism of *The Cherry Orchard*. John Palmer in the *Saturday Review* (June 3, 1911) analysed the same play, with similar emphasis on its social meaning, symbolically conveyed, 'not a thesis but a picture'. The play is original in build and method, 'a comedy of the ineffectual', of 'the passing of the old order', a masterpiece in the portrayal of 'disintegration and purposelessness'. The solo effect of each person thinking out loud 'fortifies the impression of shiftless and selfish individualism, the complete failure of the old social order, which is the central idea of the play'. It is not what the characters say which matters; it is what they are and what they are doing with their lives. The purpose is to convey a 'dramatic impression of irrelevance'. Chekhov is not writing in despair of his country: 'It was his task to take and picture Russia in the moment of her passage. The dark room of the empty old house contains the past and in that room we have seen it drift and break. Outside they are cutting down the trees and preparing for tomorrow; for the young have departed with the old.'

Ashley Dukes in his book, *Modern Dramatists* (1911), surveys Scandinavian, German, French, as well as English drama, and finds a place for Tolstoy, Gorky and Chekhov. But he found 'little technical accomplishment' in the Russian drama. One might quarrel with Mr Dukes over the meaning of the word *technical*, and he might insist on very precise points; but after all, Russian drama boasted of Griboyedov, Gogol and Ostrovsky, even before the three he names. None of Chekhov's plays had at this date been published in England, though *The Sea Gull*, in a translation by George Calderon, had been performed by the Scottish Repertory Theatre in Glasgow in 1909. Mr Dukes concedes to the Russians one accomplishment; they can ask questions, set a note of interrogation against life. This habit of theirs accounts for the 'appearance of incompleteness and incoherence which marks most of the plays'. Chekhov seeks the meaning of life in the 'intelligence'—that is, the intellectual class; Tolstoy, in the peasantry; Gorky, in the city proletariat. By no stretch of the imagination could Chekhov be called a great dramatist; he died '*before he could perfect the new dramatic form which he attempted to create*'. (Italics mine.) Summing up, Mr Dukes imagines Chekhov saying: We live in a civilization accessible only to the few. Here are the few. I show them to you for an hour, with their culture, their books, their plays, their theatres within the theatre, their learning and their wit. He offers fragments of a picture; piece them together as you please. The scheme grows clearer as you fit in more fragments. What is the meaning? 'Now hold it up to the light. . . . See, you have made a window of stained glass.' And that is the drama of Chekhov.

George Calderon (1868–1915), adventurer, scholar, artist, and man of action, killed at Gallipoli in World War I, decided while still at Oxford to 'take up' Russia, a neglected country. He spent two years (1895–1897) in St Petersburg, learned to read and to speak the language, and when he returned to England, held a post in the British Museum (1900–1903). Familiar with Slavonic subjects, particularly folk-lore, he published in the monthly reviews articles, stories and sketches, generally dealing with things Russian. From 1909–1913 he was associated with the Stage Society and the Manchester Repertory Theatre. He translated two of Chekhov's plays in 1912. Percy Lubbock, author of a *Memoir* (1921), describes Calderon's house in London as an unofficial legation for stray Muscovites, refugees, tourists, poets and dancers; he mixed, Lubbock says, scholarship and art, refusing to consider, in the prevailing fashion, that the art of letters was a separate and exclusive claim. In a long article in *The Quarterly Review* on the Russian stage (July, 1912), he comments on the playwrights whom we would now label the Decadents—Dymov, Sologub, Bryusov, Andreyev, Blok, and others—explaining that Meyerhold, regisseur of the St Petersburg Imperial Theatre, had pointed out the plays to him, directed his reading and outlined the development of the drama. Calderon gives summaries of some of the plays ; relates moods and themes both to the national crisis of recent years and to the foreign influence of D'Annunzio, Verlaine, Maeterlinck, Wilde, Poe and Beardsley. Though he calls these Russian playwrights neurasthenics, specializing in colour sensations, symbols, doubles and fantasies of the 'all this has happened before' type, he is not at all enthusiastic about Tolstoy and Gorky as dramatists. Gorky was calling for a new breed of men rather like himself—tough, strong-willed, patient and confident; but he left unanswered the question put by a character in a Bryusov play: 'What will people do in your new Eden, if they take you for their pattern?' That certainly remained to be seen. Chekhov's theme is disillusion, and his plays will never go out of date, since disillusion is constant and irrefragable. *The Cherry Orchard*, to Calderon, is a 'picture of the nothingness of hope in all countries and all ages'; of disillusionment painted with a melancholy grace that makes it seem more beautiful than achievement. In all the plays of the last generation in Russia, there is a cry for liberty and emancipation from every restraint; 'a fundamentally aimless and unconstructive impulse'; a let's-go-away-from-here discontent; a rebellion against the fundamental conditions of man's destiny.

This emphasis on aimlessness and disillusionment as peculiarly Russian is questioned by Desmond MacCarthy in a review of *Uncle Vanya*, produced by the Stage Society (*New Statesman*,

May 16, 1914). The play is 'unforgettably good' and its technical qualities superb; his definition of *technical* is evidently different from that of Ashley Dukes. Relating Chekhov's themes to Turgenev's, Mr MacCarthy describes the country-house atmosphere as one of 'sighs and yawns and self-reproaches, vodka, endless tea and endless discussion', a still closer air than that of Turgenev's generation, 'still more unresponsive to effort and hope', with no Bazarovs or Insarovs left. There is 'a warm muffling mist, narrowing the world to garden gates'. He continues: 'We have no right to label this atmosphere "Russian" and regard it with complacent curiosity. Have you not felt that fog in your throat on English lawns, in English houses? Indeed the main point of difference between this spell-bound cultivated Russian society and the English variety is not in our favour. If Chekhov's intellectuals are half-dead, the other half of them is very much, painfully much, alive. They suffer more consciously; there is intensity in their lassitude; at least they torture themselves and each other by displaying each his own bankruptcy. They are not comatose and outwardly contented, but sensitive, self-conscious and critical.' They are not, like Wordsworth's family circle in Hades, 'all silent and all damned'. Damned the Russians may be, admits Mr MacCarthy, but silent, no. He recognizes that this wail, responsive to their own frustration and life's disillusionment, is part of a phase in Russian history, but it keeps Chekhov's work very fresh. After a spirited account of *Uncle Vanya*, he begs Mr Granville Barker, 'put this play in your repertory'.

This was in 1914. After the war, James Strachey, reviewing a performance of *The Sea Gull* in London (*Athenaeum*, June 13, 1919), notes that the critics are still struggling to get used to its peculiarities, with results as curious as some early English criticism of Ibsen: '*The Sea Gull* is a low-spirited play'—'the sea gull is a symbolic fowl'. The root of the difficulty he found to be in Chekhov's use of an entirely new dramatic technique that would have made the play seem queer even if written by an Englishman, and that required the efforts of a Stanislavsky to render acceptable even in Russia.

An important aspect of the new dramatic technique came to be understood as the dramatization of group emotions, the creation of an 'ensemble of solitary souls', in Gerhardi's phrase, the playing off of one mood against another. The Moscow Art Theatre players succeeded in carrying across to the audience what Sir Oliver Elton called Chekhov's 'peculiar strain of poetic musing' and his picture of an action in which externally nothing is accomplished. It was not only Chekhov among the Russians who had command of this technique, as Londoners discovered when Turgenev's *A Month in the Country* was performed in 1936, and the dramatic critic of the *Manchester Guardian* called it 'the most exquisite thing that Chekhov never wrote'.

Understanding of Chekhov in the United States is bound up with the history of the 'little theatre' movement. When Gertrude Besse King saw a performance of *The Cherry Orchard* in Petrograd in the war spring of 1915 and sent a two-column account of it to the *New Republic* (June 26), she began with the question, 'who is Chekoff?' She knew that he 'stood with Pushkin and Turgenev' and had reached England 'in a virulent form' about five years before, and would strike America some few years hence, and one of his plays had recently been given in Boston. In a somewhat complacent tone, with a typically American moral viewpoint, she said that the play made her interested in the commonplace and induced a tolerant kindliness, enabling you to face sorrow 'not because another such as you is receiving his deserts, but because pain is part of a larger reconciling experience'. From 1916, with the founding of such little theatres as the Washington Square Players and the Neighbourhood Playhouse, the list of performances of Russian plays in English begins to grow. Chekhov's *Sea Gull* and *Marriage Proposal* were seen in 1916. To measure the progress of interest in Chekhov, look forward to June, 1930, when Jed Harris produced *Uncle Vanya* and the *Theatre Arts Monthly* recorded: 'With *Uncle Vanya*, *The Cherry Orchard* and *The Sea Gull* all over our most popular and effective stages, it is difficult for a person who knows what life is, what theatre is, and what is the perfect measure of the distance between them, to recall the time when Chekhov was considered as much a stranger to both life and art as today he seems a master of both.'

The precise sense in which Chekhov was the master of life and of art was usually blurred by the customary phrases about melancholy, the fragrance of human despair and aspiration, the veil of detachment and the like. An encouraging hint of precision appears in a remark by one of the authors of *Deep Are the Roots*, a Broadway success of 1946: superficially, he says, there does not seem to be anything we can take from Chekhov, but underneath we see that there is—'the character always seen in a social context; the personal and historical dilemma depicted as one'.[13] That, we may assume, is what D'Usseau and Gow were aiming at in their play; it is what Lillian Hellman achieves in *The Little Foxes*, and may represent a deeper Chekhov influence than those parallels in dialogue or mood, which usually impress critics.

Many such parallels have been detected between Chekhov's plays and those of Paul Green and Clifford Odets, and the parallels are sometimes very close; between the ending of Odets's *Paradise Lost* and that of *The Cherry Orchard*, for instance. Tennessee Williams has been said to create the Chekhov mood in *The Glass Menagerie*. And in one of his short plays, *The Lady of Larkspur Lotion*, concerning a battered and dubious lady who dreams of a non-existent plantation in Brazil, Williams makes an equally futile writer pretend to believe in the dream, and at the end introduce himself as Anton Pavlovich Chekhov. It is not surprising that both Paul Green's *House of Connelly* and Odets's *Paradise Lost* should have been described as Chekhov plays, with their themes of middle-class family decline. It would be more accurate to say that Chekhov's manner of dramatizing the slow collapse of a class or a tradition became, as soon as he was known and played and interpreted, an available model for any American playwright who may have observed something similar going on in the Bronx or in the South. But to trace the historical and social and economic changes in the United States, which may bring the plight of a Jewish family in New York or a Southern family about 1930 close to that of a Russian landowning family in the 1890's, is a more difficult job for a critic than to paste on a convenient label. It was said that *The House of Connelly* killed two birds with one stone: the Seagull and the Wild Duck. That at least suggests the interaction of 'influences'.

[1] 'Obviously inspired by Turgenev', says the *Concise Cambridge History of English Literature* of *The Untilled Field.*

[2] *New England: Indian Summer*, pp. 237-238.

[3] 'The Influence of Turgenev on Henry James', by Daniel Lerner, in *Slavonic Year-Book*, American Series I, being Vol. xx, 1941, of the *Slavonic and East European Review*. Pp. 28-54.

[4] See F. O. Matthiessen, Newton Arvin, Clifton Fadiman, and others, in introductions and notes to collections of James's short stories, American novels, etc.

[5] See Lord David Cecil, in *Poets and Story Tellers*, Macmillan, 1948, and Alfred Kazin in the *N.Y. Times* Book Review section, March 12, 1950, 'The Un-Russian Russian'.

[6] Reprinted (with some slight revisions of phrasing) in *The Captain's Death Bed and Other Essays*, 1950.

[7] Henry James's preface to *Portrait of a Lady.*

[8] The quotation is from an essay on the art of Henry Handel Richardson by her husband, J. G. Robertson, included in her autobiography, *Myself When Young*, 1948.

[9] George Sainsbury: *The Later Nineteenth Century*, 1907. P. 332. f.

[10] Quotations are from James's *Notes on Novelists*, chapter on 'The New Novel', 1914, and from James's *Letters*, of May 19, 1912 and August 21, 1913.

[11] *Britain Today*, June 1950. See also Mr Phelps's article, 'Russian Realism in English Fiction', in the *Cambridge Journal*, Vol. iii, No. 5, Feb. 1950.

[12] Later reissued under the title *The Greatest Stories of All Time.*

[13] Arnaud D'Usseau, 'The Theatre Critic as Thinker', in *Mainstream*, Vol. i, No. 1, 1947.

all well-known actors, playing at leading New York theatres. In 1908 the Yale University Dramatic Association produced a good amateur *Revizor* (Gogol's *Inspector General*).

In 1905 the Russian actor Paul Orleneff with a company of fourteen players came to New York from London, where they had attracted favourable notice from Irving, Beerbohm Tree, Kropotkin and Jerome K. Jerome, the last of whom had called them to the attention of an American manager. Orleneff, roused by the treatment of the Jews in Russia—these were the days of the pogroms and the Black Hundreds—brought with him a play called *The Chosen People*, written in prison by Eugene Chirikov (who was not himself a Jew). Gorky had advised taking it abroad to show how Jews were being persecuted. The company performed once at the Herald Square Theatre, then at the Murray Hill Theatre and at several Bowery theatres. The appeal was largely to the cultivated Russian Jews of the lower East Side; 'the taste in this quarter', noted Florence Brooks in the *Century Magazine*, 'is rather hungry for the best things in art'.[1] Orleneff's company also played in *Tsar Feodor Ivanovich* (or 'The Sin of Ivan the Terrible'), in versions of *Crime and Punishment* and *The Brothers Karamazov*, and in Ibsen's *Ghosts* and Strindberg's *Countess Julia*—the last as a benefit for Mme Alla Nazimova. An ambitious plan was drawn up for a full season of Russian and Scandinavian drama for the following spring. But the *Century*, in June, 1907, contains the obituary: 'owing to divided responsibility and an ignorance of theatrical exploitation' the venture was doomed and the company sent back to Europe by private subscription, leaving Mme Nazimova behind, to begin her career on the American stage in English, as Hedda Gabler, November, 1906. Owen Johnson, author of the *Century* article, mentions Mme Nazimova's year of study with Stanislavsky—'probably the greatest stage manager of the present time'. In 1908, the actress Vera Komissarzhevskaya presented in Russian a number of world-famous plays, among them Gorky's *Children of the Sun* and Ostrovsky's *Girl Without a Dowry*; but with little success.

There was a fine Yiddish theatre on the East Side in New

York, and Harold Clurman, one of the founders in the early 1930's of the Group Theatre, recalls in his book *The Fervent Years* that between 1913 and 1917, when he was a young boy, he saw at this theatre performances, among others, of plays by Gorky, Tolstoy and Andreyev. The actors, he says, were among the best in the world, and the audiences were most stimulating; most of them immigrants to whom the theatre was a centre of social intercourse, where the problems of their lives, past and present, were given a voice. The concern of the Group Theatre, one notes, was 'with our lives and the life of our times'.

From 1916 on, performances in English of Russian plays became more frequent, both in 'little theatres' and commercial theatres. In 1916 we have Evreinov's *Gay Death*, Chekhov's *Sea Gull* and *Marriage Proposal*, Andreyev's *Life of Man* and *Sabine Women* (this last at the Indianapolis Little Theatre); in 1918 and 1919, Arthur Hopkins produced Tolstoy's *Redemption* (*The Living Corpse*) and Gorky's *Lower Depths*, and in 1920 the Theatre Guild produced Tolstoy's *Power of Darkness*. And then in 1923 the Moscow Art Theatre came to New York.

Anyone who remembers the hysterical fear of 'Bolshevism' that prevailed in the United States after the October Revolution; who has not forgotten the lies with which the truth has never caught up; who remembers the Palmer raids against the 'reds'; who risked mob violence to go to public meetings where one might hear speakers recently returned from Russia—any of the old survivors of those days will recall the glad surprise at being able to welcome the Moscow Art Theatre. Here was a whole group of Russian actors and theatre workers actually allowed to enter the country and perform a series of Russian plays. This famous theatre had survived revolution, civil war, intervention and famine; when things were at their worst, it had gone on a European tour, and now, when conditions were improving, the American tour was undertaken. Oliver Sayler tells us that the profits of this tour went towards keeping the theatre playhouse in Moscow up to pre-war standards, when every other playhouse in Moscow was cold, dirty and out of repair.[2] Oliver Sayler's book on the Russian Theatre (1922), wrote Stark Young, 'combined with the most intelligent and effective publicity in the course of our theatre, had made us familiar with the Moscow Art Theatre before we ever saw it'.[3] And he goes on to characterize this group of sincere artists, created by their art, 'rich by their intense living in it and sure of all art's importance and duration. . . . Most significant of all, they possess a racial or popular life from which they can draw their belief and idea'.

The admiration aroused by the productions of the Moscow Art Theatre group, during their two tours in the United States (1923 and 1924) with their 181 performances, stimulated playwrights, actors, producers, directors and dramatic critics to visit Russia in the years that followed. Out of many, we may mention Lee Simonson, Hallie Flanagan, Halsted Welles, J. W. Krutch, Norris Houghton, Elmer Rice, Harold Clurman and Stella Adler. They found Soviet theatre a flourishing and complex institution. Lee Simonson, in 1926, went to theatres crowded with proletarians in shabby jackets, 'absorbed in performances of opera, ballet, Russian classical comedies, dramas of the Soviet Revolution, a revival of *The Blue Bird* and of *Anna Christie*, superbly acted without exception and brilliantly staged, whether with meticulous realism or on constructivist trestles'.[4] When he was in Leningrad and Moscow, in September, 1932, during the famine in the Ukraine, he had to go to two theatres a night in order to see a fraction of the plays being given, ranging from Shakespeare and Schiller to Ostrovsky, Chekhov, Tolstoy and the newest proletarian playwrights. The enthusiasm of the earlier visitors persisted, but became more discerning, more aware of where the strength of the Soviet theatre lay. Mr Krutch, for instance, stressed the 'intimate relation with the life of the community which constitutes the essential characteristic of the Russian theatre'. (*Nation*, July 11, 1928.) Halsted Welles, director of the Yale Dramatic Association, wrote in 1935: 'The Soviet theatre is tremendous and inspiring. It is, on the whole, a solid vital form of theatre. It serves its age and society on a gigantic scale and in a manner far better than the American theatre serves us. The credits run into enormous figures and the currency is sound. Within the Soviet Union they are real credits. They are not, however, transferable to New York. Artistically the New York theatre worker has little to learn from Moscow. The matter of theatre organization is another story and a long one. Briefly, the set-up of Soviet theatre on this side is almost pure gold. We shall work long and hard before we can open the September season with twenty sell-out shows, before we can take a superb piece of work like *The Lower Depths*, and keep it going for ten or fifteen years, and before we can let our actors play together for some twenty or thirty years, giving them year-round salaries, but above all, giving them a year-round chance to play. . . . There would be no stopping us if somehow we could give our theatre artists just this one thing—a chance to work and our public a chance to see them.'[5]

Both American and English observers learned to see the Soviet theatre as distinct from dramatic literature; to see it as a consciously fashioned social instrument for cultural development in the widest sense, as distinct from an entertainment business, in which cultural development might be a happy accident—or a casualty. The plays that excited their admiration as literature are likely to be the older plays, especially those of Chekhov. The newer Soviet plays, if seen in Russia with all the advantage of stage design, song and dance and direction, sometimes impress the critics. But if read, in imperfect translations, or interpreted by non-Russian actors and adapted to American taste (or politics), they seemed to be a falling-off from pre-Revolutionary standards. It is usually forgotten that the older plays were often published before they were performed, if they were performed at all; several of Gorky's dramas waited many years before they were produced, in an atmosphere more favourable to their ideas than when they were written. The playwright had time to concern himself with the literary values of 'closet drama'. But, as H. W. L. Dana points out in his *Handbook of Soviet Drama*: 'The Soviet theatre is looked upon as a composite art, in which the art of the playwright is only one of the many component parts in the composition of a dramatic production.' And Norris Houghton makes the same point: 'With the tremendous theatrical activity of the U.S.S.R. and its emphasis on acting, direction, design; with the vast public flocking to the playhouses nightly to *see* the play, the Soviet dramatist writes in terms of the stage and production, and has little time for the perfection of literary style; his plays are chiefly skeletons which depend on the other artists of the theatre to be filled out.'[6]

Between 1920 and 1947, some fifty-odd Russian plays, old and new, were offered to American theatre-goers; plays by Chekhov, Pushkin, Tolstoy, Gogol, Andreyev, Turgenev, Gorky, Kataev, Tretyakov, Kirshon, Pogodin, Bulgakov, Simonov, Ivanov and others. Chekhov and Andreyev had the greatest number of performances. The productions were in commercial theatres, little theatres, university and community theatres, and the Federal Theatre. As students of the Russian language increased in number, plays in Russian, both classic and modern, were produced by special groups, usually in universities. In the early 1920's the Stanislavsky method began to be taught by the Russians Boleslavsky and Ouspenskaya, in courses at the American Laboratory Theatre. The story can be followed through the years in the *Theatre Arts Monthly* (first christened *Theatre Arts Magazine*). Take for example Volume xiv, 1930. There are photographs of scenes from productions of the Moscow Kamerny Theatre, and the Azerbaijan State Art Theatre in Baku; of the Pasadena Community Playhouse production, for the first time in America, of *The Armoured Train*, described as a 'melodrama of the recent Russian revolution', by Ivanov; and of a production at the American Laboratory Theatre of *The Three Sisters*, with Maria Germanova and Maria Ouspenskaya, both formerly of the Moscow Art Theatre, in leading roles. In this year Gorky's *Lower Depths* (under the title *At the Bottom*) was played at the Waldorf Theatre under Leo Bulgakov's direction; *He Who Gets Slapped* was revived by the Palmetto Players of the University of North Carolina; the Civic Repertory Theatre in New York produced *The Living Corpse*; the Theatre Guild, *A Month in the Country*, and *Roar, China*; and the Gloucester School of the Little Theatre,

The Sea Gull. Anna Louise Strong reported from Russia on the Theatrical Olympiad in Moscow, noting the emergence of local dramatic clubs in factory and village, preparing the soil for a nation-wide appreciation of the drama, which would nourish more significant art than crude amateurish propaganda-drenched productions.

It has obviously been possible for a variety of influences from the Russian theatre to affect the American theatre. But just because there are so many possibilities and so many channels, the connection between causes and effects is a tricky business to establish. Furthermore, people most open to Russian influences are sometimes least helpful in such an inquiry. In recent years Congressional investigations have put a very high survival value on the discovery of other than Russian influences in cinema, theatre and elsewhere in the arts, sciences and professions. Naturally enough, when some members of Congress in 1938 were seeking to put the Federal Theatre Project out of business, the director, Mrs Hallie Flanagan, emphasized the fact that out of over a thousand plays, the Project had done only two Russian dramas—'both farce-satires on the present Russian regime'. (*Arena*, page 360.) Senator Reynolds was determined to save America from the danger of 'red' propaganda being broadcast by the 'majority of plays'. Senator McCarran challenged him: 'There are those who for ever use the bugbear of Communism to scare someone in order that they may themselves rise up and thus be held up as champions against the so-called danger of Communism.' This is an interesting prophecy of the senator's own later and highly successful career. Among the plays that, to Senator Reynolds, bore the 'trade-mark of red Russia in their titles, plays spewed from the gutters of the Kremlin', were *Love'em and Leave 'em*, *Up in Mabel's Room*, and *A New Kind of Love.* Disavowal of production of Russian plays did not save the Federal Theatre, and Mrs Flanagan puts her finger on the real error of the Project: it was, among other things, educating a vast new audience on some of the important issues of government and politics; and though less than ten per cent of the plays produced dealt with such issues, that was simply ten per cent too many, in the opinion of certain politicians who did not care for thinking voters. By neat manoeuvring, the Project was killed; and as Mrs Flanagan records in an amusing anecdote, congressmen who voted to kill it did not in some cases even know that it was the Federal Theatre Project that they had killed.

Another example of playing down the Russian influence is Harold Clurman's rejection of the idea that foreign aesthetic theories affected the Group Theatre: 'The almost inevitable mention of the Moscow Art Theatre in relation to our first production was in some respects unfortunate. For the importance of *The House of Connelly* as a production lay in the fact that it was an American production—that is, a play and a performance that sprang from circumstances and conditions peculiarly indigenous at that time. To speak of Russian influence, as some did, because we had learned certain things of general technical or artistic value from the best practitioners of contemporary theatrical art was as pointless as it would be to view Sherwood Anderson's novels or Edgar Lee Masters's verse as offshoots of Dostoevsky's work.'[7] Pointless indeed, and illustrative of semantic confusion; the sun certainly influences the growth of a plant, but the plant is no offshoot of the sun. 'Circumstances and conditions peculiarly indigenous' to Russia favoured certain developments in the arts of the theatre. Once developed, there they were, for any other society to adapt to its own uses, whenever its own indigenous circumstances were favourable. Is there influence of the earlier upon the later? If there is any circulation of ideas, there will be contagion. And that is why politicians in many countries have realized the necessity of stopping the traffic.

Mr Clurman and his Group Theatre colleagues, Stella Adler and Lee Strasberg, visited Moscow in 1934, and Mr Clurman again in 1935, and they had many talks with Stanislavsky in Paris. Lee Strasberg studied at the American Laboratory Theatre where the Moscow Art Theatre techniques were taught. The Group actors practised exercises in 'affective memory', the root discovery that led Stanislavsky to the elaboration of his system. During one of their early summer-camp interludes, Mr Clurman tells us, social, economic and political preoccupations intruded. Lee Strasberg had copies of publications about the Soviet theatre, which a Russian acquaintance who worked in the camp kitchen translated; this Russian happened to be a philosophical anarchist himself, with a particular dislike to the Soviet system. The books were mostly aesthetic and technical, but the Group was fascinated by a phraseology that smacked of science. Behind the words of Vakhtangov was 'the authority of a great historical event—a Revolution—the brilliant example of a theatre carried on in days of upheaval and starvation and, above all, something that seemed very strong and definite compared with our verbose incantations. What ideology cemented our collective? Nothing that could be put in a single phrase, only things that could be set down as "mysticism"; whereas the Russians, no matter how vague or foreign their terms, had the prestige of a whole world behind them.' (Page 92.)

What impressed Mr Clurman on his first visit to Moscow was the variety and scope of theatre repertoire, the incredible richness of the productions and the excitement and enthusiasm of the audiences. On his second visit he met Meyerhold, Eisenstein, and Afinogenov, and saw thirty-five productions; but he did not wish to remain, realizing that to yearn for the Soviet Union was just a way of avoiding the difficulty of life by escaping into something not altogether real to him. He carried away the sense of a *sane* people; returning to New York in 1935, he felt he was living in a mad world. The Left movement in the theatre, he realized, was only one response to a general dislocation of which others were the organization of the C.I.O., the passing of the Wagner Act, and a Marxist drift in economic interpretation.

Two aspects of Soviet theatre particularly impressed American observers: the experiments in production and organization and the relation of the theatre to the life of the community. As for the experiments, many were tried out, in our little theatres or laboratory groups, and adopted or modified or rejected; and to discuss them would require a technical study. As for the place of the theatre in community life, the Soviet example counted significantly in some developments that can be summarized.

The New Playwrights Theatre, organized in 1927 by five young playwrights, including John Dos Passos and John Howard Lawson, devoted itself to the defence of the underprivileged, but the effort ended with the depression of 1930. A new impetus then came from the amateur stages of the foreign language workers' groups; hundreds of dramatic clubs, attached to the organizations of foreign-born workers, put on performances in a dozen different languages. Cut off though they were from the main stream of the American theatre, they were stimulated by the economic crisis to new efforts, and some of them adopted the motto of the Soviet drama—'theatre is a weapon'. They called themselves 'agitprop' troupes (agitation-propaganda). The first group to inaugurate the new method was German; then an English-speaking agitprop troupe appeared—the Workers' Laboratory Theatre. These troupes were patterned after German mobile stage units and the Blue Blouse troupes of the Soviet Union. As early as 1926 the *Theatre Arts Monthly* published photographs of the Living Newspapers enacted by the Blue Blouses. Blue Blouses of Chicago and Los Angeles joined with those of New York and elsewhere to create the League of Workers' Theatres in 1932. Some of the young actors pooled their resources and devoted all their time to dramatic production, and one of these groups became the Theatre of Action of New York, which had a play staged on Broadway. Odets's *Waiting for Lefty* was successfully produced by individual members of the Group Theatre during a taxicab strike in New York. By this time—1935—the influence of workers' plays was evident on Broadway and even a little later in Hollywood. The earlier alliance of workers' theatres had broadened to include middle-class and community theatres; and the League of Workers' Theatres gave place to the New Theatre League, with a liberal programme calling for a mass development of the American theatre to its highest artistic and social level.

All these efforts at experimenting with new techniques, reaching new audiences, and integrating the theatre more closely with community life, were strengthened by the Theatre Union of New

York, an organization that, beginning in 1935, produced both American and foreign plays, many frankly propagandist. Among them was Bertolt Brecht's version of Gorky's *Mother*. This theatre in the old playhouse on Fourteenth Street attracted both sympathetic intellectuals and large working-class audiences, and enriched and deepened the earlier agitational plays. Then there was the Labour Stage of the International Ladies' Garment Workers' Union, whose satirical review, *Pins and Needles*, presenting the workers' outlook on current affairs, had over 1,100 performances between 1937 and 1940. The Labour Stage was an outgrowth of the educational department of the union, which had organized over sixty amateur dramatic groups in fifty-two cities.

Finally the Federal Theatre Project had its brief but very significant career between 1935 and 1939. It was one of the many New Deal efforts to deal with depression and unemployment, particularly acute among theatre workers of all sorts. Mrs Hallie Flanagan who organized the project had studied in 1926–1927 comparative methods of play writing and production in Europe, including Russia; in 1931 she was again in Russia. Among the most successful of the Project's productions were the Living Newspapers, dealing with such issues as housing, power, agriculture and labour. According to Mrs Flanagan, the Living Newspapers borrowed from many sources, native and foreign; among the latter, from the Blue Blouses of Soviet Russia. It was Mrs Flanagan who called attention in 1931 to the fact that a theatre of workers was being born in the United States, with the object of creating a national culture by and for the working class. She tells the story of the Federal Theatre Project from start to finish—from birth to assassination by act of Congress, June 30, 1939—in her book *Arena*, the title symbolizing an arena packed with huge audiences in nearly every part of the country, many of whom had never seen living actors performing before.

'The Federal Theatre at its best was working toward an art in which each region and eventually each State would have its unique, indigenous dramatic expression, its company housed in a building reflecting its own landscape and regional materials,

> producing plays of its past and present, in its own rhythm of speech and its native design, in an essentially American pattern.' (*Arena*, page 371.)

With a change of the adjective *American* to *Russian* (or *Soviet*) one has here a statement of the aims of Soviet theatre, as thousands became acquainted with them both at the theatre festivals and through innumerable reports and articles. The Federal Theatre, for all its mistakes, proved what the Soviet theatre had proved: that millions of people want to go to the theatre, 'if it can be brought geographically and financially within their range'. The greatest achievement, writes Mrs Flanagan, of these public theatres was in 'their creation of an audience of many millions'.

ii

England

THAT AUDIENCE, the English theatre workers, were most envious of this aspect of the Soviet theatre. An impression derived from reading English comment, especially in the 1930's, is that the Russian influence was chiefly that of arousing the English interested in the theatre to reflect upon their own problems—and to come to rather gloomy conclusions. Could the good things in the Soviet theatre somehow be transplanted, without the basic social changes?

Though the process had been slow, Chekhov's plays had finally been accepted in England. In the 1926 season, three of them were running in London and the suburbs of Barnes and Hammersmith—*The Cherry Orchard*, *Uncle Vanya* and *The Three Sisters*. Ashley Dukes commented on the London scene for the *Theatre Arts Monthly*: 'In one year Chekhov has done more to form a distinguished public taste than all the repertory theatres have done in a generation.' But scarcely had the Chekhov play come to be appreciated by English theatre-goers than the Russian theatre was transformed by the Revolution. Not that important established traditions were overthrown, but the entire theatre was taken over by the Government and put under the direction of the Education Department, with Lunacharsky, himself a writer of plays and a theatre specialist, at the head. The great directors, Stanislavsky, Tairov, Meyerhold, continued their work under the changed conditions. But a strange new audience began to throng into the theatres. What this was going to mean is strikingly foreshadowed in the account Stanislavsky gives in *My Life in Art* of a performance of *The Cherry Orchard* by the Moscow Art Theatre on the very eve of the October Revolution in Moscow. Soldiers were gathering around the Kremlin, the city lights were out, the police patrols removed, grey-clad crowds milling around the streets; and a thousand-headed crowd of the common people were pushing into the theatre to see this play, 'in which the life of that class against whom the common people were preparing for final revolt was painted in deep and sympathetic tones. The auditorium, filled almost exclusively with the common people, buzzed with excitement. The mood on both sides of the footlights was one of worry.' The actors were afraid of being attacked, and the crowd was new to theatres. 'But the lyricism of Chekhov, the eternal beauty of Russian poetry, the life mood of country gentility in old Russia, caused a reaction even under existing conditions.' It seemed to the actors as if the spectators wished 'to wrap themselves in the atmosphere of poetry and to bid peaceful farewell to the old and beautiful life that now demanded its purifying sacrifices'. When the final curtain fell, there was an ovation—and then many went from the theatre to the barricades.

It was this new audience, steadily growing through the years after the Revolution and encouraged to grow by every conceivable device, that aroused the longing and envy of English observers. In the early days of the new order, Huntly Carter, like the American Oliver Sayler, showed tireless enthusiasm in reporting what he found. Before the Revolution he had been writing about the 'new spirit' in the European theatre, and developing his own theories about making the theatre a functional part of the life of the people. Going about Europe in search of support of his theories, he discovered the Soviet theatre, and for several years in the 1920's he was almost the only thoroughly qualified interpreter to the English public, in his books and articles, of all its different aspects. 'The present-day theatre,' he wrote, 'stands for the collective spirit of the age, especially the mass production of the sentiment of liberty, mass social construction and synthesis, guided by a clear conception of the social problem.' In simpler words, the theatre, to the people, was becoming 'a place for putting their house in order', and it was this fact that helped to explain the themes of the new plays, the changes in the organization of the theatre, the conflict in ideas, and so forth.

In England it was easiest at first to arouse interest in Soviet films, although a censorship operated against their importation. Many intellectuals admired the technique of the Russian revolutionary films. The Film Society secured the admission of Gorky's *Mother*, but for all its efforts, the list of Russian films shown in England up to the date of Mr Carter's survey (1928) is meagre. It was usually the aesthetic values that were acclaimed. The social content and the propagandist aspect of the films were ignored, according to Mr Carter; 'a white herring was drawn across the path of common sense' when Russian films were said to contain no more propaganda than Keats's verse about miners in his *Isabella or the Pot of Basil.* There were three channels through which the influence of the Soviet theatre reached England in the earlier years: intellectuals who were opposed to Bolshevism and repudiated the social revolution, but were attracted by an aesthetic which they considered revolutionary, and fought the censorship for the sake of the new techniques, most of these intellectuals being technical specialists; then there were the 'go-betweens' who worked both with the English intellectuals and with Moscow, and fought for wide distribution precisely because of the revolutionary content which the aesthetes rejected; and finally there were the purely Bolshevist agencies, that is, certain theatre directors and proletarian theatrical organizations, hostile alike to the intellectuals and the go-between compromisers.

After the inauguration of the Theatre Olympiads and then of the Festivals in the Soviet Union, and the encouragement of foreign visitors, there is a great variety of comment from more or less qualified English observers of most shades of political opinion. John Strachey, for instance, saw *Roar, China*, *The Armoured Train* and *The Days of the Turbins* in Moscow, but thought no masterpiece had yet appeared. (*Spectator*, May, 1928.) The critic of the London *Observer* was depressed in 1930 by the uniformity in the subjects of the plays which he saw at a festival of the theatres and arts of the different peoples of the Soviet Union; but he was rebuked by Tom Thomas in the *Labour Monthly* (October, 1930): 'One must make allowance for the mentality of a bourgeois critic; the absence of "Eternal Triangle" dramas and crook plays . . . is enough to throw any one of them off his balance', and lead him to overlook the fact that the Soviet theatre is 'an open and avowed social weapon, just as the bourgeois stage in capitalist countries is a social weapon cunningly concealed'.

Gordon Craig, who had been in Moscow from 1909 to 1912, listened to the Russian delegates (Tairov and Amaglobeli) at a drama conference in Rome in 1934, and found that they talked the best sense of any: 'They were to be expected to tell us that it was only the Soviet Republics which could do the trick—for not to say so would have been an affectation. And they said so with all becoming emphasis. Then they went farther. They spoke of a new theatre public, a public which was to be counted by millions, and not by a few hundred thousands—of a public which had rid itself of apathy and cynicism—and of this public of millions flocking night after night to theatres for relaxation and inspiration.'[8] When he had visited Moscow before, there had been but one experimental theatre and a comparatively small public. Invited to Moscow, he went in 1935, was greeted by actors, dramatists, producers and designers, and not surprisingly in such company found Moscow 'the most intelligent place in Europe'. He pays tribute to Lunacharsky, who as Commissar of Education had worked to preserve the past of the theatre as well as to create the new; disagrees with the German director, Erwin Piscator, on the question of a political-propaganda theatre; and notes that all connected with the theatre have enough money and are provided with what they need for their work. The only question they need to concern themselves with is whether the work is good or bad.

Basil Wright reported the 1937 Theatre Festival on the whole favourably in the *Spectator* (September 10), finding the drama quite evidently an integral part of the cultural life of the people, with a level considerably higher than in England: 'The ordinary citizen's response to good plays, good acting and good production must come as something of an eye-opener to those who are working for the raising of the levels of the theatre in this country. It would be gratifying indeed if our new National Theatre were to infuse the same appreciation of drama into the mass of our own citizens. There is no reason to suppose', he concludes wistfully, 'that they are less intelligent, or that their appreciation of good plays is less acute than the recently emancipated population of the U.S.S.R.' The National Theatre Committee had been in existence since 1908; it is pleasant to note that the corner-stone of the National Theatre was laid during the Festival of Britain in the summer of 1951.

Barbara Nixon, who contributed the article on the theatre in the collection edited by C. Day Lewis, *The Mind in Chains* (1937), surveys the economic and social factors in the English theatre situation, and concludes that it is so bound up with the whole system of capitalist society that there is not much hope of present improvement. Miss Nixon, a Cambridge graduate who had worked as stage manager and producer at the Festival Theatre in Cambridge and the Duchess Theatre in London, was one of the founders of the Left Theatre. Her interest in Soviet drama is shown in her translations and adaptations of Tretyakov's *Roar, China*, Afinogenov's *Fear*, Gorky's *Mother* and Dostoevsky's *Crime and Punishment*. She was under no illusion that a change to Socialism would immediately provide a vital *drama*, but she thought it would produce a vital *theatre*: 'The workers and peasants of the U.S.S.R. who never before saw a play now fill the theatres to capacity.... When the majority of the people are given the facilities, and when the State realizes that the entertainment and artistic education of the public is a duty, there will be more than sufficient support for both art forms—i.e. cinema and drama—and this support will in turn assure that the quality of the plays themselves will be progressive and no longer decadent.'

The Left Theatre was a group of young actors and dancers who performed plays of 'social significance' in both working-class districts and in the West End of London, with some support from trade unions. Miss Nixon compares it with the Theatre Union in New York.[9] The Unity Theatre and the Group Theatre had back of them the support of private clubs and a subscription membership, for it was still necessary to circumvent the Lord Chamberlain's censorship. The theatre in which the Unity group played was a converted Non-conformist chapel in Goldington Street. *Waiting for Lefty* and Pogodin's *Aristocrats* were both produced there; and, according to John Lehmann, it was 'inspired' by American and Russian models.[10] Unity Theatre is still, in 1953, in Goldington Street. It is still an amateur theatre, a co-operative society; it has a school of acting and a school for producers, links with similar acting groups in other parts of London and the provinces, and good relations with the Co-operative Movement. *People's Theatre*, a sixpenny pamphlet recording the story of fifteen years, refers to Unity Theatre's debts to American, Spanish and Russian theatre, insisting, however, that it has remained very English. Of 'the impact of the Soviet Union' on Unity, it states: 'The Socialist example and cultural regeneration have been as a torch held high for the encouragement and inspiration of Unity's young pioneers.' Harold Hobson, dramatic critic of the London *Sunday Times*, in his book *The Theatre Now* (1953), mentions Unity in a chapter on 'The Involved Theatre' as an example of politics using the drama, rather than the drama using politics; 'No one can accuse the lively and tendentious Unity Theatre of political indifference.'

Among Unity Theatre's productions in 1938 was Stephen Spender's *Trial of a Judge*, which contained nothing particularly revolutionary or Russian, except that it implied the existence of a working-class. An article in *New Writing* ('Politics on the London

Stage', Spring, 1939) explains that the working-class does not have to be brought upon the stage, provided its pressure on other classes, its determining influence on events, are part of the dramatic situation, 'for politics without the working-class is like shadow-boxing as compared with a prize fight'. In Mr Spender's play it appears 'only under the form it takes in the mind of the liberal, just and humane judge, that is, as an object of pity, compassion, and sympathy. . . . It plays a passive role'. And that is a very satisfactory role, in the eyes of a Liberal. About all the Judge and the Liberal middle class can do is 'to lick and explore' their wounds, and the play dramatizes the 'mental tortures of a class in decline'.

What did working-class audiences think of these plays? John Allen, writing on the theatre in *Fact*,[11] reports what they thought about Auden and Isherwood's *Dog Beneath the Skin* and Auden's *Dance of Death*; it was, in effect, that if Mr Auden feels that way about things, he should write that way—which seems to be a very nice tolerant British point of view. But he is speaking a different language and writing for a different class, and what he says for the dissatisfied bourgeoisie has little interest for the fighting spirit of the working-class. Mr Allen concludes: 'The future of the Socialist theatre depends upon its ability to solve two straightforward but immensely difficult problems: how to get plays and how to organize an audience.'

The Soviet idea of the place of the theatre in the community was widely accepted at this period by those politically tinged with pink. But Soviet plays, being rarely produced, could exert very little literary influence. A high-spirited comment on that situation was contributed to the *Labour Monthly* in January, 1942, by Sean O'Casey. By that date a little note of jubilation had crept into the dismal atmosphere which had prevailed on the Left since the 1939 agreement between Germany and the U.S.S.R. O'Casey had seen a performance in London of Afinogenov's *Distant Point*. 'Soviet plays and Soviet films haven't been very plentiful here. Secretly, at night, and in odd corners, they have appeared, but they are seen by the few, for most of the people were terribly afraid at any hint of the existence of such a power as the Soviet Union. To them, proud of their ignorance, the Soviet land was where massed executions took place at every tick of the Kremlin clock; where everyone spent their little leisure hunting for crusts of bread; where every glance upward meant instant arrest by a prowling machine called the O.G.P.U.; and where the mass of people were rapidly becoming deaf and dumb mutes, losing the power of speech because for years and years they had been terrified into keeping their mouths closed; while the splendidly housed, richly clad, full-bellied Briton strolled around, doing whatever he listed, under the kindly and safe shelter of Neville Chamberlain's umbrella.'

It is very unlikely that Sean O'Casey's play, *The Star Turns Red* (1940), is indebted to any Soviet play, but its sympathy with Communism is obvious. Some critics prefer not to see it, others see nothing else in the play. Jules Koslow, in a recent comprehensive study of O'Casey,[12] offers an amusing list of critical samples. Stephen Spender, for instance, claims it is straight Party-line propaganda and concludes that 'the play must be bad, because the Communists are shown as good'. G. J. Nathan fears that Communism 'has now adversely affected Sean O'Casey as a dramatic artist, as a perusal of his latest play, *The Star Turns Red*, disturbingly hints'. And B. G. Brooks, commenting upon a performance in London, says that many in the audience felt that Mr O'Casey 'in his zeal for Communism had allowed his art to be sacrificed unforgivably'. Other critics avoid the issue. The play is certainly about politics, stylized and simplified in his later expressionistic manner; about the dynamic issues of 'Communism, Fascism, Trade Unionism, the role of the State and religion in politics, and the individual as a political being'. It dramatizes 'a world of opposites in which the middle way has ceased to exist'. Back of his choice of a political theme lay his long years of toil and poverty, his interest in the social problems of the dwellers in the Dublin slums, his experience in workers' organizations, his secretaryship of a workers' military organization, the Citizen Army. More recently, the political events of the 1930's had pushed him farther to the Left: 'in the play he has several passages on the civil war in Spain'. Mr Koslow sums up: 'the Nazi seizure of power in Germany is mirrored in the characters, organizations and events of the drama; alignment of the Catholic church with the Franco forces finds its parallel in the alignment of the Catholic church with the Saffron Shirts in *The Star Turns Red*'. The play is dedicated: 'To the men and women who fought through the great Dublin lock-out in nineteen hundred and thirteen', and the time is 'Tomorrow or the next day'.

But what of that Red Star? That Russian influence? For that we can turn to the autobiographical volume *Inishfallen, Fare Thee Well* (1949).[13] In the period just after the October Revolution, during the days of foreign intervention, O'Casey was in sympathy with the revolutionists, with their victory over a world in arms against them; with them, in pushing away 'the ruin they were rising from, the ruin from which all the people would one day rise'. 'The terrible beauty had been born there and not in Ireland', where the cause of the Easter Rising had been betrayed. 'The Red Star shines over the Kremlin, once the citadel of the Tsars. Those who tried hard to shake it down have fled homewards, helpless against the might and good courage of a half-starved people.' And he goes on (painting the very image of the fears of the western world), 'The Red soldiers with their Red cavalry are on the frontiers, are on the sea-edges of their vast land. Socialism has found a home and has created an army to patrol around it. The Red Star is a bright star . . .' This may be disturbing, but it is not a mere hint. In another and longer passage in the volume, where he is explaining why a certain Nora 'was not for him', he writes: 'Never once had he mentioned the Bolshevik Revolution to her, though it was ever in his mind; never once had he tried by a word to attune her ear to an echo of the march of the Red Guards, though he himself had followed, with quaking heart, the advance of Kolchak from the east and the advance of Denikin from the south. . . . The Press was full of the death and defeat of the Red madmen; then suddenly they fell silent, and Sean knew that the Red Flag was high in Moscow and Petrograd.'

This quotation cannot be carried on to its triumphant close; the often magnificent outbursts in these O'Casey books take one to exhilarating climaxes that cannot possibly be lifted out of their context.[14] Mr O'Casey is indeed 'a great hand with words', as the writer in the London *Times Literary Supplement* observed, in a recent appraisal of his genius ('The Paradox of Mr O'Casey', September 21, 1951); considering his genius as unquestioned as his judgment was dubious. As to *The Star Turns Red*, it is a play 'which, in form and apparently in purpose, had already been written many times before by less well-equipped propagandists of Communism'; but even here was 'one marvellous scene—that in which priests, cruel and gentle, politicians, spirited doctrinaires, mothers, daughters, and the nondescript poor of the streets meet in finely balanced contention about the corpse of brutality's victim'.

[1] *Century Magazine*, Dec. 1905, 'The Russian Players in New York'.
[2] *Theatre Arts Magazine*, vol. ix, 1925.
[3] *New Republic*, Feb. 28, 1923.
[4] Lee Simonson, *Part of a Lifetime*, 1943.
[5] *Yale Review*, Winter 1935, 'Red Theatres and the Green Bay Tree', by Halstead Welles.
[6] Norris Houghton, in a review of Anita Block's *Changing World in Plays* and Theatre, in *Soviet Russia Today*, May 1939.
[7] Harold Clurman, *The Fervent Years: The Story of the Group Theatre and the Thirties*, 1945.
[8] *The London Mercury*, vol. xxxii, Oct. 1935.
[9] *Left Review*, Dec. 1935.
[10] See Critics Group Pamphlets, Critics Group Press, N.Y., No. xii, 'New Writing in England', by John Lehmann.
[11] *Fact*, No. 4, July 15, 1937, 'Writing in Revolt'.
[12] Jules Koslow, *The Green and the Red: Sean O'Casey: The Man and His Plays*, 1950. Arts. Inc., New York. Quotations from Chapter vi, 'The Red Horizon'.
[13] Sean O'Casey, *Inishfallen, Fare Thee Well*. Macmillan, 1949. Pp. 220-222, and pp. 318 ff.
[14] For a later expression by O'Casey on the subject of Communism see the discussion with W. B. Yeats in *Rose and Crown*, the fifth volume of O'Casey's autobiography, pp. 148-151. (Macmillan, 1952.)

CHAPTER XII

THE PINK DECADE

i

The English Rudins

DURING THE 1930's the question of the theatre became part of the much larger question of revolutionary literature. The decade has been christened Pink. However difficult it is to isolate and to define the specifically Russian and Soviet share in the currency of certain opinions, the dissemination of certain ideas, and the form and content of certain literary productions, there can be no doubt that the influence was at work. It was only one of many; had there been no others, there might have been a Red Decade. In England—and it is to the English scene that the expression usually refers—the Pink Decade opened with the Depression (1929) and closed just before the outbreak of World War II, with the signing of the non-aggression pact between Germany and the Soviet Union in August, 1939. The climax of the European political drama of those years was the Spanish Civil War, 1936–1938. A number of Left writers volunteered on the side of the Loyalists; several of the most gifted were killed; others went at least so far into action as to attend the Writers' Congress in Madrid in 1937. Both in literary expression and in deeds, it was a feverish period. When we read the pronouncements in *Left Review* and *New Writing*, the manifestoes at the congresses for the defence of culture, the poems and the critical articles, we are reminded of that earlier age of revolutionary excitement hailed by Wordsworth—

> 'Bliss was it in that dawn to be alive,
> But to be young was very heaven.'

Yet there was a significant difference between the emotions of the two periods. It was fear quite as much as hope that stirred the

Pink Decade young men; fear and insecurity, a sense of guilt and a reluctant acceptance of social responsibility; with a readiness to fall back on Freud (who had not been available to the earlier Romantics), in order to escape from Marx (who was almost too available to the later generation). But they could not escape from Marx, because they were acutely conscious that a powerful Socialist state had been established on the basis of Marxist theories. It was no longer a spectre that was haunting Europe—it was a fact: the existence and growing strength in international affairs of a Government born in a mighty revolution, and committed to realizing, with whatever corrections and delays, the prophecies of the Communist Manifesto. The Russian influence on English writing at this period is not that of Soviet literature, as in the past it had been that of the great nineteenth century novelists. Rather it is the influence of Communist theory and Soviet practice in politics, economics and especially in the arts.

We have seen how writers interested in the theatre accepted or were tempted by the Soviet conception of the place of the theatre in the building of a new culture. There was much less agreement and less clarity about the role to be played in social change by poetry and fiction. The would-be revolutionary novelist puzzled over 'Socialist realism', which was often confused with the 'social realism' of the English tradition. And no wonder, when Soviet critics had arrived at a satisfactory definition only after years of arguing over the implications in theory and practice of this new brand of realism. What the Pink Decade really accepted was the rather vague conception of 'art for the sake of life', which they were aware had guided the major nineteenth century Russian writers, and which was not easily distinguishable from the English tradition of the humanitarian novel. But in the Soviet Union, it meant not only that the artist must have a social point of view, but that he must abandon his Ivory Tower, and take his part in the political struggles of his time. This view of the writer's duty intensified the feeling of urgency aroused by the ever more threatening international developments. The young men felt that they must act. When they volunteered to fight in Spain, they were (probably unknowingly) following in the footsteps of Turgenev's hero, Rudin, that gifted young intellectual of the 1840's, who, unable to find a way to act in Tsarist Russia, went off to France and died on the Paris barricades of the 1848 Revolution. Young English Rudins, finding no barricades in England, went off to fight on those in Madrid. 'I first read *Rudin*,' recalls Mr V. S. Pritchett in 1942, 'during the Spanish Civil War; and dying on his foreign barricade, Rudin seemed to me (and still does seem) one of "the heroes of our own time".'[1]

Mr Pritchett did not follow Rudin. Ralph Fox, Christopher Caudwell and John Cornford did, and suffered Rudin's fate. These three were convinced Communists, and their poetry, fiction and criticism is a clear and uncompromising expression of their revolutionary faith. They and the other young Rudins were not primarily interested in the civil struggle in Spain; but accepting the analysis of the world crisis that bore the stamp of Left thinking, they saw it as the overture of the world struggle against Fascism, and they saw the Soviet Union as the leader in that struggle. Mr C. Day Lewis gave vivid poetic expression to their compulsion to choose and to act, in his poem *The Conflict*, with its stanzas:

'Yet living here
As one between two massing powers I live
Whom neutrality cannot save
Or occupation cheer.

The innocent wing is soon shot down
And private stars fade in the blood-red dawn
Where two worlds strive.
For where we used to build and love
Is no man's land, and only ghosts can live
Between two fires.'

It was an uncomfortable position. Mr Lewis analysed the predicament of many writers in his pamphlet *Revolution in Writing* (1935).[2] Influenced by Freud and the psychological masterpieces of Kafka, Proust, and Joyce, they were torn between their political sympathies and their desire 'to stand up for the unconscious'. Freud's stress on the individual fitted in with the English writer's traditional individualism. The talented vaguely revolutionary young writer belonged to a generation that 'automatically applies the principles of psycho-analysis to its own motives'. The result is that he is 'seldom gravely neurotic or a self-deceiver'. Satisfied with the explanation of his individual impulses, he feels as yet little need of a 'philosophy co-ordinating these explanations', or of a scheme of values 'built out of the interpretation of individual motives and relating them to social necessities'. Generally free from those sexual conflicts 'with which orthodox Christian morality tormented his forebears for centuries', he finds the sense of guilt delivering its main attacks 'not on the sexual but on the social front'. His conscience is troubled about the miseries of his fellow men, and this creates in him the revolutionary bias; 'just as his own comparatively tolerable economic environment restrains the life-instinct from pushing him on to the final revolutionary position'. If he wishes to express the life of the workers, 'as opposed to merely exploiting it for literary purposes, the bourgeois writer must share it'. But how? Often in the pages of *Left Review*, the problem is posed in one way or another: how to synthesize working-class sympathies with middle-class background. Mr Lewis's own hero, Anthony, in the novel *Starting Point*, finally goes off to Spain, when he is no longer able to reconcile his privileged position with what he understands about the social question. And the tutor, in Edward Upward's *Journey to the Border*, makes up his mind in the end to 'go to the people', where the book does not follow him and where, one suspects, he is going to have a pretty unsatisfactory time—like Turgenev's hero Nezhdanov, in *Virgin Soil*. The hard fact is, as Mr Lewis admits (*Revolution in Writing*), this vaguely revolutionary writer can still get an adequate living out of the present economic system, and from this point of view has no incentive to be a revolutionary.

The three Communists—Fox, Caudwell and Cornford—

apparently had incentive enough. The work of Caudwell has been considered able Marxist literary criticism—at least until lately (1951), when Communist critics in the *Modern Quarterly* have been making or denying a charge against it of Freudian deviations. Fox's *The Novel and the People* has had somewhat less acclaim, but this book, his life of Lenin, his reportage and his fiction are good literature and (one speaks under correction) good Communism. He first went to the Soviet Union in 1920, to help in the hard-hit famine area, and followed every stage of development during the next fifteen years, believing that there man was becoming 'sovereign of circumstance'.[3] The youngest of the three, John Cornford, is least known, and it may be interesting to tell something of this English Rudin, for the light his brief life throws on the artist as a young Communist at this period.

A *Memoir*, edited by Pat Sloan, and including extracts from Cornford's poetry, prose articles and letters, was published in 1938, two years after his death.[4] His story, according to Mr Sloan, 'reflects the problems which a whole generation is having to face, and it points clearly to one solution of these problems'. He was the son of a Cambridge professor, and one of his teachers at Cambridge, Professor Ernest Barker, writes briefly of his first-rate mind and his deep convictions, and of 'the ultimate testimony which a man can give to his conviction'. Cornford was twenty-one when he gave this ultimate testimony; and he had been very busy since he was sixteen, forming his convictions. Ready at sixteen to enter the university, but being too young, he studied for two terms in the London School of Economics, joined the Communist party, worked in its Labour Research Department, and spoke to working-class audiences. His letters at this time mention his reading of Chekhov's plays, which somewhat puzzled him; he knew they were good, but how good? In 1932 he was learning Russian—'or going to when I find time'. His friend Tristram Jones went to Russia in August of that year, and Cornford had long political discussions with him, both before and after the visit. He was beginning to read Marx and to think of Communism, not as inevitable like measles or war, but as necessary. When his mother expressed anti-Russian views, in terms of the threat of a mechanized humanity, he thought she had somehow confused Communism and mechanization, 'though God knows that happens fast enough in capitalist countries'. Writing to her about Jung and Adler, he says (being young and untender), 'in general they only get the dregs of the unemployed rich to work on, who aren't a representative cross-section of humanity and who are mostly incurable from birth'. In his teens—and indeed he scarcely got out of them—he was reading Robert Graves, Eliot and Auden, Tolstoy and Dostoevsky. His brother tells us that he felt much current literary criticism was meaningless, because it assumed the poet or artist to exist in an aesthetic vacuum unrelated to the world around him. John's characteristic gesture in argument was to force a point home with bended arm and clenched fist; his father remarked that it combined the hammer and the sickle.

In Cambridge, where he studied history, noting that it was *class* history of a confused national variety, he found a lively Socialist movement already under way. A group of his contemporaries in the second half of the *Memoir* tell about this Cambridge socialism of the 1933–1936 period. Communists began work in the town in 1931–1932 among the working-class, organizing the unemployed and protesting against high rents. Up against a deadly indifference in the universities, they tried various kinds of shock treatment. And by 1936, 'far more "normal" young men were coming towards Communism, not because they were in revolt against social convention or cultural emptiness, but because they enjoyed life and were panicky at the thought of having it cut short. The Communist solution seemed to them not merely heroic, but common sense'. We can gain an idea of Cornford's thinking from papers published in the Cambridge *Left*, some of which are reprinted in the *Memoir*. One of them analyses some of Stephen Spender's ideas: 'Spender adheres to the doctrine that has become fundamental to the bourgeois writers of our epoch—the contradiction between art and life, between the life of the artist and the life of society. The world of the artist is considered as a metaphysical abstraction, unrelated to the world in which he lives, which produced him and his art. In so far as he is related to it, it is as the impartial observer.' There is a fundamental confusion between the 'impartiality' of the bourgeois writer and the 'objectivity' of the revolutionary writer. Bourgeois impartiality is a denial of the objective fact of the class struggle, 'a deliberate self-protection from the conclusion to which an objective study of the world today will lead'. He quotes from Spender's poem, *The Funeral*:

'They walk home remembering the straining red flags,
And with pennons of song still fluttering through their blood
They speak of the world State
With its towns like brain-centres and its pulsing arteries.'

Cornford calls this the poetry of revolution as a literary fashion, not as an historic reality, and finds it not at all surprising that Spender is a favourite with bourgeois-liberal critics: for if this is the revolution, there is no need to fear. But it isn't; 'this is only the intelligentsia playing at revolution'. One of Cornford's own poems, entitled *Sad Poem*, written at Cambridge, has a fine cluster of revolutionary images:

'You know at what forge our purpose was steeled,
At what anvil was hammered the hammer we wield,
Who cut the sickle to a cutting edge.
And under the light of our five-point star
The faces you see here are different far
From those at the closed works or fallen bridge. . . .'

The moral of Cornford's life, as Pat Sloan sees it, is pointed out in the preface: 'To middle-class readers this story may throw new light on the world in which they live and on the part which they can play in such a world. To the working-class reader, it will bring confidence, for it shows how an honest thinker, brought up in conditions in which contact with people is impossible, nevertheless decides to ally himself with the working-class movement as the only force that can save human civilization and carry it to a higher stage. Thus the professor's son becomes at the same time the holder of a First Class Honours degree and the leader of the

Communist and Socialist movement among the students of his generation.' When Cornford left for Spain, to train at Albacete and form a company that became the nucleus of the British section of the International Brigade, he took with him the first volume of *Das Kapital* and the tragedies of Shakespeare. An old war veteran, an Irishman who was with Cornford in Spain, said of him, 'He was a lovely soldier'.

Beside the young poet-Communist, let us place the old economist, turned Communist. Both portraits belong to the 'thirties, and to the Russian influence. It was at this time that Beatrice Webb (according to her biographer Margaret Cole) began to see that 'gradualness' was coming very near to meaning complete immobility, and she turned her eyes and her attention to what was happening in the East. 'She turned from journalistic accounts to absorbing the solid facts of consular reports. . . . "Old people," said Beatrice upon one occasion, "often fall in love in extraordinary and ridiculous ways—with their chauffeurs, for example: we feel it more dignified to have fallen in love with Soviet Communism." It is a good defence; and as the years went on, they only fell in love more deeply.'[5] The love affair had solid consequences in the publication of their book *Soviet Communism: A New Civilization?* (1936).

ii

A Voice from Scotland

THE 'THIRTIES, according to a writer in the London *Times Literary Supplement* (September 28, 1946), was an era above all of 'messages' in literature. 'They resounded to Mr Spender's chilly statement that "different living is not living in different places", and to the almost embarrassing helpfulness of Mr Day Lewis's "I am here to show your own divided heart". Seldom, perhaps, has the creative imagination been so anxious to illuminate as during those years, and seldom have technique and vocabulary been more opaque.' The key-book of the 'thirties was Mr Auden's *The*

Orators—'a summary of the messages which were being flashed to the public by the rival literary battle-squads: the wit, the mockery, the seriousness, the highly personal amalgam of inherited styles'. But for the particular battle-squad we are concerned with, in the effort to hold on to the slender thread of Russian influence, a key poem is Hugh McDiarmid's *First Hymn to Lenin*, which was published in a limited edition in 1931, with a dedication to D. S. Mirksy and an introduction by 'A.E.' A *Second Hymn to Lenin* appeared in the *Criterion* (July, 1932). Hugh McDiarmid is the pen-name of Christopher Murray Grieve, a Scotsman—and no nonsense about that.

Horace Gregory wrote of him in the *New Republic* (May 26, 1937): 'To the London journalist sent up to Scotland to cover reports of strikes and riots, Hugh McDiarmid . . . has been a mysterious force behind hatred of the British Empire and all its works, including capitalism. Quotations from his verse are words on banners carried by workers through the dark streets of Glasgow.' His poetic vocabulary draws upon ancient and modern Scots and English, but, according to Mr Gregory, its principal origins are in the spoken word of the Glasgow and London streets; and he speaks directly to the intellectual Scot as well as to Scotch workers. In 1943 he published *Lucky Poet: A Self-Study in Literature and Political Ideas*, where he speaks for himself with a vigour that leaves nothing for an interpreter to do.

Mr C. Day Lewis (*A Hope for Poetry*) records how the *First Hymn to Lenin* was followed by a rush of poetry sympathetic to Communism, or influenced by it; *New Signatures* (1932) marked the beginning; *New Country* (1933) followed and continued the trend. Both of the hymns are in Scots (more or less). The first has eleven six-line stanzas; we quote the first and the ninth to suggest the quality of the poem:

'Few even o' the criminals, cravens and fools
Wha's voices vilify a man they ken
They've cause to fear and are unfit to judge
As they're to stem his influence again,

But in the hollows where their herts should be
Foresee your victory.

. . . .

Christ said: "Save ye become as bairns again."
Bairnly eneuch the feck o' us ha' been!
Your work needs men; and its worst foes are juist
The traitors wha through a' history ha' gi'en
The dope that's gar'd the mass o' folk pay heed
And bide bairns indeed.'

In one stanza the poet brushes off the activities of the Cheka with what must have seemed rather startling ease to some of his readers. The second hymn makes comparisons between the work of a poet and that of Lenin, in which the poet yields nothing of final importance:

'Ah, Lenin, you were richt. But I'm a poet
(And you c'ud mak allowances for that!)
Aimin' at mair than you aimed at
Tho' yours comes first, I know it.

Poetry like politics maun cut
The cackle and pursue real ends
Unerringly as Lenin, and to that
Its nature better tends.

Wi' Lenin's vision equal poet's gift
And what unparalleled force was there!
Nocht in a' literature wi' that
Begins to compare.

. . . .

Your knowledge in your ain sphere
Was exact and complete,
But your sphere's elementary and sune by
As a poet maun see't.'

In another poem, entitled *The Seamless Garment*, the poet speaks with a cousin in a cloth mill, comparing Lenin's work with that of Rilke in his different sphere, and both Lenin's and Rilke's with that of a weaver:

> 'His secret and the secret o' a'
> That's worth ocht
> The shuttles fleein' owre quick for my een
> Prompt the thocht.
> And the co-ordination atween
> Weaver and machine.
> Lenin was like that wi' the workin' class life
>   At hame wi't a'.
> His fause movements couldna been fewer
>   The best weaver earth ever saw.'

Philip Henderson, in his book *The Poet and Society* (1939), considers McDiarmid's *First Hymn* 'the nearest that we have come to a genuinely Communist poetry, because it gives the impression of arising out of immediate contact with the working class and their lives'; and he notes a certain affinity with *The Vision of Piers Plowman.*

iii

Left Review. Fact

LITERARY-POLITICAL phases of the Left movement can be followed in *Left Review*, which ran from October, 1934, to May, 1938. The date of the first number is significant. By that time the importance of the Soviet Union in European affairs had been emphasized by its entry into the League of Nations, where the collective security policy of its representative, Litvinov, gave great impetus to 'united front' movements. The European crisis had been sharpened by the Fascist-inspired riots in Paris during February, 1934, and by the crushing of the militant Vienna workers in that same month. The editors of the new review, Amabel Williams-Ellis, Montagu Slater and T. N. Wintringham, hospitably invited many English writers, whose names had power in more than one generation and more than one class, to 'express their opposition to the warlike plans of the Imperialist Governments'. A British section of the Writers' International had been formed at a London conference in February, 1934; on its executive committee were Ralph Fox, John Strachey, Michael Davidson and Edgell Rickword, with Wintringham as secretary. The International Association of Revolutionary Writers, with which the British group was affiliated, had among its many well-known members Maxim Gorky, Romain Rolland, and Upton Sinclair. While the first issue of the new review was in press, a conference called by the Soviet Writers' Association was being held in Moscow, to which Amabel Williams-Ellis was a delegate, and which was reported in the November issue of *Left Review*.

The editors make their appeal to all writers who see in Fascism 'the terrorist dictatorship of dying capitalism', and who 'will use their pens and their influence against imperialist war and in defence of the Soviet Union, the State where the foundations of Socialism have already been laid', and who will expose the hidden forms of war against Indian, African, Irish and Chinese peoples; and to working-class writers who wish to express more effectively the struggles of their class.

Favourable responses came from Storm Jameson, Naomi Mitchison, Sylvia Warner, Ralph Bates, Winifred Holtby, Edward Upward and many others. By January, 1935, the editors can report a general agreement that the review is filling a gap in English journalism and has come to stay. Stephen Spender contributes some reflections on the Socialist artist and is pleased about those conditions in the Soviet Union which permit writers to reach a wide audience and write about matters that passionately concern the people, but he is worried over RAPP (the Association of Revolutionary Writers, which had been dissolved nearly three years before), and is inclined to hearken to Max Eastman on the subject of 'artists in uniform'. Whereupon he is taken to task by Mr Wintringham, who, though scornful of the Eastman book, recognizes that it crystallized feelings and ideas implanted in people by a long process of suggestion. And he criticizes Spender's poem *Vienna*—one of the first expressions of actual contact which the new group of poets had had with a working-class revolution—for the remoteness and coldness of its imagery in the celebration of the greatness of the defeated fighters.

The Russian novelist Sholokhov, then in London, is interviewed in March, 1935; Ralph Fox is advertised to lecture on Soviet literature in February and March at the Chantecler Restaurant in Soho; and writing contests are announced for workers on the job: narrative-descriptive passages which sound like assignments in Freshman English in American colleges. There were play-writing contests, too, and a report on the theatre season in Moscow. Sylvia Townsend Warner, hitherto rather remote from politics in her delightful fantasies, contributes a poem with the refrain 'Red, Red', which is a rousing challenge to action:

> 'Comrade, are you cold enough,
> Lean enough, bold enough—
> Hush—to march with us tonight
> Through the mist and through the blight?
> Dare you breathe the after-damp?
> Can your cunning foot the swamp
> Where you tread on the dead?
>   Red, Red . . . '

In the next few months the quality of the literary criticism becomes quite good. Alick West points out the very weak spots in D. S. Mirsky's book on the Intelligentsia of Great Britain, and is especially disturbed by Mirsky's inclination to call everybody a Fascist; for we have allies everywhere, Mr West feels, if we know how to enlist them, and we must show the past in its best light, since we need it to fight the present; Mirsky will not face the contradiction that 'we need the thought of bourgeois society to destroy bourgeois society'. A pleasant note from across the sea is the report of efforts to deport Mr John Strachey, who had gone to the United States to lecture; a Chicago paper is quoted, describing Mr Strachey as an author with forged mental credentials: his mask is literature, but his face is the face of Stalin. (May, 1935.) Mr Spender is again the target of criticism in August, when Edgell Rickword finds *The Destructive Element* lacking in clarity; Mr Spender is always inventing a Communist siren whose advances he repels. The trouble with the English intellectual is his hesitancy to recognize the class struggle; the more nakedly it declares itself, the more elaborate are the unconscious defences woven against this recognition. The backwardness of the intellectual is ascribed to the inferior mental training provided by the English school system. One wonders whether Mr Spender had this in mind when he entitled his first novel *The Backward Son*. By the end of the year there is an appeal, dismally familiar to readers of Radical magazines, for more subscriptions and help to meet debts.

As the months go on and the crisis deepens, the list of native and foreign contributors becomes more notable: Malraux, Silone and Aragon from abroad, Jack Lindsay, Bernard Shaw, Edwin Muir, Calder-Marshall, among the English. There are articles, stories, reportage, poetry, sections devoted to the cinema, the theatre and art; more competitions; reports of the achievements of the Group Theatre, the Left Theatre, the Left Book Club (40,000 members) and the Left Book Club Theatre Guild. March, 1937, marked a high point, when the Second National Congress of Peace and Friendship with the Soviet Union was held in London, with delegates said to represent some two million English men and women. Alexei Tolstoy attended. And on May Day a great celebration was advertised: 'Contributors and readers, rally to the *Left Review* banners on the Victoria Embankment.' After the international gathering of writers held in Madrid, a questionnaire sent out by the *Left Review* to every author 'of standing or promise' in England—'Are you for or against Franco and Fascism?'—brought answers published in a pamphlet called *Authors Take Sides* (November, 1937). The 'enormous preponderance of opinion' was against Fascism. Encouraged by this showing (as C. Day Lewis reported in a letter to *New Masses*, July 5, 1938), a great meeting of writers was organized in London on June 8, 1938—'the biggest and most significant meeting of writers ever held in England', with speakers and supporters whose names read like an English *Who's Who* in letters. 'At first sight, the platform looked like a living tableau of the miracle of the healing of the blind. When the speeches started, however, it soon became apparent that some of the patients had only reached the stage of seeing men like trees walking. The traditional attitude of the English writer was well exemplified by Walpole, who said that he liked to be left alone, that Fascism disturbed the writer's peace of mind, and that he would say of both Fascism and Communism, "A plague on both your houses."' Fine resolutions were passed, but Mr Lewis admits that the meeting showed the writers of the Left, in microcosm, 'all the intellectual and emotional obstacles to a popular front which exist among the intelligentsia'. They realized that they had a great deal of patient explaining to do to their colleagues about the need of a mass movement of the people 'to which writers must give both imaginative understanding and practical support.'

Many of the writers associated with *Left Review* also contributed to *Fact*, a sixpenny monograph published on the 15th of each month, under the general editorship of Raymond Postgate, with such contributing editors as Margaret Cole, Storm Jameson, George Lansbury, Francis Meynell, Stephen Spender and Arthur Calder-Marshall. Number 4, 'Writing in Revolt' (July 15, 1937), is particularly interesting for its division of material into Theory and Examples. Under Theory, Storm Jameson discusses Documents; Stephen Spender, Poetry; John Allen, Theatre; and Calder-Marshall, Fiction. Among the examples of 'writing in revolt' are *Colliery Disaster*, by J. E. Samuel, *On the Road*, by Leslie Halward, *Episode*, by James Hanley, *The Deserter*, by Stephen Spender, *I Want My Suitcase Back*, by Arthur Calder-Marshall, and two pieces from abroad: *Machine*, by the Indian writer Mulk Raj Anand, and a story by the Soviet humorist, Zoshchenko.

Storm Jameson does not like the expression 'proletarian literature', preferring 'Socialist literature'—that is, 'writing concerned with the lives of men and women in a world which is changing and being changed'. The difficulty presented by such writing is no excuse for retreating into a world 'made artificially static by excluding from it all the facts of change'. She speaks of 'the dreadful self-consciousness which seizes the middle-class writer who hears the command to sell all he has and write a proletarian novel'; when he begins to observe, he thinks of himself: 'What things *I* am seeing!' So she calls for the 'fact', and away with self-analysis, 'since that is to nail himself inside his own small ego at a moment when what is individual to each man is less real, less actual, than that which he shares with every other man—insecurity, the need to become a rebel for the sake of human dignity'. Writers should be willing to go and live for a long enough time 'at one of the points of departure of the new society . . . willing to sink themselves for a time, so that they become conduits for a feeling which is not personal or static'.

To Arthur Calder-Marshall (*Fiction*), hope for the English novel lies in the alliance of writers with the working-class and the recruitment of writers from that class. Writing about the working-class in the bourgeois tradition, showing workers to be exploited, may well provoke them to say—we don't need to be told that; what we want to know is how not to be exploited. An editorial sets forth a plan of documentary surveys, social and anthropological, of typical sections of Great Britain, including both conditions and their results on the minds and hopes of the people who live under them. The first number of *Fact* offered a study of hotel conditions, 'Behind the Swing Door', of which 2,000 copies were presented to the Transport Workers' Union and 1,000 to the National Union of Distributive Workers, as a contribution to their organizing plans. This encouragement to produce documents, to record the results of Mass Observation, has an interesting similarity with efforts in the Soviet Union, especially in the years 1928–1932 during the First Five-Year Plan. Two processes were set going: first that of making observers, and then active factory and farm workers, out of professional writers; and second, the reverse process of turning workers into literary shock-troops. Contact with the masses had to be developed, Socialist competition stimulated in this field, collective writing projects organized. Writers went off on observation tours, singly and in squads. Mass participation in journalism, to develop writers out of workers and peasants, produced by the end of 1931 two million journalistic novices, and it was hoped that new forces would pour into literature along the channels of the mass Soviet Press. The idea was that those worker and peasant correspondents who were 'capable of proceeding from factual reporting to thinking in images—from casual journalism to creative writing—would rise to the next phase, creative art'. The discussions of the period constantly stress *creativeness* as the goal.[6]

Maxim Gorky, who approved of these efforts, had, himself, 'participated' by economic necessity in the life of the working class. Whether English proponents of this method of learning about the society we live in were in any precise way acquainted with the Russian experiments is a subject for research. Similarly in the United States, under the New Deal, writing projects resulted in documentary books of great sociological and sometimes literary value, such as *These Are Our Lives*. The movement comes out of a very laudable ambition that writers should know what they are talking about, and from the suspicion that many of them don't. Many American writers, not held so closely within class compartments as in England, had what seemed to the English enviable job experience of the most proletarian sort, whether they wanted it or not. It is amusing to find in an article in *New Writing* (spring, 1941), 'Artist of the 'Thirties' by Walter Allen, a statement that Henry Green was able to write a novel about a foundry, because his father owned one and he could 'move up and down the social scale as he pleased'. Christopher Isherwood had to go to Berlin to see some working-class life, whereas Mr Green just had to go to Birmingham, and enjoyed 'some of the advantages of the Americans'. Mr C. Day Lewis pointed out to *New Masses* readers the disadvantages under which the English novelists laboured; and showed how it was partly 'this dearth of experience outside a class which they have now rejected' that had turned two remarkable writers to allegory—Rex Warner and Edward Upward.[7] A turn in that direction, one may add, would certainly lead them to Kafka rather than to Gorky.

In a review of Gorky's novel *The Spectre* in the *New Statesman and Nation* (May 14, 1938), there is an interesting equating of the plight of English and other Western intellectuals with that of the Russian intellectuals in the period covered by Gorky's book: 'What Gorky intended was to expose the paralysis that attacks the majority of intellectuals when once they realize that the system in which they live is doomed; and he has succeeded so well that *The Spectre* seems to include portraits of a great many people one knows. It is anything but reassuring to realize that from 1905 on, educated political discussions in Russia were absolutely indistinguishable from those in Paris and New York and even parts of London today. . . . Problem for problem, the situation is derisive in its similarity and nothing could be more instructive than Samghin's scrupulous, helpless, fatal havering.'

iv

Analysis and Retrospect

THE SITUATION after September, 1939, and before the Nazi invasion of Russia in June, 1941, created ideological confusions among the intellectuals in England and the United States that still divide them and embitter almost every area of discussion—not least, the literary. During the four years that followed till the end of the war, the atmosphere cleared a little, only to become increasingly murky, with new confusions to complicate the old. As the writers of the Pink Decade looked back from 1939 upon their activities, they may have pondered Christopher Caudwell's analysis, in *Illusion and Reality*, of the artist in times of change. For the artist in bourgeois society, he wrote, there were three possible roles in relation to the working class: opposition, alliance, or assimilation. Among those of his contemporaries who were trying the role of alliance, there was a realization that they must somehow work with the proletariat and engage in united action, but they were reluctant to join a political party, like the Communist. 'They announce themselves as prepared to merge with the proletariat, to accept its theory and its organization, in every field of concrete living except that of art. Now this reservation—unimportant to an ordinary man—is absolutely disastrous for an artist, precisely because his most important function is to be an artist. It leads to a gradual separation between his living and his art—his living as a proletarian diverging increasingly from his art as a bourgeois . . . this separation cannot take place without a mutual distortion. His proletarian living bursts into his art in the form of crude and grotesque scraps of Marxist phraseology and the mechanical application of the living proletarian theory. . . . They often glorify the revolution as a kind of giant explosion which will blow up everything they feel to be hampering them. But they have no constructive theory—I mean as artists: they may as economists accept the economic categories of Socialism, but as artists they cannot see the new forms and contents of an art which will replace bourgeois art. They know something is to come after this giant firework display of the Revolution, but they do not feel with the clarity of an artist the specific beauty of this new concrete living, for they are by definition cut off from the organization which is to realize it; and which therefore alone holds in its bosom the nascent outlines of the future.'[8]

Looking back to the poets of the Industrial Revolution period, who, like Byron and Shelley, did in a sense come over from their own class to another, Caudwell says: 'These deserters are in moments of revolution always useful and always dangerous allies. . . . They are always individualistic, romantic figures, with a strong element of the poseur. They will the destruction of their own class but not the rise of the other, and this rise, when it becomes evident and demands that they change their merely destructive enmity to the dying class to a constructive loyalty to the new, may, in act, if not in word, throw them back into the arms of the enemy.'

How Caudwell, had he lived, would have interpreted the changed scene is a fascinating, but fruitless, speculation. He died —perhaps another example of the love the gods are supposed to have for the young. Those who did not die were spurred to self-examination by their own honesty as well as by the criticism that came from outside their group. Some of this was witty, but superficial or contemptuous. Malcolm Muggeridge, in one of those 'only yesterday' books on the ideas and activities, fads and follies of a period, *The 'Thirties: 1930–1940 in Great Britain* (1940), wrote: 'Young men with beards sold the *Daily Worker* in the streets; novelists led their heroes by devious ways to solidarity with the toiling masses, and poets sang in *vers libres* the praises of the Soviet Union. The Film Society strenuously applauded the storming of the Winter Palace at Petrograd in the many versions of it presented; and the Unity Theatre was satirical to the delight of largely unproletarian audiences. Fathers in clubs complained that their sons had become Communists at Oxford; and well-brought-up daughters announced sometimes in the presence of servants that they proposed henceforth to devote themselves wholly to the Class War.' (Page 201.) 'To the Left Book Club's standard flocked Friends of the Soviet Union, Popular Front advocates, near and actual Communists, all the restlessly progressive who have nothing to lose but their hopes.'[9]

Virginia Woolf was analytical and compassionate. She made the plight of the sad young men the subject of an address before the Workers' Educational Association in Brighton, in May, 1940, which was printed in *New Writing* (Autumn, 1940), under the title *The Leaning Tower*. English writers for generations, with very few exceptions, according to Mrs Woolf, had surveyed the world of which they wrote from a tower built upon privileges of class status and education—a tower so steady until about 1914 that the writers were scarcely conscious that theirs was a tower view. The generation that grew up during the First World War and began to write in the middle 'twenties—Lewis, Auden, Spender, MacNeice, Isherwood, Rex Warner—were all in her view tower-dwellers, sons of the well-to-do, educated at private schools and universities. But their tower view showed changes in the social landscape; neatly marked class hedges were being uprooted, structures of privilege falling down; and their books were written under the threat of change and war. As their own towers began to lean, they became acutely tower-conscious. First they felt discomfort, then self-pity, then anger against the society which had built the towers, then guilt because they continued to enjoy the privileges, however insecure, of the tower—this tower founded upon injustice, giving a small class privileges for which other people paid. But how to right the injustice? With their minds full of discord and bitterness, confusion and compromise, Mrs Woolf found it not surprising that their plays, poems and novels were not great. 'When everything is rocking around one, the only person who remains comparatively stable is oneself.' So they wrote about themselves, and she thought that they wrote honestly and creatively on that theme.

Elizabeth Bowen expressed her opinion of the group in a review of a Pelican *New Writing*, in the *Spectator* (January 17, 1941). The literary movement represented in the *New Writing* volumes of the 'thirties was, Miss Bowen wrote, the Romantic Movement of our century. She stressed its explicitly political direction, its youthful and masculine quality, and its European character; it was active in France and Spain and Italy and pre-Nazi Germany and Left-wing America; and it was 'towered over by an idea, *its* idea, of the U.S.S.R.' The war in Spain was its rallying-point and symbol. The prose adventures of the English movement were happiest in the realm of Kafka-like fantasy, rather than in the realistic reportage efforts. The writers had complete integrity, but were unable to generalize or synthesize and lacked irony. Illustrating a common tendency to idealize some world to which one does not by birth belong, the young men of middle-class origin sought an idealized proletariat. Calling themselves intellectuals, they located themselves, whether abroad or in England, inside the intellectual world; isolated, special, charged with personal feeling, they were in the long run as 'claustrophobic as any middle-class home'. 'Would it be unfair to say,' she concluded, 'of this group of writers that, though they changed their milieu, they never fully emerged, but remained life's delicate children after all?'

Some of life's delicate children answered their critics, and then answered each other's answers. Arthur Calder-Marshall, reviewing a Penguin *New Writing* in the *New Statesman and Nation* (February 15, 1941), wrote: 'I think that most writers who began their careers in the 'thirties are like me in looking back on that decade with a sense not of triumph but of shame and failure. We accomplished something, but how little it was compared to what was necessary.' But there had never been a decade in which so large a body of dissident writers felt enough unity to refer to themselves in the first person plural. 'We believed in the necessity for social revolution, in the common humanity of the artist and the identity of his ultimate good with that of the working class. We differed considerably about means, but our social analysis had enough in common for us to be able to agree.' There were minor successes: the writer's isolation was broken down, his claim to active citizenship renewed; writers showed themselves more sensitive to events in Europe than any other professional body, and mixed more freely than their predecessors with people of every class. 'Yet as a group of writers, we shall probably be judged by posterity as moral, political and artistic failures, each aspect of that failure being implicit in the whole. . . . The certainty of what was wrong with the middle-class was stronger than its corollary, the need to join with the working class.' Their financial success depended on the controllers of middle-class opinion, and they did not have courage enough to break away from this middle-class book market. They also refused to work in close co-operation with any political party. 'The pattern of the growth of Fascism, which obsessed the work of the 'thirties, was an intellectual formula, evolved by schoolmasters who knew no Fascists or Communists, no armament manufacturers or international gunmen.' He agrees with Virginia Woolf that their autobiographical work has value. 'Their political writing is bad, not because it is political, but because it was never lived.'

Stephen Spender, answering next week in *New Statesman and Nation*, modifies but does not really disagree with this verdict. The writers of the 'thirties suffered from two intuitions: a sense of what was going to happen, in most of which he considers them completely justified; and a sense of being outside the social machinery of their time. They felt that 'the inexorable machinery of doomed politics was beyond their reach', and that they were 'equally shut out from the life of the people at the level of most compressed living: the workers, socially fettered, who alone might have stopped the political machine, to release forces of joy within themselves and within us'. They knew what was happening; 'why go to Spain to prove it, unless one really was qualified to act there? Why have to seek the corroboration of the moral support of one small politically conscious section of the working classes, before "we" dared put what we knew down on paper? The fact is, we lacked confidence in our own humanity. We did not believe even that we really lived until we had it proved to us by someone else. We thought that we were isolated; but if we had accepted that isolation, it might have been a shaft leading deep down into the sources of a common humanity including all classes and all countries.'

John Lehmann, editor of *New Writing* from its first number in 1936, delivered a lecture in Czechoslovakia in 1945 on 'English Letters and the European Vision: 1930–1945',[10] in which he refers to the upsurge of innovating zeal among a group of young writers in the 'thirties, turning to a more and more political and revolutionary temper; until, with 'the disappointment of the Left-wing dreams of the period, the original fervour burnt itself away'. After Munich they began to wonder whether, by their political activites, they were truly fulfilling their responsibilities as artists —'more important than anything else'. The desire to play an ever more busy role in purely political agitation frequently led to a writer's allowing himself to be 'manipulated by unscrupulous politicians for their own ends in their own complicated and not entirely spotless game of party intrigue and party vendetta'. When the war with Germany broke out, 'the ebb was complete except among those who had always been politicians first and artists second'. Mr Lehmann's definition of the English tradition to which these writers returned includes, among other fine things, a hatred of political expediency; it is a tradition always inspired, as he understands it, 'by the basic values of our common Christian and classical civilization'. And so Mr Lehmann leaves the politicians to their own inspirations and expediencies, which are perhaps classical, if not always Christian.

A younger literary generation, expressing its views in *New Writing and Daylight*, during the war years, passed a harsh judgment on its Pink Decade predecessors: it was a myth that the 'Auden-group' were rebels, a myth fostered by the group itself, prompted by 'nothing more substantial than the transient ebullience of political enthusiasm'; the effect of the group on the next writing generation was 'appalling'; the movement of the 'thirties had a 'baneful influence'; the incursion of Left-wing politics into literature was 'disastrous'.[11] But the last word should, in courtesy, be given to one of the 'rebels'. Mr C. Day Lewis, in his lectures at Cambridge in 1946, spoke of functional imagery in relation to the achievements of his own and the later group:

> 'Functional imagery—the use of images to underline and bring home generally accepted ideas—produces its own kind of image pattern. It is a clear-cut lucid pattern, because images best serve ideas by being so disposed within it as to muffle all their associations except the one required. The danger of such a disposition is that, unless the ideas are passionately realized by the poet, it tends to produce conventional ornament, as it sometimes did with the Augustans; and unless the ideas are also generally accepted, it will produce hollow conceit. The latter failing is to be found in much of the verse written by the so-called "political" school of the thirties. The ideas they sought to illuminate in their verse, whether Marxist or Freudian or formed by an attempted synthesis of the two, were not in fact generally accepted, and therefore the images they gave off were impaired by that fancifulness, that emotional thinness, we associate with conceits. In reaction from this, the youngest

generation of poets today have swung right away from what they call the classicism of their immediate predecessors; to generalize, their verse is more sensuous, which is all to the good, and more personal; but on the other hand it either shies away from ideas altogether, or else uses them as convenient nails from which to hang festoons of imagery.'[12]

[1] *New Statesman and Nation*, Jan. 17, 1942.

[2] *Revolution in Writing—Day to Day Pamphlets*, No. xxix, by C. Day Lewis. Hogarth Press, 1935.

[3] See *Ralph Fox: A Writer in Arms*, edited by John Lehmann, T. A. Jackson, C. Day Lewis. With introductions by Harry Pollitt, Sidney Webb, Ralph Bates, Michael Gold, John Lehmann, T. A. Jackson, and Dona Torr. London, Lawrence and Wishart, 1937. The volume contains extracts from Fox's work as historian, of past and present, imaginative writer, political theorist and literary critic.

[4] *John Cornford*. Memoir by Pat Sloan. London, Jonathan Cape, 1938.

[5] *Beatrice Webb*, by Margaret Cole. Longmans, Green & Co., 1945. Chapter xv.

[6] See *Soviet Literary Theory and Practice during the First Five-Year Plan 1928-1932*, by Harriet Borland. King's Crown Press, Columbia University, 1950.

[7] *New Masses*, June 7, 1938. 'A Letter from London', by C. Day Lewis.

[8] *Illusion and Reality*, by Christopher Caudwell, 1937. New edition 1946, Lawrence and Wishart, London. For quotations, see pp. 282-285, and Chapter v.

[9] An erratum slip, pasted in on the title-page, suggests that on this topic the author was more witty than accurate: 'Mr Stephen Spender wishes to deny the accuracy of the author's statement regarding him on page 248.' The statement reads: 'Spender announced his departure for Insurgent territory, where he proposed to operate as a spy.'

[10] See *Review* (a quarterly of literature, art and science, G. Allen & Unwin, London), vol. ii, Winter 1945-46.

[11] See, for example, *New Writing and Daylight*, summer 1943, 'The End of an Impulse', by Henry Reed; and Winter 1943-44, 'Decline and Future of the English Novel', by Philip Toynbee.

[12] *The Poetic Image*, by C. Day Lewis, Oxford University Press, 1947. Pp. 81-2.

CHAPTER XIII

ART FOR LIFE

i

'An Artist Caste'

'IN ISOLATING the concept of literature,' to quote Mr T. S. Eliot, 'they destroy the life of literature. . . . Even the purest literature is alimented from non-literary sources and has non-literary consequences.'[1] Literature plays a role in social systems that I have heard discussed by a sociologist under the headings of *integration*, *isolation*, *opposition* and *conformity*.[2] If we think of the major writers at any specified period in the history of a social system, we find them either whole-heartedly pulling with the team, or standing aloof, or actively in opposition, or conforming—conformity often implying acquiescence with some inner reservations. In some periods, literature seems, as we look back, to be harmoniously integrated with the social order. Most of the great writers in nineteenth-century Russia were in opposition; whereas the aim for writers under the Soviet régime is integration, although the achievement, so far, as most Western critics see it, is conformity. But both under the old and the new régimes in Russia, writers have been conscious to an unusual degree of obligations to their society, *as artists*.[3] During the 1930's in England and the United States, many writers were acutely conscious of their obligations. The question was forced upon them by the uneasiness of the times, and given a special pertinence by what seemed to be happening to art and letters in the Soviet Union. It was not a new question. An excellent statement of the problems involved appeared in a London *Times Literary Supplement* article on September 28, 1946—somewhat retrospective in tone—of which the opening paragraph reads:

'There is no sign that the debate on the obligations towards society of the artist or scientist is coming to an end. Argument round and about the subject, however, proceeds all too often at a platonic level, whereas it can be pursued with advantage only by reference to specific historical conditions. For there are no absolutes of social function. Different phases of material organization in the history of Western society have carried with them different conceptions of the balance of rights and obligations of the individual, and in that context the supreme instance of the individual in society is the creative artist or scientist. So far as the historical evidence goes, the degree of freedom which either has enjoyed to follow his own bent in isolation from the needs or desires of the community seems to have depended upon the relative stability of social and political institutions. On the whole, greater stability favours "pure" art and "pure" research. In the marked absence of stability there is intensified discussion of the responsibilities of the creative intelligence to society and the State, and from this discussion spring *la littérature engagée* and, in more recent times, the conception of "planned" science. The simple fact is that writers, artists, thinkers, scientists, research workers—in a word, the general body of intellectuals—have always been specially involved, and are perhaps more intimately involved today than at any time before, in the changing relationship of the individual towards the authority of the State.'[4]

The relative stability of social and political institutions in Victorian England as compared with Tsarist Russia, and the difference in the degree of freedom for writers, would certainly not have been questioned by Turgenev, talking with Thackeray or George Eliot; or Herzen, editing his paper *The Bell* in his London exile; or Kropotkin, lecturing and publishing freely in England at the end of the century. Up to 1914 the sharp contrast continues; after that, stability ceased to characterize the political situation anywhere. But Russia was particularly troubled, struggling to build a new society on the ruins of the old, and never free from the actualities or the fears or both of hostile attack from without. Russian writers, then, had developed through many decades a characteristic attitude of *opposition* to the State; but after the Revolution, if they remained in Russia, they were drawn by one means or another into *co-operation* with the Government. The changed situation is often stated in what is inevitably an over-simplified form: before 1917 the writer was told what he *must not do* and afterwards, what he *must* do—a positive control thus replacing a negative one. That, at least, is the way in which the West has understood the situation. In the first period the opposition may sometimes have been reluctant and, in the second, the co-operation may sometimes be half-hearted and uneasy. But an attitude of artistic detachment and political indifference was much more rare in Russia than in the West, and much more subject to criticism. Chekhov was accused of being 'indifferent' by politically-minded contemporaries because he refused to be labelled. 'I am not,' so he answered the charge, 'a Liberal, not a Conservative, not a believer in gradual progress, not a monk, not an indifferentist. I should like to be a free artist and nothing more, and I regret that God has not given me the power to be one.'[5] Neither God, nor, we may add, society; for hating 'lying and violence in all their forms', he had to fight against them in his own way, which was less direct than Tolstoy's way, though of all beliefs Chekhov considered Tolstoy's the nearest and most akin to his own.

ii

'*What is Art?*'

MUCH OF the late nineteenth-century English and American debate over realism, French and Russian, was a groping after a valid distinction between art for art's sake and art for life's sake. There was something in the realism of the great Russian novelists that eluded precise definition. A clue lay in the school of Russian criticism that was scarcely known except to a few scholars like Turner and Isabel Hapgood. Had it been known, Tolstoy's *What is Art?* (1898) would have seemed less eccentric, immodest and wrong-headed than it did to many people, and more in accord with Russian critical tradition.

The close working together of creative writer and critic marked Russian literary history to an unusual degree. This co-operation (by no means always smooth) began with the critics Belinsky and Dobrolyubov, and the novelists Gogol, Turgenev and Goncharov. Famous essays were Belinsky's *View of Russian Literature for the Year* 1847, and Dobrolyubov's *What is Oblomovism.* English readers, until very recently, knew of the work of these critics only from brief and incidental reference and short extracts in such anthologies as Wiener's. Sir John Maynard (*Russia in Flux*) speaks of 'the frequently recurring strain in Russian thought which, long before the Bolsheviks, demands social value from art and condemns art for art's sake'. At a memorial meeting in Moscow in 1948, marking the centenary of Belinsky's death, he was proclaimed the 'founder of the aesthetics of classical realism'. Belinsky considered literature as a product of society, reflecting and expressing its development, influencing and educating it; a work of art must be seen in relation to the historical moment in which it appears, and the attitude of the artist to society; consideration of aesthetic values must be combined with an analysis of social and historical significance. But art must first of all be art, for only then can it be the expression of the spirit and direction of society in a given epoch. Belinsky's famous analysis of Gogol's work seems to have been something of a surprise and a shock to Gogol himself, who was not a realist and a social critic by intention. When later he went his own way through a religious crisis and destroyed some of his own work, he was soundly rebuked by Belinsky in a public letter for his apostacy to the cause of human progress. Turgenev was both more aware and more docile. One of his biographers, Mr Yarmolinsky, notes how seriously he accepted the admonition: study the times in which you live; give us recognizable types of men and women; show us how they affect and are affected by our immediate social problems. His friend Flaubert had never been told that he must convey the body and pressure of his own time. 'This insistence on the writer's civic responsibility worked upon the diffident and malleable man that Turgenev was. It led him to fasten his attention upon the social and contemporary aspect of life with greater concentration than if he had followed the promptings of his own unpolitical mind.'

As the years went on, authors and critics agreed and disagreed, but by and large the tradition of realism and of art for the sake of life grew stronger. When Tolstoy's essay *What is Art?* was translated, it shocked many Western minds because of what seemed its capricious and dogmatic dismissal of much art hitherto considered sacrosanct; but to Russians his ideas were familiar, though they had never before been expressed so uncompromisingly and so brilliantly.

Art, wrote Tolstoy, is a human activity, and as such must have a clear purpose and aim; it cannot exist for its own sake alone. Its value must be weighed in proportion as it is serviceable or harmful to mankind. It is not only certain people with trained sensibilities who can respond to art; the response is latent in the peasant child, and Tolstoy knew this from his experience many years before in teaching the peasant children on his estate. Art is not the production of pleasing objects; it is not pleasure, but a means of union among men, joining them together in the same feelings and indispensable for the progress towards well-being of individuals and of humanity. Bad as well as good feelings may be contagious, and of course the better the feelings in which art unites men, the better for humanity. When hostile people are united by music or story or picture, and feel union and mutual love, 'each is glad that another feels what he feels; glad of the communion established not only between him and all present, but also with all now living who will yet share the same impression; and more than that, he feels the mysterious gladness of a communion which, reaching beyond the grave, unites us with all men of the past who have been moved by the same feelings and with all men of the future who will yet be touched by them. And this effect is produced both by religious art which transmits feelings of love of God and one's neighbour, and by universal art transmitting the very simplest feelings common to all men.'[6]

Foreign critics were not surprisingly annoyed by the notion that a simple folk-tale or song which delights millions is 'better' art than an opera or symphony or novel which diverts a few members of a privileged class especially trained to enjoy them. Art accessible only to members of such a class was, to Tolstoy, as perverted as the social system that exploited the many for the benefit of the few. But the importance of *What is Art?* does not lie in the immodest judgments upon some works of art, but in the expression of Tolstoy's faith in the innate artistic instincts of men, uniting them in a community of feeling, making for the brotherhood of man.

It was in that Christian sense of the brotherhood of man that William Dean Howells accepted Tolstoy's views; it was Tolstoy whose supreme art 'had its highest effect in making me set art for ever below humanity'.[7] The dean of American letters, in this undogmatic and, one must admit, rather vague way, placed himself in the 'art for life' camp. He was not among those who regretted that Tolstoy had turned to prophesying, and he declared in 1908, in an article on the occasion of Tolstoy's eightieth birthday, that no fiction Tolstoy might have written would have consoled him for the loss of *My Confession*, *What Is to be Done?*, *The Kingdom of God* and *What is Art?* Tolstoy's work, both ethically and aesthetically, had been like the experience of a religious revival to Howells: 'things that were dark or dim before, were shone upon by a light so clear and strong that I needed no longer grope my way to them'.[8]

Paul Elmer More, reviewing *What is Art?* in the course of an essay in the *Atlantic Monthly* (September, 1900) entitled 'The Ancient Feud between Philosophy and Art', was impressed by its 'terrible and relentless logic', but he considered Tolstoy's answer to the question 'a denial of all that has made art noble in the past, and a challenge to those who seek to continue that tradition in the present'. More then goes back to Plato, 'himself a renegade from among the worshippers of beauty'; he examines the various concepts of truth and beauty among the Greeks, the early Church fathers, the men of the Reformation and of the Renaissance;

always the same unending conflict is revealed, in which a shrewd stroke has now been delivered by 'one of the barbarians of the north'. 'The true balance was never attained, or if attained, was held but for a moment; and the sensuous love of beauty severed from the deeper moral instincts of humanity, dragged out a spurious existence, until now it is seen in the most degraded forms of modern French art.' Tolstoy is the spokesman for that humanitarianism which is a religion of our age; art for art's sake is a revolt against that religion. Examining Tolstoy's test for art—the communication of feeling—More notes the implications of sympathy, not judgment, as the goal of culture. How can the feeling of the common Russian peasant be the touchstone of art? But this Russian fanatic is a man of our age, and 'hidden in the heart of each of us lies this same curious deference to the untrained individual'. Yet More is willing to admit that the acceptance of humanitarianism in its crudest form is an advance over the exclusiveness of art for art's sake; and the celebration of humility, purity, compassion and love is better than that of pride, sexual desire and weariness of life. When Tolstoy says that art is not a pleasure, a solace, an amusement, but a great matter, More forgives him much for that trumpet call. But when your goal is brotherly union among men, are you not moving in a vicious circle, attempting to unite men for the mere sake of union?

Bernard Shaw reviewed *What is Art?* in the *Daily Chronicle* (September 10, 1898)[9] and, like More, is dubious about testing art by its accessibility to the Russian peasant. Perhaps the Russian peasant is a better touchstone than the English labourer, but 'there is nothing whatever to choose between the average country gentleman and his gamekeeper in respect of distaste for the Ninth Symphony'. Shaw brushes off Tolstoy's attacks on Wagner, Beethoven and other idols, as 'the inevitable obsolescence of an old man's taste in art'. But he is in basic agreement with him on communication of feeling as the function of art, and on the social importance of art. 'Art is socially important—that is, worth writing a book about—only in so far as it wields that power of propagating feeling which he adopts as his criterion of true art.

It is hard to knock this truth into the heads of the English nation. We admit the importance of public opinion, which, in a country without intellectual habits . . . depends altogether on public feeling. Yet instead of perceiving the gigantic importance which this gives to the theatre, the concert-room and the bookshop, as forcing houses of feeling, we slight them as mere places of amusement and blunder along upon the assumption that the House of Commons and the platitudes of a few old-fashioned leader writers are the chief fountains of English sentiment. . . . Our artistic institutions are vital social organs.' Tolstoy probably did no more than confirm Shaw's already formed opinions. But confirmation by an artist of the first rank, and a man of the world besides—a point emphasized in Shaw's article—must have been very reassuring.

On another occasion when Shaw expressed himself with vehemence on the subject of art and life, he aligned himself with the native Puritans. 'I have,' he is quoted as saying in *Table Task*, 'always been Puritan in my attitude to art. I am as fond of fine music and handsome buildings as Milton was, or Cromwell, or Bunyan; but if I found that they were becoming the instruments of a systematic idolatry of sensuousness, I would hold it good statesmanship to blow up every cathedral in the world to pieces with dynamite, organ and all, without the least heed to the screams of the art critics and the cultured voluptuaries.' This attitude is in accord with Shaw's view of Tolstoy's purpose, as Shaw interpreted it in the preface to *Heartbreak House*, of tearing down the house in which Europe was stifling its soul. Puritanism dies hard. The article on an artist caste, quoted earlier in this chapter, refers to 'the new Puritanism of the younger generation of poets' of the Pink Decade, who put 'social salvation before art'.

iii

Responsible and Irresponsible Artists

THE PRE-REVOLUTIONARY Russian literary tradition was not, of course, all of a piece. In the 'nineties and later, there were modernist movements, stressing aesthetic and individual values in preference to political and social; there were distinguished spokesmen for mystical and religious values in literature. Poets were influenced by the French Symbolists; there were Symbolist, Imagist, Futurist and other movements. Mayakovsky, who became the poet of revolutionary Russia, was a Futurist before 1917.[10] After an upheaval like the October Revolution, no inherited tradition survives unchanged. There are dependable accounts in English of Soviet literary history, from which we can infer that a synthesis has been taking place since 1932 between the young literature founded in the 'twenties and the great traditions of the nineteenth century. A process of re-evaluation and assimilation has been going on, jerkily at first, steadily since 1932; what is called 'the literary heritage' has received the devoted attention of scholars; the Russian classics have been issued in editions of increasing size with the spread of literacy. Soviet literature, in the words of Professor Ernest J. Simmons (*Outline of Modern Russian Literature*), is 'thoroughly penetrated by a social consciousness and a profound responsibility to the people'; and what is called *Socialist realism* 'attempts to integrate literature and life, to direct the creative present towards a more meaningful creative future'.[16]

Put in these general terms, this attempt to integrate past and present and direct the present towards the future, sounds simple. How complicated it actually is, how entirely unlike a crude process of coercion, of issuing directives and putting on uniforms, can be discovered by the curious reader of Harriet Borland's study of the first five-year plan in Soviet literature, 1928–1932.* No one, especially if he has read the over 700 footnotes that support the text, will be much disposed to easy generalization. To make creative work in literature a form of participation in the class struggle was the objective of that Association of Revolutionary Writers, known as RAPP, which was finally dissolved in 1932, after the trying out of all sorts of experiments and of many varieties of control. Gorky was one of the leading advocates of the final dissolution. But Gorky, according to Miss Borland, ex-

* See footnote [6] to chapter xii.

pressed the sentiments of the majority of writers in believing that they must make sacrifices to the revolutionary demands of the epoch, and so re-educate themselves that they would find service to the social revolution also a source of gratification to them as individuals. The idea of RAPP was not so much to dictate as to help the writer to perceive 'the social command'. There is no doubt that he was helped. But Miss Borland justly comments: 'Many Soviet writers undoubtedly did feel so thoroughly in harmony with the existing order of things that they were conscious of no repression.'

This matter of a 'social command' is not easily disposed of by regarding it as characteristic only of authoritarian societies. An author in England or the United States is helped to perceive the social command in ways that are often powerful, even if indirect or hidden; when for example he cannot find a publisher (we assume here an able writer with minority views about morals or economics or politics), or when because of his opinions or his associations he loses his job or his reputation in some of the more disturbed periods of our history. To be quite unconcerned with the 'social command', a writer must be economically independent of returns from his writing. One recalls Virginia Woolf's plea for a 'room of one's own' and an income of 300 pounds a year. All the writers ask for, observed Stephen Spender in 1936, is a 'little annuity that will enable us to live as civilized people—to go to concerts, buy a piano, live in a room of one's own, take a holiday by the seaside, entertain our friends, be free from the anxiety of not knowing where the next meal will come from', and they think that has nothing to do with politics; politics concerns just the life they want to escape.[11] But where does the little income come from?

In the 1920's, while the Soviet writers within their change-rocked country were struggling with their obligations to society as citizen-artists, writers in England and the United States were, many of them, in a mood to shake off responsibilities. The picture in the United States is perhaps over-familiar. The Irresponsibles were later castigated by some of their fellow-writers—Van Wyck

Brooks, Archibald MacLeish, and others—for their indifference to politics, for their absorption in their own specialties and their own coteries. The castigators did not make it very clear how a writer was to shoulder his responsibility, how distinguish between 'servitude' to the Fascist or Communist State (by 1940 the two were usually presented as identical), and the political activities of a Milton (in co-operation with a régime) and a Voltaire (in opposition). 'Why,' wrote Mr MacLeish in 1940, 'did we, scholars and writers in America in this time, we who had been warned of our danger not only by explicit threats but by explicit action, why did we not fight this danger while the weapons we used best—the weapons of ideas and words—could still be used against it?'[12] This brief cry of anguish in the form of a Declaration throws out only a few interesting suggestions in answer to the question it raises. Kenneth Burke, several years earlier when the threats were not so explicit, raised the issue of responsibility in discussing 'pure' art, in an article, 'The Nature of Art under Capitalism', in the *Nation* (December 13, 1933). 'Pure' art promotes a state of acceptance and becomes a social menace in so far as it assists us to tolerate the intolerable; it may thus help to uphold an unethical state of affairs. When there is something pretty unsound in the social system, art should not be content merely with using the values arising out of that system and integrating their conflicts. It must be partially forensic, and have a definite hortatory function and an element of suasion. But so long as a given state of affairs—even though found on intellectualist grounds to be intolerable—is with us, we have to contrive to tolerate it. Hence, along with our efforts to alter it, must go the demand for an imaginative equipment that helps to make it tolerable while it lasts. 'Much of the pure or acquiescent art of today serves this invaluable psychological end.'

Artists, then, may be fulfilling their social responsibilities in very different ways. But when there is a very widespread impression that things are most unsound indeed, the emphasis on the writer's obligations tends to shift from making the intolerable as tolerable as possible, to helping to change the intolerable to something more bearable. That was the emphasis in the Pink Decade.

Stephen Spender, often criticized in the 1930's for uncertainties and reservations in his efforts to be the 'responsible' artist, was less inclined later than some of his fellow Leftists to wash his hands of politics and denounce the politicians for exploiting his innocence. He continued to ponder over the problem of artist and society, and to see the artist's responsibility as part of the responsibility of all citizens. In his book *European Witness* (1946)[13], written after some months of travel on special missions in France and Germany in 1945, he speaks of the fascination over many minds today of the idea of destruction; 'many sensitive people begin to abandon ideas of reconstruction for the acceptance of the idea of a destructive fate'. We have the choice of making a heaven or a hell of the world in which we live, and cannot evade the act of choosing. 'We are confronted,' he continues, 'with this choice between creation and destruction immediately after a period in our history when it had seemed that morals were simply an affair of private conduct and that no necessity of making a moral choice confronted the whole of society. The characteristic of modern industrial society was surely the transference of responsibility for government first away from kings and aristocracies, then away from governments, classes and even nations, to a mechanical interaction of forces directed by certain interests of class and wealth. No individual was wholly responsible for events in a world where policy was the direction of many inter-related actions, and where any one act produced such widespread repercussions throughout the entire world that it became absorbed at once into results which developed beyond and in different directions from the initial action.' After a further analysis of this society of competing self-interested motives, Mr Spender notes that although many people had a sense of guilt for the injuries it inflicted and although there were acts of atonement and reform, no one felt personally responsible for the events around him. As for the artist, 'a sense of enlightened social irresponsibility became a sign of the intelligent adaptability of artists. It became stupid to think, for example, that literature could exert an influence to change society; books can perhaps influence the hearts of men, but they cannot influence a social automaton. All the arts could do was to save a few individuals from becoming as mechanically-minded as other people in the age in which they lived, by opening their eyes to other kinds of reality.' But now this automatism of conflict has developed means of destroying itself, 'unless a majority of the peoples of the world assumes complete and conscious responsibility for the future pattern of the world. . . . Since we have become accustomed to accepting the idea that all arrangements are adjustments of existing interests, which can be calculated in terms of power and wealth, the step before us seems almost impossibly difficult to take. We have got to set the whole *human* interest in front of the existing power-and-wealth interests, at a time when we have almost abandoned thinking of politics in terms of humanity.'

Politics indeed has been in very ill odour during the past decade among many English writers, both of the older and the younger generation. Some of them express extreme anarchist views. Alex Comfort, in a collection of papers under the title *Art and Social Responsibility* (1946), dedicated to Herbert Read, declares the artist to be 'ultimately the enemy of society'—a position the artist himself finds it hard to realize in periods of social expansion when progressive aspects of society are uppermost. He is, therefore, totally unprepared to grapple with the idea when, in a disintegrative phase such as the present, 'the necessity for accepting the role of masterless men in the face of total war and total society' has been sprung upon him. Art is in essence 'the act of standing aside from society', until or if a state of affairs develops in which art could become a part of all daily activity, and all activity would be potentially creative. This would be a 'free community', not a 'society'—such a community, one recalls, as William Morris dreamed of in *News from Nowhere*. In the meantime, while we still have a 'society', Mr Comfort points out a value of Marxist criticism: its 'perpetual emphasis on the environmental concern of the artist'. When an artist is fortified with this conception of humanity and his knowledge that he is a part of it, not merely an observer, he is under an obligation to concern himself with the entire environment of the times, both by interpreting it and by modifying it. Artistic responsibility consists in 'providing voices for all those who have not voices. The romantic ideology of art is the ideology of that responsibility, a responsibility born out of a sense of victimhood, of community in a hostile universe, and destined like Prometheus, its central creation, to be the perpetual advocate and defender of Man against Barbarism, community against irresponsibility, life against homicidal and suicidal obedience.'[14]

George Woodcock, author of a biographical study of William Godwin, has a view of society 'not far removed from Godwin's'. His essay on Kropotkin in the volume *The Writer and Politics* (1948) is in obvious sympathy with philosophical anarchism; and all the essays, as the introduction points out, have a social theme: the recognition that, 'beneath all the collective institutions and concepts, individual man is the one fundamental concern of society, and that our social efforts are valid only in so far as they tend to assist man's tendency towards individuation'. In the essay that gives the book its title, Mr Woodcock casually postulates 'the complete rottenness of the present social systems', and also 'the corruption implicit in power politics'. Writers are 'innocents in the hands of party leaders', and the Communists are especially to blame for the revulsion against political parties in general. 'The very nature of political groups . . . makes it impossible for the writer to remain within them and keep his integrity.' All valuable social thinking has been done outside the limits of organizations. Mr Woodcock thinks it was different in the time of Swift or of Hazlitt, who could be both political pamphleteers and literary writers; 'for Hazlitt there was never any problem of making a choice between politics and literature, like that which has faced many contemporary writers. He saw the two forms of writing merely as differing expressions of the same attitude towards the world'. One wonders whether politics had a less evil odour in those days; or whether the writers were of tougher breed;

or whether the stage was so restricted as to be in a way humanized. And one speculates on the possibility that the Swift-Hazlitt situation might bear some resemblance to that in the Soviet Union, in that an Alexei Tolstoy or a Gorky or an Ehrenburg might feel his creative writing and his politics in harmony. Mr Woodcock's views on the Soviet régime would make this speculation seem completely fantastic. But his views are not the only possible views.

As Mr Woodcock sees it, the writer's relation nowadays to movements aiming to change the social structure, in order to eliminate some of the evils it inflicts on humanity, inevitably involves him in politics. He cannot hide in the ivory tower: 'the ivory tower is as much a symptom of inescapable social problems as the air-raid shelter is of the inescapable evils of war'. In this century of ineluctable social disturbances, 'while the writer cannot avoid developing some kind of social consciousness, either positive or negative, he finds his values as an artist, as an intellectual, so strongly opposed to those of society in general that it is almost impossible for him to engage in politics in any ordinary sense of the word'. What then must he do? One of Mr Woodcock's answers would be unacceptable to those who, in one sense or another, believe in original sin. The writer's task, he says, is to make men aware of 'the natural and harmonious laws that already exist within them'.

iv

A Question for the Future

RECALLING THE quotation at the beginning of this chapter, we can agree that the debate on the obligations towards society of the artist shows no sign of coming to an end. But it has in recent years been most often pursued with reference to specific historical conditions, and the Russians of the new régime have had much to do with removing it from a platonic level. There is nothing platonic about the Soviet charges that Western artists are decadent, or the Western charge that Soviet artists are slaves. What about the future? Rex Warner risks some speculations in an essay on Freedom of Expression in *The Cult of Power* (1946), which take us a little above the battle into a less murky atmosphere, more favourable to thought.

Mr Warner wonders, to begin with, what a conversation between Virgil and Horace, towards the end of Virgil's life, would have been like. 'How would they feel and speak if they were to look back together on the early days—when each of them was financially embarrassed, when Virgil's farm was taken from him by soldiers returned from civil wars, when Horace in the name of liberty fought against the present régime: the days before they became acquainted with the Emperor and with his great Home Secretary, Maecenas, a man whose original mind perceived that the support of literary men would be valuable to the new order, who saw to it that Horace had his farm near Rome, Virgil his villa in Campania? Since then these great poets had lived in leisure and affluence. Their work had been officially encouraged. From time to time, no doubt, suggestions had been made to them by the Emperor, or by those who were in close touch with the court, as to the desirability of a particular ode for a particular occasion, a dedication or a general line of argument or feeling. Yet these suggestions cannot have been very burdensome. Virgil loved the country and was ready enough to compose the Georgics. True, he had had to cancel a dedicatory passage to his friend Gallus, who had died ignominiously, having in some way or other challenged the authority of the State; but he had replaced this passage by lines on a mythological subject which were, perhaps, in their sensitive, remote way, more beautiful than any which he had ever written.' Were they content as they looked back on their youth in the days of the dying Republic? Were they thankful for the security that had replaced the violence and corruption? And what would they have thought if they had been able to look into the future?

'It is interesting to imagine conversations between dead men,' continues Mr Warner, 'but one can hardly do so without referring their imagined words to the present,' and so he risks some historical comparisons and some guesses about the future. 'In our times, as in those of Virgil, countless lives have been lost or disrupted by years of economic chaos and war; and in Europe, at any rate, what the ordinary man will want most will be physical security.' The State, after the war, is certain to be Socialist, in some sense or other, and efficient, if it is to attain the aims of peace and security. 'How will literature be affected by such a State?' Perhaps the State will disregard literature, but that is unlikely, propaganda being essential, even for efficiency in production and distribution; and we have learned that a novel can exercise as much political influence as a procession or an official leaflet. 'Home Secretaries and Ministers of propaganda will find the support of literature for their new régimes just as valuable as Maecenas found it.' And if the new system solves the problems of unemployment, poverty and war, many writers will co-operate whole heartedly; and the State will probably subsidize these writers, either directly or indirectly; 'indeed, this will be a necessary step if serious literature is not to disappear entirely. Already before the war there was only a handful of writers who, without independent means, were able to live by writing alone'. If writing is considered a valuable social activity, it will probably be supported socially; then 'what is likely to be, or should be, the attitude of the State to the writers whom it supports, and of the writers to the State by whom they are supported?'

For the purpose of his speculation, Mr Warner says it matters little whether the efficient State is Republican, Democrat, Communist or Imperial. 'Under dictatorships literature has flourished, at least for a short time; and Socrates was put to death by a restored democracy. Literature may well gain force and direction and power from the new régime which we imagine. Can it also keep its integrity?' His answer is that it can do so, if it makes the same claim that Socrates made for himself: 'it should be treated with honour by the State, even subsidized, and should be not only allowed but expected to criticize the State in every way'. This is its public service—particularly necessary today, when along with the desire for food, work and peace, and the belief that they are attainable, there is great vagueness as to how they are to be secured and what, in the end, is to be done with them. 'This is what may be called the political task of literature—to hold the mirror up to nature, to show men how they live and what is meant by their own words and manners, to investigate everything under the sun, to retain the tradition of the past and to explore the future, to instruct, to criticize, to delight, to create and reveal.' The more the writer can co-operate with his society, the happier he will be; but his work, though conditioned by his social group, is not determined by it. 'And there is a sense in which it is true to say that his work must be, whether he is conscious of it or not, always disruptive of any State organization. For his loyalties as a writer are to something wider and deeper than any State can be.'

Mr Warner is well aware of the practical difficulty of convincing the politicians of a modern State 'that one of their chief services to the community is to maintain and encourage what will often appear as a revolutionary movement against themselves'. They can urge that with urgent practical tasks to be done, arguments at cross-purposes cannot be tolerated; and many other objections can be met only 'from the standpoint of a complete democratic faith, from the belief that, in the last resort, it is the individual and not the State that counts; that the State exists not only to promote the happiness but also the responsibility and goodness of its citizens'. Yet man needs, to live, a certain stability, both physical and intellectual, and 'the efficient State which we have imagined will be valued not only for its promise of economic security but also for its ability to co-ordinate national aims. And the more successful it is—in both of these respects—the more dangerous will be the position for literature. Yet also more full of promise: since if the State can be not only efficient but self-critical, not only stable but developing, the future both of the State and of literature may justify the brightest hopes. Writers, like everyone else, will welcome an ordered society of peace and plenty; and literature can collaborate with the State that achieves these ends. The State, in its turn, must admit the paradoxical nature of this collaboration

—that the writer, however he may serve the State, is still the tribune of the person, the critic of institutions, the agent of change.'[15]

[1] 'The Idea of a Literary Review', in the *New Criterion*, Jan. 1926.

[2] From lectures in a course, 'The Sociology of Literature', given at Columbia University by Dr Leo Lowenthal.

[3] We think of the writer's social responsibility as a Russian tradition established in the nineteenth century. But Professor Gudzy, in his *History of Early Russian Literature* (Eng. translation, Macmillan, 1949), states: 'Early Russian literature was fundamentally journalistic in character, concerned with the burning questions of the day, its purpose being more or less openly pragmatic. The concept of literary art as a province of culture in its own right, set off from other such provinces, did not exist for us in old times, at least if we take only written literature into account and exclude the oral tradition,' p. 1.

[4] 'An Artist Caste', London *Times Literary Supplement*, Sept. 28, 1946.

[5] *Letters of Anton Chekhov to His Family and Friends*, Macmillan, 1920, p. 127.

[6] This paragraph is taken from the section on 'The Russian Tradition', in *Modern World Fiction*, by Brewster and Burrell (1951).

[7] *My Literary Passions*, by W. D. Howells, 1895, p. 258.

[8] The *North American Review*, Dec. 1908.

[9] Reprinted in *Pen Portraits and Reviews*, vol. xxix of the Ayot St Lawrence edition of the Collected Works of Bernard Shaw, pp. 267-274.

[10] See Alexander Kaun: *Soviet Poets and Poetry*, University of California Press, 1943, for the pre- and post-revolutionary theories of the Futurists, Ego-Futurists, Cubo-Futurists, post-Symbolists, the Smithy Group, the October Group, etc.

[11] 'Liberal Individualism', by Stephen Spender, *New Masses*, Nov. 10, 1936.

[12] *The Irresponsibles: A Declaration*, by Archibald MacLeish, Duel, Sloan & Pearce, N.Y., 1940. See also *Opinions of Oliver Allston*, by Van Wyck Brooks, N.Y., Dutton & Co., 1941.

[13] *European Witness*, by Stephen Spender, Reynal & Hitchcock, 1946. Quotations and summaries from section entitled 'French Interlude'.

[14] The sub-title of *Art and Social Responsibility* is *Lectures on the Ideology of Romanticism*. London, Falcon Press. Quotations are from p. 27 and pp. 35-38.

[15] *The Cult of Power*, by Rex Warner. London, John Lane, 1946.

[16] Written in 1943. Professor Simmons surveys recent trends in the practice of 'socialist realism', and in Party control of literature, in his introduction as editor to *Through the Glass of Soviet Literature: Views of Russian Society*. Columbia University Press, New York, 1953.

CHAPTER XIV

CONCLUSION

PROFESSOR SERGE KONOVALOV, in an inaugural lecture (November 26, 1946) before the University of Oxford, where a Chair of Russian was established in 1945, traced the history of Slavonic studies in England, and especially the part played by Oxford. Much of the material—books and manuscripts—brought back from Russia by English travellers of the sixteenth and seventeenth centuries found its way into the Bodleian Library. He pays tribute to William Morfill and Neville Forbes and Paul Vinogradoff and others.

Russia, he reminds us, has drawn largely on Western Europe in her development, and the greatest Russian poet and humanist, Pushkin, is essentially Russian, yet truly European. 'Russia deprived of Greek and Western influences would not have had the art of Dostoevsky and Tolstoy, with its tension and duality, or have produced the Soviet interpretation of Marxism. Some would argue: The world would have been a more peaceful place without Russia. . . . Who can tell? Would the world have been any happier in 1812, 1914, and 1941 in the absence of Russia? And it would also have been poorer and duller perhaps.' In expressing the hope of mutual interchange, Professor Konovalov concludes: 'The measure of understanding between the two will largely depend on how far it will prove possible to reconcile two distinct interpretations of one notion, expressed in the one word *Humanism*—an old and venerable word here, and new in its revolutionary sense there. Here it represents the reality of tradition, the ideal of individualism; there it stands for the reality of the Soviet Revolution, the ideal of communal life. Whatever each side thinks of the realities and ideals, achievements and aspirations of the other, there is only one road to the living humanism of the future: from wars to peace, from social privilege and inequality to social justice, from darkness to light.'[1]

When mankind takes this road to a living humanism, then indeed will Shelley's prophecy be fulfilled and the world's great age will begin anew. In the story we have been tracing, of contacts and influences in one relatively narrow field of literary intercourse between Russia and the West, there have been moments when it looked as if the union of races by knowledge rather than their separation by prejudice (as Edmund Noble put it) was being furthered by Russian writers and Western interpreters. And there have been other moments when that hope seemed very dim. But in the history of culture, what are two or three centuries? The story is not ended. The attempt to tell it may prove helpful in discovering its meaning, in suggesting how and why lamentable misunderstandings arise, and in giving a hint of the reconciliation of conflicting ideals and aspirations. For those who share Professor Konovalov's hope for the humanism of the future, there is the choice of seeing the Kremlin—symbol of Russia—not with the eyes of Henry Adams, as 'Byzantium barbarized', but as Lewis Carroll saw it through his looking-glass, distorted a little like most human visions, but 'with glittering points of light on the gilded domes'.

[1] Serge Konovalov: *Oxford and Russia*, an inaugural lecture, November 26, 1946. Oxford. The Clarendon Press, 1947.

BIBLIOGRAPHY

Books and periodicals fully identified in the text are not listed in the bibliography, unless they contain material (not used in the text) of further interest to the student.

1.

The following titles are selected from early anthologies, bibliographies, literary histories, and translated specimens of Russian literature:

BOWRING, JOHN: *Specimens of the Russian Poets*. Boston, 1822.

KARAMZIN, NIKOLAI: *Tales from the Russian of Nicolai Karamsin*. London, 1804.

OTTO, FRIEDRICH: *The History of Russian Literature*. Translated by George Cox. Oxford, 1839.

SAUNDERS, W. H.: *Poetical Translations from the Russian Language*. London, 1826.

SHAW, THOMAS B.: *Pushkin the Russian Poet*. Three articles with translations from Pushkin's poetry. Blackwood's *Edinburgh Magazine*, volumes lvii and lviii, June, July, August, 1845.

Foreign Quarterly Review. Tables of Foreign Literature, October, 1842, pp. 242–250.

London Bookman. Seven bibliographical articles by E. A. Osborne. July–December, 1932, June, 1933.

2.

The following titles are a selection from early accounts of manners, customs and travel in Russia; and recent studies of such accounts:

Russia at the Close of the Sixteenth Century. Comprising the treatise 'Of the Russe Commonwealth', by Dr Giles Fletcher; and 'The Travels of Sir Jerome Horsey, Knt', now for the first time printed entire from his own manuscript. Edited by Edward A. Bond, assistant keeper of the manuscripts in the British Museum, London. Printed for the Hakluyt Society. 1856.

TURBERVILLE, GEORGE: *Certain Letters in Verse . . . out of Muscovia*. (In Notes upon Russia, Hakluyt Society Publications, London, 1851.)

MILTON, JOHN: *A Brief History of Muscovia*. London, 1682.

GOLDSMITH, OLIVER: *Letters of a Citizen of the World*. *Works*, vol. 4, New York and London, 1900. Letters Nos. lxii, lxxxvii.

CLARKE, EDWARD D.: *Travels in Various Countries of Europe, Asia and Africa*. Part I: Russia, Tartary and Turkey. London, 1810-1823.

EDWARDS, HENRY SUTHERLAND: *The Russians at Home*. Unpolitical sketches showing what newspapers they read; what theatres they frequent and how they eat, drink and enjoy themselves: with other matters relating chiefly to literature and music and to places of historical and religious interest in and about Moscow; comprising four Russian designs (in stone); a portion written by an American citizen. London, 1861.

Seven Britons in Imperial Russia 1698–1812. Edited by Peter Putnam. Princeton University Press, 1952. (The seven are John Perry, engineer; Jonas Hanway, merchant; William Richardson, humanist; Sir James Harris, diplomat; William Coxe, 'tutor on tour'; Robert Ker Porter, court painter; Sir Robert Thomas Wilson, soldier.)

Americans in Russia 1776–1917: A Study of the American Travellers in Russia from the American Revolution to the Russian Revolution. By Anna Babey. New York, 1938.

3.

Recent studies of certain phases of the diplomatic and political relations between Russia and Great Britain, and Russia and the United States, containing valuable bibliographies:

BAILEY, T. A.: *America Faces Russia: Russian-American Relations from Early Times to Our Day*. Cornell University Press, 1950.

GLEASON, JOHN HOWES: *The Genesis of Russophobia in Great Britain: A Study of the Interaction of Policy and Opinion*. Harvard University Press, 1950. (Period studied: 1815–1841.)

WILLIAMS, WILLIAM APPLEMAN: *American-Russian Relations* 1781–1947. New York, 1952.

4.

Studies of special aspects of Russian—English—American literary relationships and influences:

DECKER, CLARENCE: 'Victorian Comment on Russian Realism', in Publications of the Modern Language Association of America (P.M.L.A.). June, 1937. 'Aesthetic Revolt against Naturalism in Victorian Criticism', P.M.L.A., September, 1938.

GETTMANN, ROYAL A.: *Turgenev in England and America*. University of Illinois Press, 1941.

LEFEVRE, CARL: *Gogol's First Century in England and America*, 1841–1941. Unpublished doctoral dissertation, University of Minnesota, 1943.

LERNER, DANIEL: *The Influence of Turgenev on Henry James. Slavonic Year-Book*. American Series I, being vol. xx, 1941, of *The Slavonic and East European Review*.

MUCHNIC, HELEN: *Dostoevsky's English Reputation* (1881–1936). Smith College Studies in Modern Languages. Vol. xx, April and July, 1939. Northampton, Mass.

SIMMONS, ERNEST J.: *English Literature and Culture in Russia* (1553–1840). Cambridge, Mass., 1935.

SMITH, J. ALLAN: *Tolstoy's Fiction in England and America*. Unpublished doctoral dissertation, University of Illinois, 1939.

'VOKS' *Bulletin*, April, 1952, Moscow. (A number devoted to Gogol, on the centenary of his birth, contains articles on Gogol in England (by Jack Lindsay) and Gogol in the United States (by Dorothy Brewster).

YARMOLINSKY, AVRAHM: *Pushkin in English*. A list of works by and about Pushkin, edited with introduction. New York, 1937.

5.

Selected titles of books, essays, letters and memoirs, dealing with Russian literature, incidentally or extensively, and its effects on English and American writers and readers:

ARNOLD, MATTHEW: 'Count Leo Tolstoy', in *Essays in Criticism*, second series, London, 1888. (First published in the *Fortnightly Review*, December, 1887.)

BARING, MAURICE: *Landmarks in Russian Literature*. London, 1910; *An Outline of Russian Literature*. London, 1914; *The Mainsprings of Russia*. London, 1914; *The Puppet Show of Memory*. London, 1922.

CARTER, HUNTLY: *The New Spirit in the Russian Theatre*, 1917–1928. London, 1929.

CONRAD, JOSEPH: *Letters from Joseph Conrad*, 1895–1924. Introduction and notes by Edward Garnett. Indianapolis, 1928; *Notes on Life and Letters*. Garden City, N.Y., 1921.

ELLIS, HAVELOCK: *The New Spirit*. London, 1892 (essay on Tolstoy).

GARNETT, EDWARD: *Friday Nights*. London, 1921 (includes essays on Ostrovsky and Chekhov).

GERHARDI, WILLIAM: *Anton Chekhov: A Critical Study*. London, 1923; *Futility*. 1922; *Polyglots*. 1925.

GOSSE, EDMUND: *Books on the Table*. 1921. (Contains two essays on Russian themes: 'The Unveiling of Tolstoy' and 'The Letters of Chekhov').

HENDERSON, PHILIP. *The Poet and Society*. London, 1939.

HEWITT, DOUGLAS: *Joseph Conrad, a Reassessment*. Cambridge, Mass., 1952.

JAMES, HENRY: *French Poets and Novelists*. 1878. (Contains essay on Turgenev, first published in the *North American Review*, vol. cxviii. 1874); *Partial Portraits*. 1888: *Notes on Novelists*. 1914.

KELLEY, CORNELIA P.: *The Early Development of Henry James*. Urbana, 1930.

KROPOTKIN, PETER: *Ideals and Realities in Russian Literature*. New York, 1915. (First published as the Lowell lectures in 1905.)

LAWRENCE, D. H.: *Letters*. New York, 1932. (Numerous references to Tolstoy, Dostoevsky, Turgenev.)

MCCULLERS, CARSON: *Russian Realists and Southern Writers*. *Decision*. Vol. ii, 1941.

MACKENZIE, COMPTON: *Literature in My Time*. London, 1933.

MANSFIELD, KATHERINE: *Letters*. New York, 1929. (Numerous references to Chekhov and Dostoevsky.)

MIRSKY, D. S. *Modern Russian Literature*. London, 1925; *Contemporary Russian Literature*. New York, 1926.

MOORE, GEORGE: *Impressions and Opinions*. London, 1891; *Avowals*. 1919.

MORTIMER, RAYMOND: *New Statesman and Nation*, July 10 and August 14, 1943 (articles on Turgenev).

PARES, SIR BERNARD: *A Wandering Student*. Syracuse University Press, 1948.

PHELPS, GILBERT: 'The Teapot and the Samovar', in *Britain Today*. June, 1950; 'Russian Realism in English Fiction', in *Cambridge Journal*. February, 1950.

PRITCHETT, V. S.: *New Statesman and Nation*, October 3 and December 25, 1943 (articles on Goncharov and Aksakov). Also January 17 and April 25.

SAINTSBURY, GEORGE: *The Later Nineteenth Century*. 1907.

SCHUYLER, EUGENE: *Memoir and Essays*. New York, 1901.

SHAW, GEORGE BERNARD: *Heartbreak House*, including Preface. 1919; *Pen Portraits and Reviews*. Vol. xxix. New York, 1932. (Includes two papers on Tolstoy, pp. 267–280.)

SWINNERTON, FRANK: *The Georgian Scene*. 1934.

TILLEY, ARTHUR: 'Gogol the Father of Russian Realism', in *Living Age*, July, 1894,vol. xxiv. First appeared in *London National Review*.

TURNER, C. E.: *Studies in Russian Literature*. London, 1882; *The Modern Novelists of Russia*. 1890; *Count Tolstoy as Novelist and Thinker*. London, 1888.

VOGUE, MELCHIOR DE: *The Russian Novelists*. Translated by J. L. Edmands, Boston, 1887. (The translation by Col H. A. Sawyer, published in London in 1913, was a new one, from the eleventh French edition.)

WOOLF, VIRGINIA: 'The Russian Point of View', in *The Common Reader*. New York, 1925; 'The Novels of Turgenev', in the *Yale Review*, autumn, 1933, reprinted in *The Captain's Deathbed*. 1950.

WRIGHT, HAGBERG: 'The Meaning of Russian Literature', in the *Quarterly Review*, vol. ccxxxv, 1921, pp. 102–120.

INDEX

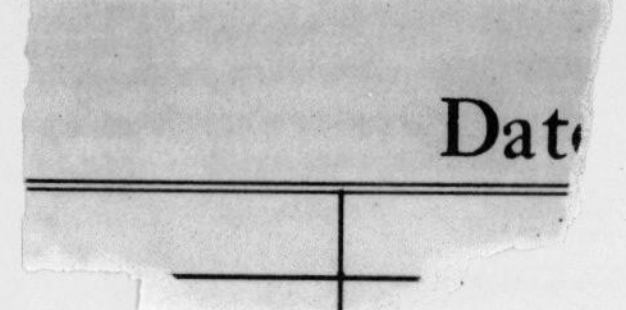
Dat